ENDURING EMPIRE:
ANCIENT LESSONS FOR GLOBAL POLITICS

An exploration of the ways in which ancient theories of empire can inform our understanding of present-day international relations, *Enduring Empire* engages in a serious discussion of empire as it relates to American foreign policy and global politics.

The imperial power dynamics of ancient Athens and Rome provided fertile ground for the deliberations of many classical thinkers who wrote on the nature of empire: contemplating political sovereignty, autonomy, and citizenship as well as war, peace, and civilization in a world where political boundaries were strained and contested. The contributors to this collection prompt similar questions with their essays and promote a serious contemporary consideration of empire in light of the predominance of the United States and of the doctrine of liberal democracy.

Featuring essays from some of the leading thinkers in the fields of political science, philosophy, history, and classics, *Enduring Empire* illustrates how lessons gleaned from the Athenian and Roman empires can help us to understand the imperial trajectory of global politics today.

DAVID EDWARD TABACHNICK is an associate professor in the Department of Political Science at Nipissing University.

TOIVO KOIVUKOSKI is an associate professor in the Department of Political Science at Nipissing University.

EDITED BY DAVID EDWARD TABACHNICK
AND TOIVO KOIVUKOSKI

Enduring Empire

Ancient Lessons for Global Politics

UNIVERSITY OF TORONTO PRESS
Toronto Buffalo London

©University of Toronto Press Incorporated 2009
Toronto Buffalo London
www.utppublishing.com
Printed in Canada

ISBN 978-0-8020-9762-0 (cloth)
ISBN 978-0-8020-9521-3 (paper)

Printed on acid-free, 100% post-consumer recycled paper with
vegetable-based inks.

Library and Archives Canada Cataloguing in Publication

Enduring empire: ancient lessons for global politics/edited by David Edward
Tabachnick and Toivo Koivukoski.

Includes bibliographical references and index.
ISBN 978-0-8020-9762-0 (bound). – ISBN 978-0-8020-9521-3 (pbk.)

1. Imperialism – History.   2. United States – Foreign Relations.   I.
Tabachnick, David   II. Koivukoski, Toivo

JC359.E57 2009   325'.3209   C2009-901713-X

This book has been published with the help of a grant from the Canadian
Federation for the Humanities and Social Sciences, through the Aid to
Scholarly Publications Program, using funds provided by the Social Sciences
and Humanities Research Council of Canada.

University of Toronto Press acknowledges the financial assistance to its
publishing program of the Canada Council for the Arts and the Ontario Arts
Council.

University of Toronto Press acknowledges the financial support for its
publishing activities of the Government of Canada through the Book
Publishing Industry Development Program (BPIDP).

Contents

Preface

DAVID EDWARD TABACHNICK
AND TOIVO KOIVUKOSKI

Words had to change their ordinary meaning and to take that which was now given to them. Reckless audacity came to be considered the courage of a loyal ally; prudent hesitation, specious cowardice; moderation was held to be a cloak for unmanliness; ability to see all sides of a question, inaptness to act on any.

Thucydides, *History of the Peloponnesian War*[1]

In this remarkable passage we are reminded that times of political disorder can give rise to questions about the meanings of political terms, establishing a tension between the novelties of the present and the accumulated history of past interpretations. The meaning of the term 'empire' is presently encountering such a contested interval, one that in many ways is a reflection of an imperial setting, with all of the connotations of unsettling violence and revolutionary change that Thucydides describes. Such crises of common sense represent moments of theoretical opportunity to reflect on political phenomena with a renewed openness, testing present experiences against the lessons of the past. From Thucydides to Herodotus, Cicero to Caesar, Machiavelli to Titus Livy, ancient encounters with empires contribute the critical steadiness of 2,500 years of political philosophy and history to what can be disorienting times of crisis, while enabling us to re-evaluate the tradition in a new political context.

The authors of the essays that follow consider ancient articulations of empire in an effort to better understand the meaning of empire today. The aim of this book, then, is to lay foundations of political philosophy and ancient history beneath a lively contemporary discourse on empires

– a discourse that seems to have tended towards either hyperbolic, academic condemnation or embedded, patriotic reportage, alternating sentiments of fury with those of awe, or terror, or amazement. The United States of America is now commonly referred to as an empire in the same general sense as the Roman Empire, the Athenian Empire, or the Persian Empire. But what do such diverse political organizations have in common? Here the original clear-minded reflections of the ancients can add substance to an idea that is too easily reduced to a term of either approbation or glorification. The question of whether empire is a good or bad thing for America and the world is a matter for political debates to decide. If scholarship on empire has any purpose, it is to supply the ballast of historical perspective for those debates on contemporary imperial projects, be they imagined or real.

This book raises more questions than it settles, asking not simply whether the United States is an empire, but how we are to understand empire in the first place. How can various forms of empire – tyrannical, totalitarian, hegemonic, democratic, and republican – be distinguished? What uneasy mediations can be formed between democratic republics and imperial power? What drives empires to expand, and what limits are there to an expansionist dynamic? Our authors set out to ask such political questions in a spirit of philosophic openness, while suggesting lessons about empire drawn from the study of ancient history and political philosophy. Obviously this is not just a matter of direct applications, since the circumstances for judgement and political action are varied and particular to the time, place, and people involved. Yet simply asking such fundamental questions that were not settled in the fifth century BCE (and that won't likely be settled in the twenty-first century either) encourages one to step back from the insistent demands of the present so as to moderate those political judgements that have arisen from knee-jerk reactions. If we could suggest one classical virtue of particular relevance to a time of perceived crisis such as our own, it would be moderation, and there is an element of this in the moment of calm that is prerequisite to philosophic reflections on ancient empires.

Needless to say, contemporary discussions of imperialism have been inspired by recent events in American foreign policy. The American invasion and occupation of Iraq was said to be part of broader effort to destroy the tyrannies of the Middle East and replace them with democracies. Supporters of this project argue that the United States has a moral right to force democracy upon the region. Critics say that while they support the spread of democracy, it should be developed by indigenous populations rather than imposed by a foreign power. Both groups, however, seem to agree that for good or ill, the United States is behaving like an empire – that is, using its superior power to control and direct other countries. The question is this: How did a country founded on anti-imperialist principles become an empire?

David C. Hendrickson begins his chapter by exploring this very question. As he notes, many neoconservative supporters of the Bush administration see no disagreement between the goals of empire and those of democracy. In effect, they have co-opted the left-wing critique of American imperialism as an accurate description of American foreign policy – a policy, moreover, that merits praise. Hendrickson's account of American history reveals a long history of empire building; that said, the Bush Doctrine suggests a revolutionary new effort towards 'universal empire' or the domination by one power of the state system as a whole. According to Hendrickson, though, 'American policy … is imperial in aim but likely to fail.' He suggests that those who craft American foreign policy would be wise to follow the example of the American founders, who, when considering the republic's future, took many lessons from ancient Greece and Rome, including these: aspire to peaceful order rather than domination; and avoid overextension abroad lest one suffer domestic decline.

Laurie Bagby continues in this vein by pointing out that ancient and modern democracies are more different than is commonly held. In part, this difference can be attributed to the fact that Athens practised direct democracy – something viewed as dangerous by the moderns. As Thucydides makes abundantly clear in *The History of the Peloponnesian War*, it was the empowered, fickle, glory-seeking, and materialistic Athenian people who led their city into both ill-advised military adventurism and domestic political infighting. From Thucydides we can learn that democracy is not itself opposed to imperialism; rather, it is modern 'liberal' democracy that opposes imperialism with its emphasis on individual rights and self-determination.

Similar to Bagby, David Edward Tabachnick compares ancient Athens with contemporary America. Ruminating on Thucydides' account of Athens' transformation from a respected regional hegemonic power into a brutal empire during the Peloponnesian War, he wonders whether we are not now seeing a similar transformation of the United States. His survey of post–Second World War American foreign policy suggests that the United States was at one time a welcomed world leader but that its efforts to eradicate first its communist and then its terrorist enemies have seen it become far more coercive as well as interventionist in the sovereign affairs of other countries.

Ryan Balot also examines the relevance of Athens as an imperial democracy to the contemporary United States. Initially, the Athenians required courage to maintain their freedom from foreign enslavement as well as from domestic tyranny; this gave them autonomy, democracy, and (ultimately) a sense of superiority over other, 'unfree' city-states. As Balot notes, this sense of superiority led these same self-described 'courageous freedom fighters' to 'subject other Greeks to their own power.' Because of their own emphasis on freedom, the Athenians became especially sensitive to the obvious charge that they had become tyrants themselves. And because they were now so hated by the rest of Greece, they had no choice but to maintain their empire out of fear that losing it would result in their own destruction. Unfortunately, imperialistic foreign policy damaged democratic ideals at home, leading to the rise of domestic tyranny and the erosion of the very freedoms for which the Athenians had fought so bravely.

Using Herodotus as his guide, Clifford Orwin considers how the free people of the ancient world were able to defeat the much larger armies of despots. The despotic Persians based their right to rule on a belief in their own innate superiority, whereas the Hellenic peoples were motivated to fight by the far more powerful and universal idea that they were protecting their own freedom. Problematically, though, this very same impulse also led them to enslave others in order to preempt any future threats to their liberty. Put simply, what began as an effort towards self-determination and the destruction of tyranny was transformed into imperialism.

Leah Bradshaw worries about an even more profound consequence of universal empire. Her chapter begins with this provocative statement: 'Empire may be triumphant in modernity. Politics may be over.' She observes that, while ancient Athens may have inspired contemporary democracy, our now globalized world bears a far stronger resemblance to the expanding, universalistic, and materialistic character of empire than to the self-sufficient community of the Greek *polis*. Considering Aristotle's idea that we are only fully human when in the *polis*, the rise of a global empire may signal the end not only of politics but also of our very humanity.

A certain compulsiveness underlying reactionary imperialism is the topic of Toivo Koivukoski's chapter, which examines the motivations of honour, interests, and fear, which Thucydides considered the causes of Athens' dynamic arc of expansion, overstretch, and retreat. These apparently discrete motives take on a uniquely open-ended character in an imperial republic, in which interests cannot be clearly distinguished from the state of the world as a whole, in which honour drives towards universal recognition, and in which fear is experienced as dread of civilizational collapse. The author argues that in efforts to understand the sorts of imperialist compulsions that one sees embodied in the restless spirit of, for example, Alcibiades – who was the most vocal proponent of Athens' imperial wars – something like Nietzsche's self-overcoming will to power may provide deeper insights into imperial striving than the outward motivations of fear, honour, and interest identified by Thucydides; such will to power may also explain the 'fight for the dominion of the earth – the compulsion to large-scale politics' that Nietzsche presaged would characterize post-national (i.e., global) politics.

Moving from ancient Greece to ancient Rome, Art Eckstein challenges the notion that empires must always be built and preserved through a culture of war. According to Eckstein, unlike its rivals, which were led by bloodthirsty kings, the Roman Republic mitigated the overemphasis on militarism and predatory manliness by limiting the terms of its leaders and by subordinating the personal behaviour of those leaders to the law. This bred a culture of cooperation in the centre of Rome. It was only with the rise of Caesar, ruling on the periphery of the empire beyond the pacifying influences of Senate limits and laws, that we see the rise of a dangerous authoritarian counter-culture, one that threatened the stability of the empire and that drew Rome into civil war. Thus Eckstein advises that if the United States hopes to carry out its imperial ambitions without experiencing a similar fate, it will have to impose and maintain strict limits on the power of its leaders.

In her exploration of Roman imperial power, Susan Mattern questions the notion that the empire was expanded and maintained solely through military might. Indeed, it was its ability to navigate complicated networks of alliances that made Rome such a successful political entity. Using examples from Caesar and Cicero, Mattern concludes that instead of simply physically dominating newly taken territories and peoples, Rome wisely recognized the importance and legitimacy of existing social, bureaucratic, and legal institutions, working with and through them, 'understanding both stories, that of their own nation and that of the one they are invading.'

The sometimes ruthless requirements of 'founding' raise particular challenges for republican empires. To reconcile this apparently necessary ruthlessness with a republican political philosophy, Geoffrey Kellow examines Cicero's invocation of a harmonic historical order – 'the music of the spheres' – to uplift civic spirit in the Roman Republic and to simultaneously veil its brutish origins (as in a founder suckled by wolves). Kellow views this invocation as a rite of passage on the way to a cosmopolitan project. A empire cannot claim the natural right to rule over territories based on original possession, so it substitutes an overarching historical purpose as a locus for republican civic virtues. Kellow considers whether a similar sense of historical purpose can uplift the spirit of an expanding American republic, offering Martin Luther King's appeal to the revelatory and sanctifying qualities of history as a model for the reconciliation of remembered origins and for the ideals that sustain hope for the future.

Waller Newell's chapter emphasizes the dynamic character of liberal empires. He contrasts a classical preference for the stable, relatively autonomous *polis* with Machiavelli's praise for the invigorating effects of empire building, during which times 'growth is always accompanied by danger.' There is virtue of a kind in attuning oneself to the chaotic field of happenstance that underlies a political order; that is how republics arise and empires fall. The expansionist drive to control chance and bring order to the world is what inspires liberal empires such as Rome (in the eyes of Machiavelli) or America (as Newell sees it) with a common purpose that engages individual energies in a uniquely imperial conception of civic spiritedness.

One of the noteworthy aspects of empires relates to the violent levelling that always accompanies aspirations to construct a new civilizational order. Whether these aspirations are fulfilled in a new unity of humankind, and to what extent this is so, may be a function of the limits of human comprehension and technical accomplishment. Taking as his point of departure Eric Voegelin's 1961 declaration that the 'age of empire is coming to an end in our time,' John von Heyking considers to what extent contemporary candidates for imperial status – from a supposed American Empire, to an imagined global restoration of the Caliphate, to a 'global civil society' – actually succeed in their projects of world creation. He suggests, following Voegelin, that attempts to organize humankind into a political whole amount to little more than intellectual swindles, in that they deliberately distort human participation in a divine order that no earthly analogue can stand in for. Von

Heyking suggests that even during times of crude totalitarian domination, a sense of suspense about the future remains, and that in this possibility of surprise, humankind is held out towards the possibility of
participation in a beyond that is beyond human powers to control.

How imperial power should be exerted is a question that segues from
the ethical towards the strategic. In practical terms, ethical priorities
must be considered alongside an honest appraisal of the force necessary to address those priorities. In considering Athens' use of maritime
power, Barry Strauss contends that the empire declined not so much
through imperial hubris as from a lack of resolve, complicated by moral
agonizing over the difficulties inherent in maintaining a Hellenic empire. Judged against the alternative – Persian domination – the
Athenians' rule over a league of Greek cities seems measured, when
one remembers that it brought the benefits of democracy, security, and
material well-being. According to Strauss, the choice was clear: foreign
despotism (Persia), or hegemonic empire (Athens). He makes the radical suggestion that Athens' mistake, if indeed it made one, was that it
did not employ its naval forces decisively enough. 'If that is a morality
story,' Strauss concludes, 'it is not a comforting one.'

Strauss's concluding sentiment echoes lessons learned from 2,500
years of rising and falling empires, a chronicle that registers the vicissitudes of power, the changes invited into the centres of imperial republics, and the violence visited on their fluctuating peripheries. But then,
after optimism and in that moment before the pessimism accompany-
ing tragic decline sets in, there is a purpose to be fulfilled simply in
bearing witness to the changes taking place in our world with an honest clarity owed to philosophic reflection on empires past. In this apprehension of both the time-bound, fragile character of empires and
their enduring legacies, there is embedded a promise that is beyond
either false comforts or counsels of despair. So our reflections begin
with recollection, and here with a question: What remains of ancient
empires in the form of enduring lessons for understanding an imperial
global politics?

NOTES

1 Thucydides, *History of the Peloponnesian War*, trans. Richard Crawley
(London: Everyman, 1993), 3.82.

ENDURING EMPIRE:
ANCIENT LESSONS FOR GLOBAL POLITICS

1 In the Mirror of Antiquity: The Problem of American Empire

DAVID C. HENDRICKSON

We have been asked to compare the experience of empire in antiquity with contemporary articulations of empire and to consider whether lessons drawn from the ancient past may shed light on the imperial trajectory of contemporary international politics. The Western imagination has long been troubled by the question of how we moderns stand in relation to antiquity; indeed, it is possible to write histories of modern political thought in terms of that question.[1] To think of the matter in this way is to essentially ask what we and our forebears think and have thought about antiquity; but in the way the editors of this volume have posed their own question, there is also a hint of another perspective, one that might be somewhat crassly summarized by this question: What would antiquity think of us? Put differently, are there enduring lessons in ancient political thought that speak to the present moment? Are we to be either fortified or struck down in our imperial ambitions by the wisdom of the ancients?

This chapter ventures some observations with respect to these differing approaches to the subject. The first question is whether the United States today may fairly be considered an empire. I believe the appellation to be just, though there are certainly good reasons why American policy makers do not like the term. Second, I will be examining how the contrasting experiences of Greece and Rome entered into the American imagination in such a way that the lessons drawn from antiquity formed an essential aspect of what may be termed 'the American project.' Finally, I will consider the question of American empire from the vantage point of the lessons implicit in Thucydides' masterful account of the great war between Athens and Sparta.

The American invasion of Iraq in March 2003 and the development by the Bush administration of a new national-security strategy provoked an enormous volume of commentary – a flood of books, essays, and op-ed pieces – on the theme of American empire. The terrorist attacks of 11 September 2001, wrote one critic, 'produced a dangerous change in the thinking of some of our leaders, who began to see our republic as a genuine empire, a new Rome, the greatest colossus in history, no longer bound by international law, the concerns of allies, or any constraints on its use of military force.'[2] The question urgently demanding attention, wrote another critic, 'is not whether the United States has become an imperial power [but] what sort of empire [Americans] intend theirs to be.'[3]

It was not only critics of American foreign policy who found 'empire' to be the most apt label for what the United States had become. Neoconservative supporters of the Bush administration did so as well. Columnist Max Boot insisted that 'Afghanistan and other troubled lands today cry out for the sort of enlightened foreign administration once provided by self-confident Englishmen in jodhpurs and pith helmets.' Other neoconservatives, such as Charles Krauthammer and Tom Donnelly (the latter of the Project for the New American Century), agreed that it was time to come out of the closet on the subject of American empire. Of the supporters of the Bush's Iraq policy, perhaps the most brazen was British historian Niall Ferguson, who not only came out of the closet but nearly burned down the house. His argument was 'not merely that the United States is an empire but that it always has been an empire.'[4] Ferguson, like others, insisted that the United States should step up to the imperial responsibilities that fall to it as a conservator of world order, and he feared that it would not.

Thirty-five years ago, in the ideological heat generated by the war in Vietnam, few defenders of that war spoke of it as an imperial venture.[5] The charge of American empire was an indictment, an ascription of hidden intent used to encourage a repudiation of the forbidden temptation. That charge arose on the left and was condemned on the right. 'Once,' wrote critic Jonathan Schell, 'the left had stood alone in calling the U.S. imperial and was reviled for defaming the nation. Now it turned out to have been the herald of a new consensus. Yesterday's leftwing abuse became today's mainstream praise.'[6]

Or so it seemed. In fact, as time went by, observers on both the right and the left developed second thoughts. The Bush administration never accepted the 'imperial' label and repeatedly insisted in its public pronouncements that the United States was not and had never been an empire. 'We have no empires to establish or utopias to promote,' Bush declared. An academic proponent of the Bush Doctrine, who later joined the administration, denounced the 'imperial' label as reflecting a total misunderstanding of the purposes of Bush's national-security doctrine. 'Let us stop talking of an American empire, for there is and there will be no such thing.'[7] Victor Davis Hanson, another strong supporter of the Bush Doctrine, denounced the 'imperial' moniker as a gross misrepresentation of reality. '"Imperialism" and "hegemony,"' wrote Hanson, 'explain nothing about recent American intervention abroad – not when dictators such as Noriega, Milosevic, the Taliban, and Saddam Hussein were taken out by the U.S. military. There are no shahs and Your Excellencies in their places, but rather consensual governments whose only sin was that they came on the heels of American arms rather than U.N. collective snoozing.'[8]

The neoconservatives' reconsideration of empire ultimately has a very simple explanation: at the beginning of the twenty-first century, imperialism is widely viewed as bereft of political legitimacy. In a democratic age in which legitimate government is held to rest on the consent of the governed, to avow an imperial project is to draw attention to oneself as pursuing aims that will be widely regarded as illegitimate. The instinct of the Bush administration – to deny that the United States wants anything to do with empire – was undoubtedly much surer and more deeply attuned to public sentiment than the excited proclamations of a few intellectuals. *Pace* Schell, the 1960s denunciations of empire were not the advance wave of a new consensus. That does not mean, however, that there is no such thing as the American empire. It does mean that its architects will henceforth not be so obtuse and unfeeling as to denominate it as such. That will be left to its critics.

Yet the critics also developed second thoughts. The dominant leitmotif of critics was that Bush had abandoned the honourable traditions of American internationalism to chase after the elusive and disreputable goal of an American imperialism. Instead of leading the world in cooperative enterprises, as post–Second World War American internationalists had done, the United States under Bush now proposed to dominate the world. This theme, however, sat uneasily alongside the conviction – pronounced on the left since Vietnam – that the United States had long entertained imperial ambitions. On this view, Bush could scarcely be said to represent something new under the sun, though critics differed as to when the transformation from republic to empire had taken place. Some writers detected the change as having arisen with the end of the Cold War and the elimination of a geopolitical counterweight to the United States. Others followed the lead of J. William Fulbright, who wrote in the midst of the Vietnam War that America had succumbed in Southeast Asia to the lure of empire and who insisted that such a course represented a grave departure from American traditions.[9] If a vast complex of overseas bases and standing military establishments was the decisive development, perhaps the most logical date was 1945, when the United States first emerged as superior to all other states in the various dimensions of power.

Once the search began for precedents to 'empire as a way of life,' however, it became apparent to many that 1945 marked merely the ascendancy of the United States to 'global empire,' in the words of historian Ronald Steel. The imperial urge, these historians believed, long predated the moment of global ascendancy. It could in fact be traced to the beginnings of the nation's history, if not before. 'The American nation was no sooner founded,' wrote Steel, 'than its leaders embarked on an energetic program of expansion that – through diplomacy, conquest and theft from its original inhabitants – brought into the ever-expanding Union all the lands east of the Mississippi, then the vast territories of Louisiana, followed by Texas and a third of Mexico, the Pacific Northwest, Alaska, Caribbean and Pacific islands seized from Spain, and the once-independent kingdom of Hawaii.'[10] Historians Fred Anderson and Andrew Cayton also emphasized 'the centrality of imperial ambitions to the development of the United States.'[11] According to this view, only a kind of profound historical amnesia prevents Americans from appreciating how *traditional* and *characteristic* are the ambitions of the Bush administration. The Bush Doctrine, on this view, was no wayward eruption of a revolutionary president but a logical working out of propensities well established from the outset.

It would be difficult to deny that the United States, at one time or another, has acted in an imperialist manner. If empire is defined as the domination of one people by another state separate and alien from it, then assuredly there have been episodes in which one can speak confidently of an American empire. In the 1830s an opponent of Indian removal, Congressman Henry Storrs, declared that he would not sacrifice the reputation of America's founders, who had counselled just treatment of the native inhabitants, 'for all the Indian lands that avarice ever dreamt of, and all the empire which ambition ever coveted.' Of course he lost that argument.[12] The Cherokee and other southern tribes were removed. So, too, America undoubtedly acquired an empire in the war against Spain at the end of the nineteenth century. The regeneration of the Philippines and the acquisition of protectorates over various Caribbean islands followed an imperialist script. 'Has it ever occurred to you,' asked the *Missionary Journal* in 1899, 'that Jesus was the most imperial of imperialists?'[13] When facing peoples outside the society of states (then European and Christian in character), the United States did indeed act so as to displace peoples in its path. Thus far, then, those who would insist on a long imperial pedigree for America are adducing facts that cannot be denied. It is also true, however, that when America faced towards Europe and the society of states, its message was avowedly anti-imperial.

Several pertinent distinctions, moreover, are lost if the Bush Doctrine is seen as simply the latest instalment in a long imperial project. If it is true that there are precedents for an American imperialism, it is also true that Bush raised the empire business to an entirely new level. At its core, the Bush Doctrine proposed that the United States extend the position of military domination that fell to it as a consequence of victory in the Cold War; and that same doctrine was unafraid and unapologetic when it came to using force to reshape the international system. In embracing a doctrine of preventive war, the United States was abandoning the policies of containment and deterrence that it had followed during the Cold War. In announcing that it intended to preserve against all rivals its preeminent military status, it was jettisoning its previous commitment to arms control. In its insistence that it would no longer be bound by the laws traditionally governing the use of force – laws that forbid preventive war, torture, and the violent overthrow of regimes for the purpose of changing their political form – the United States had come to breathe a spirit of defiance towards international law. Especially in the early years of the Bush administration, America seemed recklessly indifferent to the views of traditional allies and airily dismissed the importance of showing a decent respect for the opinion of mankind.

In its pure form, as it were, the distilled essence of the Bush Doctrine was undoubtedly an imperial project, one that was far in advance of America's Cold War policy. It proposed a mastery of the state system by one power that recalled what Schell termed 'the hoary old nightmare of the ages, the always feared but never realized project of universal empire.'[14] Whereas empire signifies the domination of one people by another, universal empire had traditionally signified the domination by one power of the state system as a whole. This vision could only really take root in circumstances of unipolarity. In this regard, a new vista had opened after the collapse of the Soviet Union that created an entirely different milieu from that which existed during the Cold War. Those observers (among both supporters and critics) who insisted that the Bush Doctrine represented a revolutionary change in American policy were closer to the mark than those who emphasized continuity.

Though various critics err in downplaying the novelty of the administration's grand design, the more telling objection is that these imperial ambitions are doomed to frustration. The essential paradox is that the more ambitious and arrogant the United States becomes in its conduct of statecraft, the less likely it is to succeed in its aims. The Iraq war, of course, is the classic example of this phenomenon. It was this war that, above all else, earned the United States the appellation of an imperial power; yet by the same token, it is the Iraq war that has most clearly illustrated the limits of American power. At the outset of the war, one commentator insisted that 'the extent of American military superiority has become almost impossible to overstate.'[15] Subsequent years have shown that it is very possible to do so. The fact that the United States enjoyed a remarkable technological advantage over any other state; the fact that its military expenditures were larger than those of the next fifteen nations combined, equal to approximately half of total world military spending; the fact that it had accumulated since 1989 an extraordinary record of short, successful wars – all of this promoted scepticism towards the idea that military power has certain intrinsic limitations. The experience of the Iraq war has rightly renewed that scepticism. Though the consensus criticism of the U.S. military's performance in Iraq is that the Bush administration went to war 'without a plan,' the more telling point is that it is extremely difficult to see what combination of strategy and tactics might have enabled an occupying foreign army to impose a pacification on a refractory people.

We have here a sort of exemplification, at the level of grand strategy, of the Peter Principle – the idea that people will rise in organizations to the level of their incompetence. There is a kind of debility that attends the possession of so much power, for given sufficient time it will expand to the margins of its capability. What there is to use, gets used. Once committed, moreover, the imperial power cannot lose. It straps itself to the wheel, invests its resources in projects that will demonstrate its credibility, and persists in enterprises that ought not to have been undertaken in the first place but that, once undertaken, immediately become vital interests whose sacrifice is unthinkable. That relationship between extravagant aspiration and subsequent decline goes to the core of the American predicament today.

American policy, then, is imperial in aim but likely to fail. The Bush Doctrine represents a bid for mastery of the state system and is an authentic working out of Charles Krauthammer's call, at the end of the Cold War, 'to go all the way and stop at nothing short of universal dominion.'[16] But the verdict on this policy in the future is likely to be something on the order of Frederick Gentz's judgement on the eighteenth-century European powers: 'Our greatness occasioned our fall; our insatiable desire of advancing was the cause of our enervation; our meritorious ambition led to our present humiliation.' The causes of this Gentz traced, as might we, to 'attempts to rise from the safer paths of experience into regions yet untried of speculative politics.'[17]

The steps the United States took towards a form of universal empire actually followed an old script. Those steps had been prophesied. Few themes in the American story are of more antique lineage than the proposition that standing military establishments give rise to endless wars and that nothing is more fatal to republican government, and to liberty, than a policy that is friendly to war and to the militarized institutions that war fosters. To late eighteenth- and early nineteenth-century American republicans, the examples of England under Cromwell and France under Napoleon reflected a logical trajectory that was utterly alarming to the apostles of republicanism, and they were well aware, too, that the lines of this drama had been written in Roman history and in the subversion of the Roman republic by Julius Caesar. The belief that the military must be strictly subordinate to the civil power was a lesson drawn from the experience of ancient Rome, as from the experience of modern Britain and France. George Washington earned the undying gratitude of his countrymen by acting in accordance with that lesson and returning, like Cincinnatus, to his plough after rendering his valiant services to the republic.

In this as in other respects, the experience of antiquity hung over the early years of the American republic. To a degree difficult for us to appreciate, the mental horizons of the Founders were steeped in the experience of antiquity and the lessons drawn therefrom. The American conception of republicanism, as one observer has noted, was largely inherited from Rome: 'This included (1) pursuit of justice and the common good, through (2) the rule of law, under (3) a mixed and balanced government, comprising (4) a sovereign people, (5) a deliberative senate and (6) an elected magistracy. Americans in every faction endorsed this basic conception of republican government and the patrician vision of (7) ordered liberty and (8) public virtue it sought to preserve.'[18] The experience of ancient Greece, too, weighed heavily. Alexander Hamilton was dazzled by the 'bright talents and exalted endowments' of ancient Greece, and his eulogist, Fisher Ames, believed that 'the glory of Greece is imperishable.' It would last as long, Ames thought, 'as learning itself, which is its monument; it strikes an everlasting root, and bears perennial blossoms on its grave.'[19]

But the experiences of Greece and Rome brought forth examples not only to be emulated but also to be shunned. 'It is impossible,' remarked Hamilton, 'to read the history of the petty republics of Greece and Italy without feeling sensations of horror and disgust at the distractions with which they were continually agitated, and at the rapid succession of revolutions by which they were kept in a state of perpetual vibration between the extremes of tyranny and anarchy.'[20] In Greece, the 'want of a solid fœderal union to restrain the ambition and rivalship of the different cities [had ended,] after a rapid succession of bloody wars ... in their total loss of liberty and subjugation to foreign powers.'[21]

Rome, by contrast, was a case study of the perils of conquest and the thirst for imperial and despotic rule over distant provinces. All throughout the American Revolution the charge had been rung against Great Britain that its aspirations for the colonies were equivalent to Rome's for those 'plundered and spoiled' provinces conquered in the 'one hundred years before Caesar's dictatorship' – an experience which suggested to the eighteenth-century mind that 'though free governments have been commonly the most happy, for those who partake of their freedom, yet are they the most ruinous and oppressive to *their provinces.*'[22] Antifederalists rang the same charge in the debates over the Constitution. It required no great imagination to trace the connection between great size and despotism, to see why empire meant both the exploitation of subjects and the loss of republican liberty, to espy the fatal sequence by which Caesar had crossed the Rubicon and seized the purple. 'History furnishes no example,' wrote the eighteenth-century anti-federalist writing under the pseudonym Brutus, 'of a free republic, any thing like the extent of the United States.' Once Rome and other ancient republics grew too large, they had become 'the most tyrannical that ever existed in the world.'[23]

Greece and Rome thus entered the early American imagination in the form of minatory lessons regarding the consequences of international anarchy and universal empire. Greece had destroyed itself by falling victim to the forces of disintegration and anarchy; Rome had corrupted itself through territorial expansion and military conquest. 'Greece,' as one senator expressed the prevailing consensus, 'was destroyed by division, and Rome by consolidation.' He urged America to 'profit by their example; lest, in our zeal to perform what we cannot accomplish, we one day become what Greece and Rome now are.'[24] Americans had profited by their example by constructing a federal union that was to combine the advantages of a wide-ranging empire, one that ensured peace and order over an extended territory, with the liberty and independence of the small republic. Jefferson's reference to an 'empire of liberty' reflected this search for a form of government that would represent an elaborate counterpoise between the forces of decentralization and those of centralization, or anarchy and empire.

That elaborate construction, of course, proved impossible to maintain, and the American Civil War brought the realization of Jefferson's fear, expressed in 1821, that the United States, sundered between North and South, would see a revival of the Athenian and Lacedemonian confederacies, which would then 'wage another Peloponnesian war to settle the ascendancy between them.'[25] The ideological categories that informed the debate over federal union, however, did not disappear; indeed, they were given renewed expression in the debates over American foreign policy in the twentieth century. Like the American experiment in federal union, twentieth-century internationalism reflected the search for a middle path between the odious alternatives of international anarchy and universal empire. In the Atlantic community that emerged after the Second World War, such internationalism received its fullest expression. America was to lead in the creation of an international order that would frustrate bids for global domination by hostile totalitarians while at the same time suppressing the tendency towards international anarchy inherent in any system of sovereign states. The United States sought the creation of a preponderant power that would aggregate the forces of the 'peace-loving' nations into a system of collective security; and it believed that this power had to be expressed through international institutions that it would play a central role in creating. A peaceful world ordered by law, one in which offensive uses of force were categorically forbidden, was at the core of this scheme. This would represent an advance on the anarchical European system, one that in the American estimation had brought civilization very nearly to the brink of extinction in the course of two horrific world wars. In crucial respects this vision represented the rearticulation of ideals deeply embedded in the original conception of federal union, now to be instantiated on a planetary scale.

This was a grand and noble conception, capable of eliciting admiration and loyalty from others. It is only against the backdrop of this conception that one can appreciate the astonishment and near horror with which the world greeted the Bush Doctrine. For the United States, at the moment of its greatest power, to abandon the idea that power needs restraint amounted to an admission that its past declarations of fidelity to international law and international institutions had been a sort of mask disguising deeper impulses towards aggrandizement. America's allies began to think if not act in the fashion of the Mytileneans, who, as they contemplated their revolt from Athens, insisted that 'we did not become allies of the Athenians for the subjugation of the Hellenes, but allies of the Hellenes for their liberation from the Mede.'[26]

If an essential task of statecraft is to somehow realize the advantages of both empire and liberty without falling victim to either oppression or anarchy, it follows that empire – understood as the construction of a system ensuring peace and order over an extensive territory and a variety of peoples – is capable of providing essential public goods. Gibbon pronounced the experience of Rome in the Augustan age as the happiest period in the history of mankind. It was reserved for Augustus, said Gibbon, 'to relinquish the ambitious design of subduing the whole earth, and to introduce a spirit of moderation into the public councils.' Rome, Augustus appreciated, 'had much less to hope than to fear from the chance of arms.' In the prosecution of remote wars, 'the undertaking became every day more difficult, the event more doubtful, and the possession more precarious and less beneficial.'[27] Augustan Rome's determination to 'neither endure nor to offer an injury' must surely command admiration, as must the state of peace that resulted from this policy. But whether empire actually achieves this state of happy felicity is a contingent question. When perpetual peace is sought through perpetual war, this pleasing scene vanishes, and we are left to consider empire in its more natural and less agreeable state.

The Roman experience must also draw alarm by virtue of the relationship it shows between external aggrandizement and internal transformation – or, put differently, the effect that acquiring an empire abroad has on the empire's home.[28] That effect, perhaps more than any other, has been the one that American critics have fastened on in objecting to empire. Whatever we call the vast conglomeration of extended commitments undertaken by the United States, it is reasonable to ask what sort of effect they have had on America's domestic institutions. The classical experience suggests that they should have the effect of increasing executive power, of creating an 'imperial presidency,' and that in large measure is what has happened in the United States. It is impossible to understand the growth of presidential power in America without reference to the expansion of America's overseas commitments. So when President Eisenhower warned in his Farewell Address of the emergence of a military-industrial complex and insisted that the danger of the misuse of this power 'exists and would persist,' he was expressing a danger familiar to students of Roman history. John Calhoun identified the essential process at work in his speech opposing the acquisition of all Mexico: 'There is not an example on record of any free state holding a province of the same extent and population, without disastrous consequences. The nations conquered and held as a province, have, in time, retaliated by destroying the liberty of their conquerors, through the corrupting effect of extended patronage and irresponsible power.' It was said of Calhoun that 'it was easy to fancy, when you heard him, that you were listening to an oration from the lips of a Roman senator, who had formed his style in the severe schools of Greece.' Never more so than on this occasion. 'When the Roman power,' Calhoun warned, 'passed beyond the limits of Italy, crossed the Adriatic, the Mediterranean, and the Alps, liberty fell prostrate; the Roman people became a rabble; corruption penetrated every department of the Government; violence and anarchy ruled the day, and military despotism closed the scene.'[29]

A further illustration of this effect comes from the French analyst Emmanuel Todd, who compares the expansion of the United States after the end of the Cold War with the expansion of Rome into the Mediterranean after the defeat of Carthage: '[Rome] collected taxes or tribute throughout its empire and was able to transfer to the central capital massive quantities of foodstuffs and manufactured items. The peasants and the artisans of Italy saw their economic base disappear as this Mediterranean economy was globalized by the political domination of Rome. The society was polarized between, on the one hand, a mass of economically useless plebeians and, on the other, a predatory plutocracy ... The middle classes collapsed.'[30]

This is a disturbing parallel because globalization has undoubtedly increased returns on capital while forcing labour to compete with low-wage workers abroad, heightening the stratification of American society. That development, in turn, cannot fail to impair the republican character of America's domestic institutions, which have always been seen to rest upon the existence of a strong and vibrant middle class. For reasons not unlike those witnessed in Roman times, that middle class is becoming increasingly eviscerated.

These admonitions from Roman history suggest that the widespread evocation of America as a new Rome is to be received with decided ambivalence. For the Roman experience suggests that empire threatens the republic and that it may do so even if republican institutional forms continue in place – a phenomenon conveyed in Gibbon's description of Rome under Augustus as an 'absolute monarchy disguised by the forms of a commonwealth.' If, at its best, empire provides the basis for peace and order over expansive territories, uniting in a single system peoples who might otherwise be at one another's throats, at its worst it is a destroyer of republics and a breeder of desolation in the zones of violence that exist on its periphery. It makes an anarchy and calls it peace.[31] In early America, the experience of ancient Greece in the time of the Peloponnesian Wars had relevance because it suggested the vital necessity for union among the now independent American states. In the absence of union, the historical record suggested, America would fall prey to foreign ambition and conquest. That is a lesson not without relevance for our own day; for the internal division of Western civilization, especially if it were to lead to a fundamental split between Europe and America, does suggest an ominous future. But it is not that aspect of ancient history which excites the modern American imagination so much as the parallel between America and Athens. Athens secured its stature in the international system by virtue of its heroic victory over the Persian invader; it then established itself as the hegemonic leader of the Delian League – a sort of North Aegean Treaty Organization. Athens declared, as Americans have done, that by virtue of its power 'men in all places ... who either fear or plan aggression, from the near prospect before them, in the one case, of obtaining our intervention in their favor, in the other, of our arrival making the venture dangerous, find themselves constrained, respectively, to be moderate against their will, and to be preserved without effort of their own.'[32] With its rich cultural life and democratic institutions, Athens was the 'school of Hellas,' as Pericles said.[33] Of all the states of the ancient Greek world, it was Athens that most approximated modern ideas of liberty.[34] It was 'more like us' than any of the others, so the question arises: Are we on a similar path?

America, like Athens, established its legitimacy in the international system by virtue of heroic victories over despotic powers. Since then its conduct has suggested a shift – especially from the perspective of its allies – from hegemonic leadership towards oppressive empire. At the very least, the Iraq War bears an uncomfortable resemblance to the ill-fated Sicilian expedition. Greed for resources,[35] underestimation of the enemy,[36] credulity before the tall tales of exiles 'whose interest it is to lie as well as they can,'[37] and divided counsels at home[38] were all part the story Thucydides related. After Iraq, we may easily recognize the truth of the observation that 'it is a common mistake in going to war to begin at the wrong end, to act first, and wait for disaster to discuss the matter.'[39] After Iraq we better understand the psychological appeal of the Athenians' complaint that they were subject to a double standard on the part of their allies, who unfairly held Athens to a legal standard that they did not apply to other imperial powers. Perhaps, say the Athenians, we would have done better 'if we had from the first cast law aside and openly gratified our covetousness.'[40] It is well that Thucydides wrote his book as a possession for all time, for our time has much to ponder as it reflects on the similarities between these two imperial powers and the misbegotten enterprises on which they waste their substance.

The lessons that Thucydides sought to convey in his great work are not immediately apparent and have of course been the subject of prolonged controversy. The conventional view sees him as a 'hard realist' and assumes that the speech delivered by the Athenian generals to the Melians reflected the sort of tough-minded view that was appropriate to the combatants in a life-and-death struggle.[41] 'The strong do what they can and the weak suffer what they must.'[42] So say the Athenian generals. Yet there is little reason to assume that this view represents Thucydides' own, and much reason to think that it does not. The fact that the dialogue occurs at the end of book 5 and that book 6 opens with a consideration of the Sicilian expedition suggests a placement intended for dramatic effect, for much of what the Athenians dismiss as folly when it comes from the mouths of the Melians (we shall be saved by the gods, especially) they find themselves invoking as the Sicilian expedition turns disastrous. The reversal of fortune the Athenians experience looks suspiciously like a case of 'imperial comeuppance.'[43]

Instead of identifying Thucydides with one perspective in the eternal debate between power and justice, we might read him as saying instead that this argument between power and justice is a central and unending feature of political life and that one cannot make sense of statecraft without attending to both.[44] Certainly Thucydides recognizes that the love of power is deeply rooted in man, for in his depiction of the revolution in Corcyra he identifies that urge with the sheer anarchy of the moral life that develops as a consequence of the battles between oligarchs and democrats throughout the Greek world.[45] There can, however, be no mistaking the horror with which he views this degeneration, which he treats as the political equivalent of the plague that ravaged Athens in the second year of the war.[46] There can also be no mistaking his negative portrait of Cleon, 'the most violent man in Athens,' who urges the slaughter of the Mytileneans for their revolt against the imperial city. That Cleon calls for justice in the course of his argument shows that the appeal to justice is as capable of abuse as the appeal to power. Neither appeal can be dispensed with, as both are fundamental and point to enduring features of political life, but both by the same token may be abused.

Thucydides' view of the Athenian Empire is more difficult to make out. It would not be implausible to identify his outlook with that of Pericles, who insisted that though it may have been wrong to take the empire, it would be dangerous to let it go.[47] Thucydides' judgement of Pericles and of the strategy he recommended for prosecuting the war is a favourable one. In peace, says Thucydides, Pericles pursued a 'moderate and conservative policy' and rightly gauged the power of his country at the outbreak of the war. 'He told them to wait quietly, to attempt no new conquests, and to expose the city to no hazards during the war, and doing this, promised them a favorable result.'[48] It may convey a lesson for the present day that the Athenian *demos* proved incapable of pursuing this restrained policy but instead did the very contrary. The temptations of inordinate power proved altogether too compelling.

At the end of the day, we do not know what the ancients would have thought of the American empire, such as it is. After recovering from the shock of learning that there were such things as jet airplanes, nuclear weapons, electricity, motion pictures, and the Internet, they would no doubt marvel at the amazing constancy of moral life over the millennia. To enter the world of Thucydides' speeches is to enter our own world as well, and we find in those dialogues the same appeals, subterfuges, rhetorical tricks, self-delusions, and deep convictions that mark the ideological combat of the present day. We have our cautious generals (like Nicias), our unsentimental but humane realists (like Diodotus), and our raving ideologues (like Cleon) who are lost to the last insanities of unforgiving passion. We even have our imperial position in Iraq, which was certainly wrong to take but would undoubtedly be dangerous to let go.[49] That from these unhealthy ingredients we are going to make a good meal I sincerely doubt, but we would do well to remember, in the heat of our battles, all those things that the democrats and the oligarchs of ancient Greece forgot in prosecuting their hatreds. 'Reckless audacity came to be considered the courage of a loyal supporter, prudent hesitation, specious cowardice; moderation was held to be a cloak for unmanliness; ability to see all sides of a question incapacity to act on any. Frantic violence became the attribute of manliness; cautious plotting a justifiable means of self-defense.'[50]

NOTES

1 See especially Jennifer Tolbert Roberts, *Athens on Trial: The Antidemocratic Tradition in Western Thought* (Princeton: Princeton University Press, 1994); and J.G.A. Pocock, *Barbarism and Religion, vol. 3, The First Decline and Fall* (Cambridge: Cambridge University Press, 2003).

2 Chalmers Johnson, *The Sorrows of Empire: Militarism, Secrecy, and the End of the Republic* (New York: Metropolitan, 2004), 3.

3 Andrew J. Bacevich, *American Empire: The Realities and Consequences of U.S. Diplomacy* (Cambridge, MA: Harvard University Press, 2002), 244.

4 Niall Ferguson, *Colossus: The Price of America's Empire* (New York: Penguin, 2004), 2.

5 An exception to this rule was George Liska, *Imperial America: The International Politics of Primacy* (Baltimore: Johns Hopkins University Press, 1967).

6 Jonathan Schell, 'Tomgram: Jonathan Schell on the Empire That Fell as It Rose.' Accessed 19 August 2004 at http://www.tomdispatch.com/index.mhtml?pid=1691

7 Philip Zelikow, 'The Transformation of National Security: Five Redefinitions,' *National Interest* 71 (Spring 2003): 18–19.

8 Victor Davis Hanson, 'Cracked Icons: Why the Left Has Lost Credibility,' National Review Online, 17 December 2004.

9 See J. William Fulbright with Seth P. Tillman, *The Price of Empire* (New York: Pantheon, 1989).

10 Ronald Steel, 'Totem and Taboo,' *The Nation*, 2 September 2004.

11 Fred Anderson and Andrew Cayton, *The Dominion of War: Empire and Liberty in North America, 1500-2000* (New York: Viking, 2005).

12 *Register of Debates in Congress...*, 21st Congress, 1st Session (Washington: Gales and Seaton, 1825–1837), VI:994–1016 at 998.

13 Cited in John Judis, *The Folly of Empire: What George W. Bush Could Learn from Theodore Roosevelt and Woodrow Wilson* (New York: Scribner, 2004), 41–2.

14 Schell, 'Tomgram.'

15 Gregg Easterbrook, cited in Andrew Bacevich, *The New American Militarism: How Americans Are Seduced by War* (New York: Oxford University Press, 2005), 1.

16 Charles Krauthammer, 'Universal Dominion,' in *America's Purpose: New Visions of U.S. Foreign Policy,* ed. Owen Harries (San Francisco: ICS, 1991), 13.

17 Frederick Gentz, *On the State of Europe Before and After the French Revolution* (London: Hatchard, 1802).

18 Mortimer N.S. Sellers, *American Republicanism: Roman Ideology in the United States Constitution* (New York: NYU Press, 1994), 6.

19 Fisher Ames, 'A Sketch of the Character of Alexander Hamilton,' in *The Works of Fisher Ames,* vol. 2, ed. Seth Ames (Boston: Little, Brown, 1854), 263.

20 Alexander Hamilton, 'Federalist no. 9,' in *The Federalist,* ed. Jacob E. Cooke (Middletown: Wesleyan University Press, 1982), 50.

21 Alexander Hamilton, *Continentalist* no. 1, 12 July 1781, in *The Papers of Alexander Hamilton,* ed. Harold S. Syrett and Jacob E. Cooke (New York: Columbia University Press, 1961), vol. 1, 651–2. In describing the movement towards the Philadelphia Convention, Jefferson noted that, were the American states to be 'sovereign and independent in all things, [these] separate independencies, like the petty States of Greece, would be eternally at war with each other, & would become at length the mere partisans & satellites of the leading powers of Europe. All then must have looked forward to some further bond of union, which would ensure internal peace, and a political system of our own, independent of that of Europe.' 'The Anas. 1791-1806,' 4 February 1818, in Merrill Peterson, ed., *Jefferson Writings* (New York: Library of America, 1984), 663. The Founders, in the later summary of Rufus Choate, discerned 'perfectly that unless the doom of man was to be reserved for them, there was no alternative but to become dearest friends or bitterest enemies, – so much Thucydides and the historians of the beautiful and miserable Italian republics of the Middle Age had taught them.' See 'On the Preservation of the Union,' in *The Works of Rufus Choate,* ed. Samuel Gilman Brown (Boston: Little, Brown, 1862), vol. 2, 323.

22 John Witherspoon's Speech in Congress, in *Letters of Delegates to Congress, 1774–1789,* vol. 4, ed. Paul H. Smith (Washington: 1976–81), 585; David Hume, 'That Politics May be Reduced to a Science,' in *Essays and Treatise on several subjects* (printed for J. Jones, 1822), 14.

23 Brutus and other writers are cited in Sellers, *American Republicanism,* 156.

24 *Annals of Congress,* 16th Congress, 1st Session, Senate, 1 February 1820.

25 Jefferson to John Adams, 22 January 1821, *The Adams-Jefferson Letters: The Complete Correspondence between Thomas Jefferson and Abigail and John Adams,* ed. Lester J. Cappon (Chapel Hill: University of North Carolina Press, 1959), 570.

26 Thucydides, *The History of the Peloponnesian War*, 3.10.3. Cf. also 6.76.4.
27 Edward Gibbon, *The Decline and Fall of the Roman Empire*, ed. Henry Hart Milman (New York: Peter Fenelon Collier, 1900), vol. 1, 18.
28 This distinction is explored in Charles S. Maier, *Among Empires: American Ascendancy and Its Predecessors* (Cambridge, MA: Harvard University Press, 2006).
29 John C. Calhoun, 'Speech on Mexican Cession,' in *The Works of John C. Calhoun*, ed. Richard Crallé (New York: Appleton & Co., 1861), vol. 4, 411–12.
30 Emmanuel Todd, *After the Empire: The Breakdown of American Order* (New York: Columbia University Press, 2003), 62.
31 On this theme, see Amy Kaplan, *Anarchy of Empire in the Making of U.S. Culture* (Cambridge, MA: Harvard University Press, 2003).
32 Thucydides, *History*, 6.87.4.
33 Ibid., 2.41.1.
34 A point emphasized in Benjamin Constant, 'The Liberty of the Ancients Compared with That of the Moderns,' in *Benjamin Constant: Political Writings*, ed. Biancamaria Fontana (Cambridge: Cambridge University Press, 1988), 312.
35 Thucydides, *History*, 6.24.
36 Ibid., 6.17.
37 Ibid., 6.12. Cf. 6.46.
38 Ibid., 2.65.
39 Ibid., 1.78.3. Cf. 6.24.4.
40 Ibid., 1.76.4 & 1.77.
41 See, for example, Michael Walzer, *Just and Unjust Wars: A Moral Argument with Historical Illustrations* (New York: Basic, 1977).
42 Thucydides, *History*, 5.89.
43 Ibid., 5.104, 7.77.3–4. See further Daniel Mendelsohn, 'Theaters of War,' *The New Yorker*, 12 January 2004.
44 See the revealing discussion in Thomas Pangle and Peter Ahrensdorf, *Justice among Nation: On the Moral Basis of Power and Peace* (Lawrence: University Press of Kansas, 1999).
45 Thucydides, *History*, 3.82.8.
46 Ibid. Cf. 3.82–4 with 2.53.
47 Ibid., 2.63.2.
48 Ibid., 2.65.5–7.
49 Cf. ibid., 2.63.2.
50 Ibid., 3.82.4.

2 Democracy and Empire: The Case of Athens

LAURIE M. JOHNSON BAGBY

Old and New Questions

American democracy has often been compared to Athenian democracy, both favourably and unfavourably.[1] Many authors, for instance, have claimed that Athenian democracy provided more opportunities for genuine participation and a deeper meaning for citizenship than modern democracy. Hannah Arendt, in *On Revolution*, cited ancient democracy as the inspiration for the American and French revolutions.[2] Others, like Saxonhouse, have pointed out that there has been a tendency to view Athenian democracy in an idealized way, ignoring its many 'internal contradictions.'[3] Others suggest that ancient democracy did not have much influence on modern democracies and perhaps even had a negative influence. Hansen writes that 'in the 18th century, when the classical tradition was a strong element in the creation of public opinion, the tradition of Athenian democracy did not count for much. The ancient democracy referred to was the general type critically described by Plato and Aristotle.'[4]

Most recently, international-relations scholars have tried to discern the effects of democratic governance on war and peace in ancient Greece, with a particular eye to the behaviour of the Athenian democracy during the Peloponnesian War. Some have tried to argue that the experience of ancient Greek democracies upholds democratic peace theory, while others are more dubious but still hopeful that a general inclination towards peace can be found there.[5] Political theorists and classical scholars have weighed in on the other side, arguing that there was plenty of conflict among democracies in the ancient world and that international-relations scholars have either missed important historical

facts or defined the terms 'democracy' and 'war' too narrowly in an effort to avoid unwanted conclusions. For instance, Harvard professor
Eric Robinson, a classical historian, says of Russett and Antholis's work
that 'the authors' own quantitative data of Peloponnesian war–era conflicts shows, if anything, that ancient democracies were *more* likely to
war with each other than other governments; and the non-quantitative
testimony does little more than illustrate occasional cooperation between democracies and/or struggling democratic groups in the context
of Athenian imperial ambitions. Wars among probable democracies in
fifth century Sicily further weaken the proposition.'[6]

Robinson's work is convincing – there seems little choice but to acknowledge that ancient democracies generally did not behave towards
one another in smooth agreement with democratic peace theory. But
this does not mean the theory is necessarily weaker for this acknowledgment, because in some very important ways, ancient Athens was
far different from modern America. In this chapter I want to explore
what made Athens so different from America, through the focal point
of empire. While territorial imperialism seemed perfectly compatible
with democracy in ancient Greece, it seems both logically and politically incompatible with modern democracies – so much so that many
scholars have become convinced that the democratic regime type is the
answer to the perennial human problem of war.

First, I will briefly discuss some basic differences between ancient
and modern democracies that perhaps factor into the change in attitude
that made empire so attractive to ancient democracies and so loath-
some a proposition to modern ones. Second, I will discuss in depth
some important evidence from Thucydides' *History of the Peloponnesian
War* that might help untangle the difference in attitude regarding the
compatibility between democracy and empire. Finally, I will make some
tentative conclusions as well as some suggestions for future research.

Democracies Ancient and Modern

Some of the differences between ancient and modern democracies are
not hard to detect. We can begin to discern these differences simply by
reminding ourselves of the position of the great political philosophers
of the ancient world with regard to democracy. As Ober puts it, 'the classical theorists supposed that the democracy they experienced in Athens
was real, but undesirable; many modern democratic theorists assume
that a strong, vibrant, participatory, directly democratic political culture

is desirable in principle, but that no such culture has ever existed for long – and certainly not in the Athens of Thucydides, Plato, and Aristotle.[7]

While modern theorists may not agree that the common citizens really ruled in democratic Athens, the American founders assumed they did, and like Plato and Aristotle, they were not impressed. Quoting Federalist 14, Wolin writes: 'American democracy has always been dogged by a so-called Founding whose Fathers never intended a democracy and were scathing in their opinion of "the turbulent democracies of ancient Greece"' (and Madison adds "modern Italy"). The Federalists knew well that the ancient model was not good enough at producing stability and power in a nation to suit their needs. They pointed out the defects of these democracies by pointing first of all to their particular system of democratic decision making.

Athens, to which they looked most often for examples from the ancient world, was a direct democracy. This was made possible by its relative smallness: it probably had a total population of somewhere between 200,000 and 300,000.[8] Out of this number there were no more than 30,000 male citizens, and of these, around 6,000 to 8,000 participated in the assembly at any given time.[9] In Athens' democratic system, every male citizen could come to the assembly, listen to speeches, and cast his vote on whether to make war or sue for peace, whether to raise or lower taxes, whether to finance a construction project. This gave the citizens enormous power. But – as Thucydides himself points out, along with Plato, Aristotle, and other ancient commentators – this enormous power of the populace gave even more power, in practice, to demagogues. Madison opined in Federalist 55: 'Had every Athenian citizen been a Socrates; every Athenian assembly would still have been a mob.' Similarly, Hamilton wrote of two dangers: zeal for the rights of the people versus zeal for the firmness of government; and he showed that he had learned his ancient history well: 'History will teach us, that the former has been found a much more certain road to the introduction of despotism than the latter, and that of those men who have overturned the liberties of republics the greatest number have begun their careers by paying an obsequious court to the people, commencing Demagogues, and ending Tyrants.'[10]

A second and related characteristic of ancient democracies, which the Founders hoped to avoid, was their volatility and short-sightedness.[11] Hamilton again, pointing out the tendency of popular assemblies to 'rage, resentment, jealousy, avarice, and of other irregular and violent propensities,' questioned the view that mutual commerce softened such regimes' warlike tendencies.[12] As Thucydides points out on many occasions, the Athenian *demos* was very likely to change its mind quickly, and on the most important of subjects. When early in the war the Spartans ravaged the Athenian countryside, Pericles, till then respected as a kingly figure, was blamed, and his reputation plummeted: 'Pericles was the object of general indignation; his previous counsels were totally forgotten; he was abused for not leading out the army which he commanded, and was made responsible for the whole of the public suffering.'[13] Much later in the war the Athenians were convinced by the rhetorician Cleon to destroy the town of Mytilene as a punishment for its revolt. They ordered their generals to kill all the men in the town and to enslave its women and children. But the next day they rescinded the order when another speaker, Diodotus, came forward and convinced them that such action would not be prudent. Madison noted that this volatility was so characteristic of democratic governments that there were moments – especially during times of regime formation or reformation – when the leadership of one with 'indefinite powers' such as Draco or Solon (or Pericles) was an absolute necessity.[14]

A third distinct difference between ancient and modern democracies has to do with the liberal concept of individual rights. There was no such concept in ancient democracies. It is true that modern liberal democracies at first did not grant some or all rights to certain groups – such as women, Jews, Catholics, Muslims, African slaves, and so on, depending on the time and place; the point here is that the logic of liberal-democratic thought did not justify such discrimination. As a result, liberal ideology has been used successfully to eliminate discrimination against various groups over time. In contrast, there seemed to be no conflict in ancient democracies between equal political participation for male citizens and the total exclusion of women from the political process. Moreover, slavery thrived in Athens and throughout the Greek world, and similarly posed no ideological contradiction for those who advocated democracy. Indeed, some have argued that ancient democracy *relied* upon slavery (and imperial tribute) to provide the leisure and learning necessary for the Athenian citizens to participate in the political process.[15]

Furthermore, liberal-democratic thought supports the idea that a government's actions should be constrained by individual rights in some very important areas; there was no similar idea of limited government in ancient democracies. If a leader, such as Pericles, became unpopular, it mattered little whether or not he had committed some crime.

Whatever the majority decided could and would be done to him. So Pericles was fined and temporarily removed from command, even though the citizens themselves had previously voted for his policy. Athenians had the power to exile or even execute a citizen simply because they feared he might one day abuse his popularity, or because he was associated with some regrettable situation, or because he spoke out of turn. There was no right to free speech or religious worship or due process. This made the democracy seem more like a tyranny at times, at least for those on the receiving end of the *demos'* anger.

Athens and Empire

In addition to these general differences between ancient and modern democracies, we can look closer at how the Athenians viewed their own democracy, especially as it related to their empire. We see the Athenians justifying their empire early in the *History* during the debate at Sparta, during which the Spartans considered whether they should declare war on Athens, thus starting the war. Some Athenian envoys happened to be present. They were not there in any official capacity, but still they requested an opportunity to make Athens' case before the gathered decision makers. There they elucidated the famous 'Athenian thesis' that justified their imperialism: 'It was under the compulsion of circumstances that we were driven at first to advance our empire to its present state, influenced chiefly by fear, then by honour also, and lastly by self-interest as well.'[16] The circumstances to which they referred were those of the Persian War. The Spartans had led the defence of Greece against the Persian invasion, but weakened in their resolve towards the end of the war and were not willing to maintain the Greek alliance. They willingly ceded their position to their then-ally Athens.

The famous Athenian thesis puts forward three seemingly coequal reasons for empire: fear, honour, and interest. Yet at various points in the *History*, one or two of these reasons are emphasized and one or two are downplayed. Here I will focus on two seemingly competing reasons for empire, both of which are offered by Athenian spokesmen in the *History* at different times. One reason is that the empire is a tyranny that the Athenians sought owing to natural *self-interest* and that they now cannot afford to let go out of *fear*. The reasons of interest and fear are often coupled. The other competing reason is that the empire was sought owing to the Athenians' desire for *honour or glory*, a desire which outstripped that of their rival, Sparta. Glory is to be found not in shrink-ing from empire but in maintaining and expanding it. I will argue that the latter motivation more accurately describes what drove democratic Athens to become an imperial power and to keep on expanding. This desire for glory was so great among the Athenians that they totally dis-regarded similarities in political ideology that today seem to restrain democracies from attacking one another.

As we have seen, the Athenian envoys who happened to be at the Spartan war conference contended that Athens had naturally filled the void left when Sparta vacated the leadership of the alliance near the end of the Persian War.[17] They depicted this move (sanctioned at the time by Sparta), and the subsequent build-up of Athenian fortifications and naval power (not so sanctioned), as totally consistent with human na-ture and therefore as blameless. They depicted the allies as ungrateful for the protection that Athens provided, and they defended their less than democratic style of ruling over the allies by pointing out that people always become less satisfied the more kindly they are treated. In effect, they were admitting that at this point Athens was ruling over the allies as an imperial power. But they also argued that Athens ruled less aggressively than she might – that her empire was a gentle one in which, for instance, the allies had the same access to the Athenian judicial sys-tem as Athenian citizens themselves.[18]

Athens had relieved its allies of the responsibility of directly de-fending themselves. All they had to do in return was pay tribute to fund Athens' great military force. Of course, this would render the allies unable to defend themselves against Athens, but they were be-ing given the choice. Notwithstanding their nod to gentleness and liberality with their allies, their main message was that they were compelled to pursue power and that they were not to be blamed for taking as much as they could – anyone would. In this way the Athenian envoys were introducing the idea that the empire was a kind of tyr-anny, though they did not use that word. In 1986, Clifford Orwin wrote: 'The Athenians' presentation of their empire is without preced-ent or sequel. Unlike the Soviet Union, they do not deny that an em-pire is what they are. Nor, unlike those of the last century, do they claim that their rule is better for their subjects than freedom would be. They concede both that they rule, and that their concern for their sub-jects' good lags well behind their zeal for their own ... They admit to ruling, without asserting a right to rule. It is in this that their amazing boldness consists.'[19]

But it was the Corinthians who had spoken first at the war conference, suggesting to the Spartan leaders that the peculiar Athenian character was to blame. They made the case that the Athenians were motivated by an outsized desire to obtain more and more. They were restless, ambitious, brave, and daring.[20] Clearly, the Corinthians viewed the Athenians as glory seekers; yet they did not blame the Athenians for this – instead they blamed the Spartans for standing by and allowing the Athenians to have gotten this far without challenge. In the view of the Corinthians, then, Athens was not compelled by fear or interest. Rather, the Athenians desired glory and had the habits and frame of mind to boldly pursue their desires. In such circumstances a prudent power must try to stop them.

So even as the war began, we see these two points of view about the Athenian empire: (1) it was a sort of tyranny gotten because of interest, which then had to be maintained out of fear of the allies' revenge; and (2) it might very well have been a tyranny in the eyes of the subject states, but it was gotten for the sake of glory and so it was reasonable for the Athenians to maintain and expand it for the sake of glory. The question before us is not whether Athens' empire was a tyranny or not, but which vision of empire inspired the Athenians to maintain it, fight for it, and even grasp at more of it in Sicily. Was it the idea that tyranny was good for many useful things such as tribute and slaves, as well as dangerous to let go, but lacking any more elevated value? Or was it the idea that empire was a thing of beauty, something to be admired because it expressed the best parts of the Athenian character – boundless energy, ambition, and courage?

Pericles

Pericles was the first speaker in the *History* to use the word tyranny to describe Athenian power over the allies. But he did not make this claim until his third and final speech recorded in the *History*. In his first speech he compared the Spartan and Athenian national characters as the Corinthians had. He declared his confidence in Athens' political system, its military, and its hold on its empire. He bolstered the Athenians' confidence, in effect telling his listeners that the only thing they had to fear was their own mistakes, not the enemy's aggression.[21] He also reminded them that their navy was their most important possession and that they should be willing to give up everything else if necessary because their navy could, in effect, win it back. Finally, he outlined his war strategy, which was to bring the Athenians in the surrounding countryside within the city walls; instead of defending Athenian territory, he would use the navy to defeat the Spartans where they were most vulnerable.[22]

It was in his second recorded speech, the famed Funeral Oration, that Pericles emphasized the glory of Athens and her empire – at the expense of any description of the dead soldiers he was ostensibly there to eulogize. Pericles emphasized the glory of the Athenian regime, both its democratic processes and its democratic culture. Athens was a place where equality reigned alongside meritocracy; its citizens were tolerant and kind and, most important, equal. Athens' military strength came not from long training and discipline, as did the Spartans', but from the raw, native courage of its people.[23] He urged the citizens to be wholly absorbed in the glory of their city; to even become like erotic lovers whose beloved was Athens; to become great by sharing in her greatness, as did the fallen soldiers. 'You must daily fix your gaze upon the power of Athens,' he told them, 'and become lovers of her, and when the vision of her greatness has inspired you, reflect that all this has been acquired by men of courage who knew their duty and in the hour of conflict were moved by a high sense of honour, who, if ever they failed in any enterprise, were resolved that at least their country should not find herself deserted by their valour, but freely sacrificed to her the fairest offering it was in their power to give.'[24]

Also in his Funeral Oration, Pericles made a somewhat similar appeal to the allies (based on Athens' glory), when he argued that there was no shame in being subjected by the very best of cities.[25] Athens, he said, was the school of Hellas, an example for all others, not only then but forever. He even went so far as to say that Athens needed no poet like Homer to tell of her deeds and make them greater – Athens' deeds would stand on their own, through the lasting evidence of what she accomplished.[26] Clearly, Pericles was appealing to the people on the basis of their desire and admiration for fame, and not their fear or self-interest: 'For the love of honour alone is untouched by age, and when one comes to the ineffectual period of life it is not "gain" as some say, that gives the greater satisfaction, but honour.'[27]

Thus in the Funeral Oration, Pericles was pointing to the pursuit of glory as the chief characteristic of Athenians and as the chief motivation for engaging in war with Sparta. But in his third and final recorded speech – by which time he was temporarily on the outs as a result of military setbacks – he resorted to a new strategy for motivating his fellow citizens to stay the course. He scolded the people for being fickle

with him, and then he told them bluntly that their empire was a tyranny: 'From this empire, however, it is too late for you even to withdraw, if any one at the present crisis, through fear and shrinking from
action does indeed seek thus to play the honest man; for by this time
the empire you hold is a tyranny, which it may seem wrong to have assumed, but which certainly it is dangerous to let go.'[28]

They must continue to fight out of fear of what the allies – whom he
now assumed resented Athenian rule deeply (instead of sharing in its
glory as he had suggested they would in the Funeral Oration) – would
do to Athens if it ever loosened its grip on power. But he combined this
sobering message with yet another appeal to glory. He reminded them
of their greatness and urged them to bear their current burdens for the
sake of their great reputation.[29] He reminded them of their great navy
– even if they lost all their land they would still have this greatest of all
sources of power, through which they could win everything back. These
appeals were meant to remind the Athenians of their great deeds during the Persian War.[30] Yes, they might be hated by those over whom
they rule, but they would also be remembered for all time for what they
had achieved, thus obtaining the glory that Pericles assumed they still
craved: 'The memory of this greatness, even should we now at last give
way a little – for it is the nature of all things to decay as well as to grow
– will be left to posterity forever, how that we of all Hellenes held sway
over the greatest number of Hellenes, in the greatest wars held out
against our foes whether united or single, and inhabited a city that was
the richest in all things and the greatest.'[31]

Pericles' appeals worked – the Athenians stopped thinking about coming to terms with Sparta and resolved to continue the fight. They did fine
Pericles, but then they repented and made him their chief general again.
Obviously, Pericles had inspired them, and he did so not by stirring fear
or even prudence in them but by reviving their ambition and their sense
of self-importance – their glory and their potential to pursue more.

It is clear that Thucydides found Pericles' sort of leadership problematic. Pericles was able to use passionate rhetoric to obtain cooperation from
the Athenians for a rather moderate war strategy aimed at eventually defeating the Spartans. But after his death from the plague, future Athenian
leaders used similar appeals to make the Athenians immoderate and rash.
In a rare intervention into the narrative,[32] Thucydides wrote:

> But the successors of Pericles, being more on an equality with one another
> and yet striving each to be first, were ready to surrender to the people even

the conduct of public affairs to suit their whims. And from this, since it happened in a great and imperial state, there resulted many blunders, especially the Sicilian expedition, which was not so much an error of judgment, when we consider the enemy they went against, as of management; for those who were responsible for it, instead of taking additional measures for the proper support of the first troops which were sent out, gave themselves over to personal intrigues for the sake of gaining the popular leadership and consequently not only conducted the military operations with less rigour, but also brought about, for the first time, civil discord at home.[33]

Cleon and Diodotus

The idea of the empire as a tyranny was used explicitly again by Cleon during the debate with Diodotus over the fate of Mytilene. The Mytileneans were allies of Athens and were as independent as allies could be. Theirs was one of the few cities allied with Athens that still had its own fleet, and it was unlikely that the Athenians would have sought to subdue Mytilene, at least as long as the war with Sparta was on. They were ruled by an oligarchy, which decided to revolt against Athens, hoping to take advantage of the current instability and to shake off the yoke of Athenian imperialism by siding with Sparta. Unfortunately for the Mytileneans, Sparta did not come to their aid in time and the Athenians were able to defeat them. What price would they pay for their revolt? At first, swayed by Cleon, the Athenians voted to do the worst – to kill the prisoners who had been brought back to Athens, and to kill all the men and to enslave the women and children of Mytilene. But the next day they wavered, and held another assembly to hear more arguments for and against.

Cleon spoke first, appealing to the Athenians' anger and sense of justice – after all, the Mytileneans' rebellion had been unprovoked. Indeed, he characterized the Mytileneans' actions as aggression towards Athens, not rebellion at all. They had to be punished severely, both because they deserved it and to set an example for other cities that might be thinking of imitating them. It is interesting that both speakers (Cleon and Diodotus) described Athens as fit to rule the empire because it was a democracy, thus addressing to a certain extent the concerns of today's democratic peace theorists. In an effort to get the Athenians angry at themselves, Cleon said that Athenian democracy seemed incapable of ruling other cities effectively precisely *because* it was a democracy. He pointed out that democracy encouraged decision making by popularity contest. But his more serious criticism had to do with the type of thinking the democratic regime encouraged in its citizens. He argued that because of their democratic nature, the Athenians wanted to treat their allies the way they treated one another (something the Athenians at the Spartan war conference had earlier boasted about instead of bemoaning). 'On many other occasions in the past,' Cleon told them, 'I have realized that a democracy is incompetent to govern others, but more than ever to-day, when I observe your change of heart concerning the Mytileneans. The fact is that, because your daily life is unaffected by fear and intrigue in your relations to each other, you have the same attitude towards your allies also, and you forget that whenever you are led into error by their representatives or yield out of pity, your weakness involves you in danger and does not win the gratitude of your allies.'[34]

They had forgotten, apparently, what Pericles had earlier told them: that their empire was 'a despotism' and that the allies obeyed Athens because she could force them to, not because they admired her.[35] In this, Cleon was connecting the concept of tyranny with fear of the allies, just as Pericles had done in his third speech. Even if the death sentence they had imposed on Mytilene was unjust, they must still render it. To strike fear into other resentful allies, the Athenians must be harsh: they must rule like tyrants or be destroyed by the many who chafe under their tyranny. Diodotus, too, pointed out the weaknesses of democratic decision making. He noted that the people were likely to punish the bearer of news they needed to hear instead of thanking and rewarding them.[36] He did not reflect, as Cleon had, on whether a democracy is capable of holding an empire at all, but he did call into question how long it could continue to make good decisions, since good decisions seemed to rest on a supply of good leaders rather than the judgement of the people. Indeed, he declared that a speaker who really wanted to do the Athenians some good had to engage in deception: 'And it has come to such a pass that good advice frankly given is regarded with just as much suspicion as the bad, and that, in consequence, a speaker who wants to carry the most dangerous measures must resort to deceit in order to win the people to his views, precisely as the man whose proposals are good must lie in order to be believed.'[37]

Whereas Cleon accused the Athenians of being too soft because of their democratic ideology, Diodotus pointed to the inherent instability of democratic decision making, which could lead to bad decisions and the erosion of imperial power.

Though Cleon lost the debate, Diodotus had been unable to refute his contention that the empire was a tyranny. Indeed, much of what Diodotus said supported that impression, though he did not come right out and say so. Diodotus argued that imposing death on the Mytileneans would not deter any other city from revolting because human beings make these decisions with the confidence that they will succeed even where many others have failed. Diodotus emphasized the power of hope, or what might be called wishful thinking. He presented this way of thinking as unavoidable:

> Men are lured into hazardous enterprises by the constraint of poverty, which makes them bold, by the insolence and pride of affluence, which makes them greedy, and by the various passions engendered in the other conditions of human life as these are severally mastered by some mighty and irresistible impulse. Then, too, Hope and Desire are everywhere; Desire leads, Hope attends; Desire contrives the plan, Hope suggests the facility of fortune; the two passions are the most baneful, and being unseen phantoms prevail over seen dangers.[38]

Diodotus characterized Cleon's argument as about strict justice, whereas his own argument was about what was expedient, regardless of justice. He argued that the Athenians should choose the route that would benefit them the most in the future, even if it was not the most strictly just. So he recommended that only the oligarchs who had started the revolt be put to death and that the Mytilenean *demos*, who had surrendered to Athens when they got the chance, should not be punished. In this way, future rebels would be encouraged to lay down their arms quickly once they knew they could not succeed. Thus, Diodotus' proposal at one and the same time fulfilled the requirements of expediency and, less noticeably, fulfilled the requirements of justice better than Cleon's proposal – only the truly guilty would be punished. This recommendation comported better with the Athenians' sense to begin with: that their initial decision to punish all the Mytileneans had been too harsh. It gave the Athenians rhetorical cover for doing what they wanted to do in the first place.

Because of this rhetorical strategy, Diodotus is an intriguing figure in the *History* – one who does not fit neatly into any category. But it is safe to say that he characterized Athens' empire as a tyranny even if he did not use that term. Indeed, he argued that Athens needed to become *more* tyrannical in order to avoid future rebellions. Instead of punishing harshly after the fact, Athens should keep such a tight hold on its allies that none of them would dream of revolting in the first place. This was nothing if not admitting that Athens was a tyranny. It is impossible to know how much of this claim was rhetorical strategy and how much Diodotus thought it to be true. But clearly, he thought that at this time the Athenians could be moved more easily to make a good decision by an appeal that acknowledged the tyrannical nature of their empire rather than its noble or glorious side. He did not flatter the Athenians by telling them they were so powerful that they could afford to be more just than they had to be. He did not dwell on their generous character the way that Pericles often had. Instead he acknowledged the dark side of Athenian rule and advised how best to deal with it – saving, at least in this instance, a by-product of justice in the process.

The Sicilian Expedition

Having considered the rhetoric involved in persuading the Athenians during the Mytilenean debate, can we conclude that the possibility of imperial glory that the Athenians entertained in the early years of the war had been destroyed by the harsh necessities of war and could not have motivated the Athenians later? We cannot say this, because the Athenians' future endeavours were not simply efforts to keep their current empire in line and defeat the Spartans. Rather, those efforts were attempts to grasp for more empire even before defeating Sparta. It would seem that the Athenians were persuaded to pursue this additional conquest over democratic regimes in Sicily solely out of a desire for more glory. This overwhelming desire led them to overestimate their capabilities and underestimate their enemies' capacity to unite and fight back. It is in his analysis of the decision to go to Sicily that Thucydides' own view of the wisdom of Athenian ambition comes through most clearly. In his view, the Athenians were urged on by leaders desirous of personal glory who used the appeal to fame to capture the imaginations of the people. He seems to conclude that the Athenians gave in to their worst tendencies and that with better leadership they might have steered a more prudent course. To fully understand his conclusions, we need to cover some of the events that led up to the expedition.

In 425 BCE Athens achieved an unexpected and largely accidental victory that offered them a chance for peace with Sparta on highly favourable terms. A small Athenian fleet of twenty ships was on the way to Sicily to help the small city of Leontine against Syracuse. The fleet was put to use by Demosthenes, a retired Athenian general, who was granted permission to attack the Peloponnesian coast along the way.[39] He wanted to stop at Pylos in particular, but the generals in charge wanted to make their way quickly to Corcyra, which needed help as soon as possible. However, a storm blew their ships onto Pylos' shore, and the Athenian soldiers fortified the place because they had nothing else to do.[40] Much of the rest of the fleet sailed on, leaving Demosthenes with five ships to hold the place. The Spartans eventually sent ships, intending to block the channel between Pylos and the nearby island of Sphacteria, and sending soldiers to fortify the island. But Demosthenes sent word to the Athenian fleet, which returned and surrounded the island. The Spartans had not yet block-aded the channel, which meant that their soldiers were trapped on the island! This was a real blow to Sparta, because these were some of its best men. The Spartans sent ambassadors to ask for peace and alliance with Athens. But the Athenians turned them down. They 'be-lieved that, since they held the men on the island, peace could be theirs the moment they cared to make it, and meanwhile they were greedy for more.'[41]

Thucydides' treatment of this episode emphasizes the good fortune of the Athenians, who had achieved this military victory almost despite themselves. Yet when offered peace and alliance in exchange for the men on the island, they refused without much deliberation. Eventually they took Sphacteria (under the leadership of Cleon), but even this achievement is depicted by Thucydides as fortuitous.

In the meantime, Thucydides tells of the Athenians' experience in Sicily. They had sent forces there to see if they could disrupt grain ship-ments to the Peloponnese and also to investigate whether Sicily was a place they could hope to conquer in the future.[42] They enjoyed some mil-itary successes but also some failures, even after reinforcements arrived. The generals of the Athenian fleet, on hearing that Hermocrates of Syracuse had been able to unite most of the feuding cities of Sicily into an alliance against Athens, decided to return home. Back in Athens, the gen-erals gave the Athenians an honest assessment of the situation, but their warnings went unheeded. Indeed, two of the generals were exiled and a third one was fined, and all were accused of taking bribes to leave Sicily.

Clearly, the Athenians could not believe there was any force great enough to repel them or even to merit caution on their part. Even this long into the war, their characteristic self-confidence had not been shaken. In what followed, it was not appeals to fear or self-interest that won the people's attention. No one reminded the Athenians that their empire was a tyranny they should work hard to hold (or expand) to prevent it from collapsing vengefully upon them. What influenced their actions instead were appeals to their lofty image of themselves, not as paragons of justice to be sure, but definitely as that glorious and indestructible force that Pericles had extolled, unequalled in human history, capable of achieving anything.

In an effort to stop them from making the dangerous decision to invade Sicily, the general Nicias, whose negotiated peace with Sparta was soon to fall apart, did indeed try to strike fear in the Athenians. He urged them to take seriously the threat from Sicily, he described that island's enormous fleet, and he pointed out the amount of supplies it would take to ensure victory over that far-off territory. But all his argument did was inspire the Athenians to fantasize about going after this greatest and most glorious of all prizes, to wonder at the enormity of it, and to dream about the benefits that would come from it. Nicias' reminder that they needed to consolidate their peace with Sparta and their control over their empire before reaching 'out after another empire'[43] – advice that echoed Pericles' – fell on deaf ears. The Athenians were in a mood to dream about glory, despite all they had been through. Yet they had thrown away their chance to make peace with Sparta, which would have at least allowed them to venture forth to Sicily with undivided forces. It was Alcibiades who won the decision, and Alcibiades who most forcefully characterized the Athenian vision of imperial grandeur – though what he urged on the Athenians was more an extension of his own glory than that of the people.

Responding to Nicias' attack on his character, Alcibiades, a young and reckless general with whom the people had a love/hate relationship, did not shrink from his reputation. Instead he extolled his own virtues. Young, rich, and influential, he had racked up many accomplishments, such as his Olympian victories in chariot racing and his extravagant festivities. These, he argued, had brought fame and glory to himself and to his city. Alcibiades turned Pericles' appeal to the citizens to become lovers of Athens into an appeal to bask in his personal fame, which would then be Athens' fame. Similarly, Alcibiades noted that people always resented a leader such as himself because they were not his equal, but that when that leader died, everyone tried to prove an association with him.[44] Pericles had said the same thing about Athens and its empire that Alcibiades now said about his relationship with the Athenian people: everlasting glory is to be desired even if the price is for one to be resented by people and/or feared as a tyrant. Alcibiades urged the Athenians to think of the Sicilians as a weak 'mixed rabble' and to seek their fortune there:

> 'Calculating, then, that we shall rather strengthen our power here if we go over there, let us make the voyage, that we may lay low the haughty spirit of the Peloponnesians, as we shall if we let men see that in our contempt of our present peaceful condition, we even sail against Sicily; and that we may, at the same time, either acquire empire over all Hellas, as in all probability we shall, when the Hellenes there have been added to us, or may at least cripple the Syracusans, whereby both ourselves and our allies will be benefited.'[45]

In the end, the Athenians chose the Sicilian expedition out of self-confidence and the desire for more glory. Thucydides describes what was before their eyes and in their hearts when the fleet sailed: 'And the fame of the armament was noised abroad, not less because of amazement at its boldness and the splendour of the spectacle than on account of its overwhelming force as compared with those whom they were going against; and also because it was the longest voyage from home as yet attempted and undertaken with the highest hopes for the future as compared with their present resources.'[46]

Though the citizens attempted to recall Alcibiades, suspicious that he might indeed have tyrannical ambitions, they went ahead with the expedition anyway, with Nicias at the helm. As we know, the expedition failed utterly. The result was not only a crushing defeat and the destruction of most of the Athenian fleet, but also a defeat in the war with Sparta, which took advantage of Athens' stretched resources (and the traitorous Alcibiades' advice). Thucydides leaves us with two deep impressions: that love of glory can lead to implosion; and that this love motivated the Athenian democracy to keep grasping for more, even against fellow democracies in Sicily.

Conclusions

For modern advocates of liberal democracy, democracy and empire are incompatible. Such democracies are often supremely sensitive to charges of economic or cultural imperialism, because the liberal-democratic ideal of individual rights has become – at the level of states – the right to self-determination. Democratic peace theory points to liberal democracy as the answer to world conflict. But it is precisely liberal democracy – not democracy per se – that can strive to make this claim, as the example of ancient Athens shows. The Federalists understood ancient Athenian democracy mainly as an example of what to avoid – volatile and emotional decision making as an outgrowth of direct democracy and the demagoguery it breeds. They knew that in a direct democracy it is all too easy for the majority to become a tyranny and to subject minorities to its arbitrary will. They understood that the ancients lacked any notion of individual rights and any idea of limited government.

Once we understand these basic differences between ancient democracy and modern liberal democracy, it should be clear that the one justification for action on the international scene that is never used anymore – the quest for honour and glory – is precisely what moved the Athenian people to undertake empire, even the conquest of a fellow democracy. An American president who tried to justify a military action on the basis that it would bring honour and glory to this country, and prove its superiority to all other nations, would be anathematized both in America and overseas.

Galpin argues that the Athenians came to see their empire in a way that modern Americans cannot – as 'ideologically in a manner consistent with their democratic values.'[47] He argues that in a very real sense, the empire was necessary as a means to enact democratic reforms in Athens, including jury pay, 'peacetime pay for the Navy, for holding public office, for membership in the *boule*, and the Periclean building program as well as the relatively large land-redistribution programs in subject territories.'[48] Thus the empire 'was perceived to be necessary for the actual implementation of democratic values at home.'[49] Galpin also notes the power of the Athenian character – its love of power and glory. Athenians saw no contradiction between their freedom and the subjection of other territories, democratic or not:

> Many Americans today assume that personal liberty is universally held to be valuable; as a result, they do not believe, or would deny believing, that their own liberty entitles them to a free exercise of authority over others, who value their own freedom. The Athenians, however, considered that a free people should derive an advantage from liberty, that they should govern others, which was a true advantage that satisfied both pride and convenience. Freedom as a concept was limited to the political community of the polis rather than being extended into a 'national' Greek

community or a concern for freedom within political communities other than Athens.[50]

As the debate between Cleon and Diodotus shows, Athens (an ancient democracy) had a problematic relationship with empire: the people sometimes got soft-hearted and endangered their own gains; the people sometimes listened to hotheads and acted rashly against their own interests. Sometimes, perhaps, they even saw their allies too much like fellow citizens of a democracy and so did not understand they needed to rule harshly. But these limitations were not such as to discourage leaders from enticing the people to pursue glory through conquest. The Athenians were motivated to continue their fight against Sparta out of the desire for honour and glory. And this same desire is what made them launch the Sicilian expedition – an action that cannot be explained using current views of the power of democracy, unless we remember that Athenian democracy was not liberal democracy.

NOTES

1 See, for instance, Bernard Grofman, 'Lessons of Athenian Democracy: Editor's Introduction,' *PS: Political Science and Politics* 26, no. 3 (1993): 471–4, which begins an entire volume devoted to this general theme. The contributors include Sheldon Wolin and Arlene Saxonhouse.
2 Hannah Arendt, *On Revolution* (New York: Viking Press, 1963).
3 Arlene W. Saxonhouse, 'Athenian Democracy: Modern Mythmakers and Ancient Theorists,' *PS: Political Science and Politics* 26, no. 3 (1993): 2.
4 Mogens Herman Hansen, 'The Tradition of the Athenian Democracy AD 1750–1990,' *Greece and Rome* 2, no. 39 (1992): 27.
5 See, for example, Spencer Weart, *Never at War: Why Democracies Will Not Fight One Another* (New Haven: Yale University Press, 1998). Weart argues that the ancient Greek experience fully validates democratic peace theory, whereas Russett and Antholis make a more balanced case that there might have been a discernable but far from perfect tendency in ancient democracies towards seeking peace. Bruce Russett and William Antholis, 'Do Democracies Fight Each Other? Evidence from the Peloponnesian War,' *Journal of Peace Research* 29, no. 4 (1992): 415–34.
6 Eric Robinson, 'Reading and Misreading the Ancient Evidence for Democratic Peace,' *Journal of Peace Research* 38, no. 5 (2001): 605.

7 Josiah Ober, 'Public Speech and the Power of the People in Democratic Athens,' *PS: Political Science and Politics* 26, no. 3 (1993): 482.

8 The population of Athens in and around the time of the Peloponnesian War has been somewhat disputed by scholars. However, all we need is a rough idea of the number. Arnold Gomme in *The Population of Athens in the Fifth and Fourth Centuries B.C.* (Oxford: Blackwell, 1933) estimated 250,000 to 275,000. In studying the plague of Athens, Morens and Littman estimated the population at between 250,000 and 300,000. David Morens and Robert Littman, '"Thucydides Syndrome" Revisited,' *American Journal of Epidemiology* 140, no. 7 (1994): 621–8.

9 Hansen, 'The Tradition of the Athenian Democracy,' 24; Ober, 'Public Speech,' 483.

10 Alexander Hamilton, Federalist 1, *The Federalist Papers*, ed. Gary Wills (New York: Bantam, 1988), 4.

11 John Jay, Fed. 4, 14–15.

12 Hamilton, Fed. 6, 24.

13 Thucydides, *History of the Peloponnesian War*, ed. John H. Finley (New York: Modern Library, 1951), 2.21. Hamilton also cited the example of Pericles, whom he blamed for starting the Peloponnesian War in order to shore up his popularity (see Fed. 6, 22, as per notes 11 and 12).

14 James Madison, Fed. 38, 182.

15 See, for instance, Josiah Ober, *Mass and Elite in Democratic Athens: Rhetoric, Ideology, and the Power of the People* (Princeton: Princeton University Press, 1989), 20–35.

16 Thucydides, *History*, 1.75.3–4.

17 Forde argues that the experience of abandoning the defence of their homeland and placing all their hopes on their naval power gave the Athenians their uniquely daring nature: 'What the Athenians discovered as a body on their ships is the enormous potential of purely human power – that is, human power standing on its own and bereft of its traditional supports, terrestrial or otherwise.' Steven Forde, 'Thucydides on the Causes of Athenian Imperialism,' *American Political Science Review* 80, no. 2 (1986): 437.

18 Galpin provides contrary evidence: 'It seems reasonable to infer that Thucydides was portraying the Athenian courts as the Athenians often defended them, rather than as they seem to have been.' Timothy Galpin, 'The Democratic Roots of Athenian Imperialism in the Fifth Century B.C.,' *Classical Journal* 79, no. 2 (1983–4): 104. Also, Starr makes the case that we should stop admiring ancient Athens because its empire was tyrannical.

Chester Starr, 'Athens and Its Empire,' *Classical Journal* 83, no. 2 (1987–8): 114–23.

19 Clifford Orwin, 'Justifying Empire: The Speech of the Athenians at Sparta and the Problem of Justice in Thucydides,' *Journal of Politics* 48, no. 1 (1986): 75.

20 Thucydides, *History*, 1.70.1–9

21 Ibid., 1.144.1–2.

22 Ibid., 1.143.5. Palmer questions the wisdom of this policy, wondering 'whether what Pericles' strategy of sitting still in Athens demands of the Athenians ... something of which they are incapable, something that goes against the very temper of a city at war but especially against the Athenian temper.' Michael Palmer, 'Love of Glory and the Common Good,' *American Political Science Review* 76, no. 4 (1982): 826.

23 Thucydides, *History*, 2.37, 2.39.

24 Ibid., 2.43.1–2.

25 Ibid., 2.41.3.

26 Ibid., 2.41.4–5.

27 Ibid., 2.44.4.

28 Ibid., 2.43.2–3.

29 Ibid., 2.61.3–4.

30 Ibid., 2.62.

31 Ibid., 2.64.3–4.

32 For an excellent article on Thucydides' use of such interventions and how they should be understood, see David Gribble, 'Narrator Interventions in Thucydides,' *Journal of Hellenic Studies* 118 (1998): 41–67.

33 Thucydides, *History*, 2.65.10–12. 'Pericles' speeches and deeds were an important part of the political education of the Athenians, the few and the many alike. Could it be that the decline of Athenian political life had its roots in that civic education?' Palmer, 'Love of Glory,' 835.

34 Thucydides, *History*, 3.37.1–2.

35 Ibid., 3.37.3.

36 Ibid., 3.42.3–4.

37 Ibid., 3.43.2–3.

38 Ibid., 3.45.5–6.

39 Ibid., 4.2.4.

40 Ibid., 4.4.2.

41 Ibid., 4.21.2–3.

42 Ibid., 3.86.

43 Ibid., 6.10.5.

44 Ibid., 6.16.6.
45 Ibid., 6.18.4–5.
46 Ibid., 6.31.6.
47 Galpin, 'The Democratic Roots of Athenian Imperialism in the Fifth Century B.C.,' 106.
48 Ibid., 107.
49 Ibid., 108.
50 Ibid.

3 Empire by Invitation or Domination? The Difference between *Hegemonia* and *Arkhē*

DAVID EDWARD TABACHNICK

Academics and political commentators have routinely compared the Peloponnesian War between Athens and Sparta with the Cold War between the United States and the Soviet Union.[1] Despite the almost 2,500 years that separate these two events, the comparison is motivated by the belief that the history of this ancient war can help us better understand contemporary international relations and warfare. Indeed, this is the very kind of analysis that prompted Thucydides to write *The History of the Peloponnesian War*. Early in book 1 he admits that 'it will be enough for me, however, if these words of mine are judged useful by those who want to understand clearly the events which happened in the past and which (human nature being what it is) will, at some time or other and in much the same ways, be repeated in the future.'[2]

So, because of the unchanging warring nature of human beings, Thucydides' account of the conflict that gripped the Hellas for twenty-seven years between 431 and 404 BCE was written to be 'useful,' to instruct and perhaps to warn participants of future wars. In this it has lost none of its relevance with the passage of the centuries and the millennia.

But is reading his *History* really that useful? Right off the bat, we could challenge the 'realist' notion that human nature and thus the underlying cause and practice of war do not change. Idealist Enlightenment thinkers, for example, argued convincingly that violence and conflict could be mitigated or even eliminated through reason, education, and diplomacy. For them, war was a failure to pursue better options rather than a requisite of being human; it was not the unfortunate, constant reality of international relations as Thucydides suggested. Still, for all of the social advancements that followed the Enlightenment, the incidence of war in no way declined. If anything, the unprecedented violence of the twentieth century seems to have invalidated idealism and to have returned realism to its rightful place at the centre of international-relations analysis.

But another objection to the contemporary relevance of Thucydides can be raised. Even if war is inevitable and its underlying foundations constant, the war described by Thucydides differed in many obvious ways from how modern wars are fought. The development of nuclear weapons in the twentieth century has certainly changed things. The deterrent effect of nuclear weaponry is the main reason why the Americans and the Soviets fought a 'Cold' War very different from the 'hot' Peloponnesian War. Thus, while Thucydides helps us understand the dynamics of ancient Greek warfare, his *History* is no longer a useful document for understanding war today.

Yet Thucydides and his *History* still loom large in the field of international relations well after the end of the Cold War. Of late there has been particular interest in his warning about imperial hubris as it applies to the United States as the sole remaining superpower.[3] For those who make this link between Athens and America, Thucydides offers some sobering lessons – the danger of overextension and the threat of internal decay, to name two.[4] This post–Cold War application of Thucydides stands in contrast to earlier uses of his work. Besides accepting the inevitability of wars between states, the Cold War realists noted the persistent struggles of individual sovereign states seeking security for themselves. But because the United States is at this moment a unipolar power, having defeated its Spartan rival the Soviet Union, these rules no longer seem to apply. For obvious reasons, the total domination of the American empire over all other states represents something quite different from what the realists describe. Rather than a balance of power among competing states, global politics may now be characterized by the relationship between a singular superior and its many subordinates.

It remains to be seen whether the United States actually qualifies as an empire. For one thing, the whole idea of empire runs counter to the American ethos – the United States was founded on anti-imperialist principles and has historically supported the right to self-determination for peoples around the world.[5] In his contribution to this book, David Hendrickson points out that notwithstanding these stated founding principles, America has a long history of territorial expansion that at least suggests it *had* imperialistic tendencies (e.g., the 1898 takeover of the former Spanish colonies of the Philippines, Guam, and Puerto Rico).

More recent history suggests that American policies changed in the second half of the twentieth century. While the U.S. military regularly attacked and occupied various countries (or portions thereof) during the Cold War, it no longer annexed territory, which is what traditional empires do. But now, in the post–Cold War era, the United States may once again be an empire. The rise of a *Pax Americana* is something often talked about on both the right and the left; perhaps it is the one thing on which the neoconservative columnist Charles Krauthammer and the anarchist Noam Chomsky can agree.

Whether the United States can be called an empire depends on the definition employed. Michael Doyle, whose book *Empires* is quoted in a number of essays in this volume, provides a fairly liberal definition: 'Empire is a relationship, formal or informal, in which one state controls the effective political sovereignty of another political society. It can be achieved by force, by political collaboration, by economic, social, or cultural dependence.'[6]

From that it might seem easy to conclude that the United States was and remains an empire. In the present day it has formal control over a dozen dependencies (e.g., Puerto Rico) and maintains military bases in at least one hundred countries.[7] Furthermore, it has long been American policy to prop up pro-American regimes throughout the world while funding rebel groups to topple foreign governments viewed as anti-American. On top of all that, it has a powerful influence on the world's economy and on all societies and cultures. For many decades it was only followers of Lenin and Mao who characterized this global reach of the United States as imperialistic. And while the firebrand presidents of Venezuela and Iran, Hugo Chávez and Mahmoud Ahmadinejad, seem to have picked up where Lenin and Mao left off, there has been surprisingly strong agreement across the political spectrum that the sheer strength and influence of the United States qualifies it as an empire.

The problem with this conclusion is that the vast majority of the relationships that political societies make with the United States do not seem to result in a ceding of sovereignty.[8] While it certainly tries, the United States does not seem able to unabashedly dominate all other states or to force them to act against their sovereign interests.[9] Undoubtedly the United States has tremendous international influence, both negative and positive, but that alone does not make it an empire. If empire is primarily about political control, then American economic and cultural supremacy is not enough to make it one.[10] As the historian Niall Ferguson puts it: 'Americans, in short, don't "do" empire; they do "leadership" instead, or, in more academic parlance, "hegemony."'[11] And while Ferguson downplays the importance of this distinction, the ancient Greeks understood the significant difference between influence and actual control, reflected in their words *hegemonia* or 'leading the way' and *arkhē*, which might roughly be translated, using Doyle's term, as 'effective political sovereignty of another political society.' So what was called imperialism in the paragraph above would, for the Greeks, instead be an example of *hegemonia*. That is to say, there is a certain level of voluntary alliance or even voluntary subordination on the part of the states 'led' by America.[12]

In a sense, Thucydides' *History* is an account of Athens' movement between these two kinds of political authority: at the beginning of the book it is the respected leader (as in *hegemonia*) of the Delian League, but eventually it becomes the corrupt and vicious empire (as in *arkhē*) characterized in the Melian dialogue and the Sicilian expedition.[13] While Thucydides never explicitly makes this argument (seeming to use the two words interchangeably), it is clear that Athens' neighbours, who once willingly accepted Athenian international supremacy, eventually become unwilling and fearful captives to the despotism of Athenian imperialism.

Since the point of this book is to compare ancient and contemporary accounts of empire, it might now be asked whether something similar is happening with the United States today. Is the United States moving from *hegemonia* to *arkhē*? Is it experiencing a transformation in its relations with its allies and enemies similar to what occurred with Athens?

According to Thucydides, the Athenian empire began with the founding of the Delian League, a collective-security alliance named after the island of Delos, where the league's treasury was first kept. Ostensibly, the league was founded in order to protect the Greek world from its common enemy, the Persian Empire.[14] He does not blame Athenian ambition or aggression for the growth of the empire; instead he faults the league's other member states for not exercising their sovereignty by developing their own strong militaries and for choosing to pay tribute to Athens instead. The Athenians rightly pointed out to their Spartan rivals that because Athens was a capable and respected military leader, 'our allies came to us of their own accord and begged us to lead them.'[15] However, what began as a voluntary agreement among allies soon evolved into the domination of one state over the rest. Instead of a respected first among equals, Athens became a feared oppressor.[16]

One can argue that a similar set of circumstances led to the rise of the United States as a global superpower after the Second World War. The Americans, too, forged a military alliance to fight a common enemy. And in the same way that the defeat of the Persians in 479 BCE saw the pan-Hellenic League split into the Peloponnesian League led by Sparta and the Delian League led by Athens, the defeat of Germany in 1945 saw the quick rise of hostilities between the United States and the Soviet Union. If the United States ever hoped to establish itself as an empire, this was the chance. Immediately after the war, America was at the height of its power: it was the only country with the atomic bomb; it occupied significant parts of Asia and Europe; and tremendous wartime losses had diminished the strength of both its friends and its rivals. Yet instead of seeking *political* control over a weakened Europe, the United States introduced the European Recovery Program (the Marshall Plan), which was designed to stabilize and strengthen the economies of its allies and thereby stave off Soviet expansion. Soon after, in 1949, the Soviet threat spurred the creation of the North Atlantic Treaty Organization (NATO), a collective-security arrangement analogous to the Delian League. But unlike the Athenians, the Americans did not use their military might to bully states into staying in the alliance. For example, in 1959 France decided to withdraw its military support from NATO out of concern that the United States was becoming too powerful. Instead of using its dominant position to punish a member for insubordination, the Americans grudgingly accepted the French withdrawal.

Overall, this period of the Cold War does not seem to tell a tale of American imperialism. Instead, it appears to highlight the United States' position as an economic and military leader. The Soviets were more clearly imperialistic in their control of the Warsaw Pact countries, putting down revolts in Hungary in 1956 and Czechoslovakia in 1968 while at the same time seeking to dominate North Korea, Mongolia, and later Vietnam. Still, critics of the view that the United States was a benevolent hegemon argue that it was more of an 'empire by invitation.'[17] Unlike the Soviets, the post-1945 American empire did not have to rely on force, for it had the support of the people of Western Europe, who reaped many benefits from their acquiescence. How could this possibly be called imperialism? Quite differently, the Athenians did not seek to enrich and stabilize their colonies; instead they sought to collect tribute from them so that Athenians could live in luxury, beautify their city, and strengthen their navy. What began as voluntary contributions to the war against Persia became protection payments extracted by coercion.

Thucydides writes: 'The Athenians insisted on [the payment of tributes] being exactly met, and made themselves unpopular by bringing the severest pressure to bear on allies who were not used to making sacrifices and did not want to make them.'[18] Steadily increasing resentment against Athens eventually gave way to widespread revolts that helped bring down the empire.

Then again, Western Europe may be the wrong place to look for American imperialism during the Cold War. The war in Vietnam seemed to pull the curtain back, revealing the true, unapologetically imperialistic goals of the United States. Vietnam might be described as the American Melos. For the Athenians, the refusal of the island of Melos to join the Delian League was unacceptable, as was its choice to remain neutral during the Peloponnesian War.[19] The Athenians made it clear to the Melians that their independence from Athens might be seen as 'a sign of weakness' by the other member states,[20] which might in turn promote internal dissent. Here there was no normative concern about collective security or protecting the region against a common enemy. When the Athenians demanded that Melos join the empire or be destroyed, they did so bluntly: 'The standard of justice depends on the equality of power to compel and that in fact the strong do what they have the power to do and the weak accept what they have to accept.'[21] The Melians were being asked to acquiesce not for their betterment but for their very survival. Likewise, instead of acting as a virtuous leader standing up against Soviet encroachment in Southeast Asia, the United States chose to carry out an amoral policy in Vietnam and the greater region – a policy that seemed to reveal its vicious imperialism.

If the Vietnam War was an exercise in empire building, it was a failed one: unlike the Athenians, who crushed the Melians, the Americans lost their war on the ground and gained nothing from their defeat. Also, while the Americans' means were clearly amoral, they seem to have been motivated by what they viewed as noble ends. In 1966, President Lyndon Johnson remarked on why America was fighting in Vietnam:

If one government uses force to violate another people's rights, we cannot ignore the injustice, the threat to our own rights, the danger to peace in the entire world. And that is what's happening at this hour in South Vietnam. The North Vietnamese are trying to deny the people of South Vietnam the right to build their own nation, the right to choose their own system of government, the right to live and work in peace … And South Vietnam has asked us for help. Only if we abandon our respect for the rights of other people could we turn down their plea. (30 June 1966, speech in Omaha, Nebraska)

As it is presented here, the United States did not share the Athenians' view (in relation to Melos) that their mission was motivated *merely* by power and self-interest. Instead, they saw a clear parallel between the ideal of protecting human rights – including the right to self-determination – and their own national security. In Vietnam they would not only strike a blow against their enemies but also protect the peoples of the world from the barbarism of communism.[22] According to Johnson, the United States was not taking control of Vietnam; rather, it was giving the Vietnamese people the right to choose the kind of government they were to live under – something the North Vietnamese were not going to allow. Mind you, at the outset of the Peloponnesian War the Athenians presented a similarly noble account of their imperial ambitions. In his famous Funeral Oration, Pericles described Athens as 'an education to Greece,'[23] as an example of democracy, openness, friendship, and virtue. Pericles presented Athens as a beacon of enlightenment and prosperity, a civilizing influence that could only improve the lives of those lucky enough to be brought into her fold. So we might argue that both Athens and the United States were attempting to exercise *hegemonia* rather than *arkhē*. The problem, though, is that the United States had already helped block national elections which had been scheduled for 1956 and which would likely have reunified the country under the popular communist government of the North – so much for self-determination. With the appeal to protecting rights and democracy seemingly nothing more than a platitude, all that is left to explain the war is a national interest in projecting American power onto the region, in order to look strong and discourage dissent.

The Athenians' actions at Melos were meant to serve the same purpose. Fifteen years after Pericles' laudatory speech, they attacked the island, killing the adult male population and enslaving all the women and children – hardly an improvement. Likewise, a mere three years after his Nebraska speech, with troop levels escalating, casualties mounting, and the tragedy of the My Lai massacre coming to light, Johnson decided not to run for re-election. The new President, Richard Nixon, elected on a promise to end the war, soon had to answer why America was still fighting in Southeast Asia. In his infamous Silent Majority address he made this surprisingly candid admission: 'For the United States this first defeat in our nation's history would result in a collapse of confidence in America's leadership not only in Asia but throughout the world.'[24] In other words, the priority now was to not appear weak, rather than to ensure freedom and peace to Vietnam. The 'collapse of confidence' Nixon was referring to would cost Washington more than face and prestige; it would also embolden America's enemies. Pericles makes the same kind of warning when the Athenian *demos* has a 'change in spirit' about continuing the war with Sparta: 'There is also involved the loss of our empire and the dangers arising from the hatred which we have incurred in administering it. Nor is it any longer possible for you to give up this empire ... Your empire is now like a tyranny: it may have been wrong to take it; it is certainly dangerous to let it go.'[25] Here there is no mention of moral leadership. The Athenians may in the past have been able to justify their brutality in the name of collective security against Persia; now, there was no justification whatsoever beyond a desire to protect the empire against a growing list of internal and external enemies.

We see a similar evolution in American foreign policy as the threat of the Soviet Union recedes. For example, the United States may have been able to argue that the CIA-assisted overthrow of the democratically elected president of Chile, Salvador Allende, in 1973 was driven by a genuine fear that communists were infiltrating South America. American support for the brutal Contra paramilitaries in their war against the socialist Sandinista government in Nicaragua in the 1980s could be justified along similar lines. These interventions (and many others, including the one in Vietnam) were explained as part of a moral obligation to protect the world from Soviet totalitarianism. This seemed to be the point of Ronald Reagan's remarkable speech of 1 March 1985, during which he attempted to secure congressional support for the Contras: 'They are our brothers, these freedom fighters, and we owe them our help. I've spoken recently of the freedom fighters of Nicaragua. You know the truth about them. You know who they're fighting and why. They are the moral equal of our Founding Fathers and the brave men and women of the French Resistance. We cannot turn away from them, for the struggle here is not right versus left; it is right versus wrong.'

Of course, American policies in Central and South America were more than just efforts to protect the right of people to build their own nation, choose their own system of government, and live and work in peace. Those policies were not invitations to follow the American example; rather, they amounted to demands for acquiescence and conformity. No longer simply 'leading the way,' the United States was infringing on other countries' sovereignty and seeking political control. In contrast to the American 'empire by invitation' at the start of the Cold War, this seemed much more like a traditional empire by domination. However, as with Vietnam, one can hardly declare these efforts at empire building a resounding or long-term success.

After the Soviet Union dissolved in the early 1990s, the enemy was no longer at the gates. In the new era that was now dawning, the West's victory in the American-led and UN-backed Gulf War opened the way for a new kind of international relations – what the 41st President of the United States, George H.W. Bush, termed a new world order. In a speech to cadets at Maxwell Air Force Base in Montgomery, Alabama, he presented his vision: 'The new world order does not mean surrendering our national sovereignty or forfeiting our interests. It really describes a responsibility imposed by our successes. It refers to new ways of working with other nations to deter aggression and to achieve stability, to achieve prosperity and, above all, to achieve peace ... Never before has the world looked more to the American example. Never before have so many millions drawn hope from the American idea.'

Most certainly this was *not* a call for an aggressive neo-imperialism. Rather, Bush was casting the United States once more as the shining city on a hill, a leader among nations. America now saw itself as the 'indispensable nation,' its national interests at one with global interests, a country without which the new world order could not come together in peace and prosperity.[26] But the optimism of this 'unipolar moment' was short lived. The failure of the humanitarian intervention in Somalia, followed by inaction in Rwanda and foot dragging in Kosovo,[27] suggested that the American people were less than eager to embrace their new role as the benevolent hegemon or 'the policeman of the world.' Still, the United States had no intention of allowing the emergence of a new rival that might challenge its dominance. The problem, then, was how to justify the goal that Bush had delineated in the context of an ambivalent American public.

In a sense, the terrorist attacks of 11 September 2001 provided the solution: a 'grand cause' in the pursuit of which America could project its power around the globe. As Steven Smith predicted in 2002, 'the public reaction in the US to the events of September 11 seems likely to license a very unilateral foreign policy, which roughly translates as saying to US allies that they can join with the US on US terms, or leave the US to act alone.'[28] This set the stage for the American-led invasions of Afghanistan and Iraq.

In 421 BCE the Athenian Empire also had to consider its policy for a new world order. The shaky Peace of Nicias had been signed, which limited direct conflict between Sparta and Athens. With the immediate threat of a Spartan invasion behind them and their coffers full as a result of the truce, the Athenians decided to increase their power and position by invading Sicily. The strongest proponent of the war, the young, inexperienced, and ambitious commander Alcibiades, reassured his fellow Athenians that it would be an easy mission and that they had support among the indigenous population of Sicily: 'There seems to be, therefore, no reasonable argument to induce us to hold back ourselves or to justify any excuse to our allies in Sicily for not helping them.' He also reminded them that the invasion would prevent their Sicilian enemies from 'coming here to attack us.' He insisted that Athens ought to take 'measures in advance to prevent the attack [from] materializing' in order to avoid 'the danger that we ourselves may fall under the power of others unless others are in our power.' He concluded: 'This is the way we won our empire, and this is the way all empires have been won – by coming vigorously to the help of all who ask for it.'[29] With great optimism, the assembly voted wholeheartedly for the invasion. Those who opposed it held their tongues. Thucydides writes: 'The result of this excessive enthusiasm of the majority was that the few who actually were opposed to the expedition were afraid of being thought unpatriotic if they voted against it, and therefore kept quiet.'[30] The expedition was more than a quagmire; it resulted in the destruction of much of the navy and a cascade of internal uprisings, leading to the decline and fall of the Athenian empire.

The parallels between the Sicilian expedition and the invasion of Iraq are obvious: the erroneous declaration of a quick 'mission accomplished'; the rationalization for a pre-emptive strike; the promise to liberate a foreign population from tyranny; and the silencing of opposition. However, these are merely parallels between events separated by almost 2,500 years. It seems unlikely that the invasion of Iraq will bring down America as a nation, but it may well lead to the abrupt end of the nascent American empire.

NOTES

1 See, for example, Victor Davis Hanson, *A War Like No Other: How the Athenians and Spartans Fought the Peloponnesian War* (New York: Random House, 2005).
2 Thucydides, *The History of The Peloponnesian War*, trans. Rex Warner (London: Penguin, 1972), 1.22.

3 For example, Anne Norton's *Leo Strauss and the Politics of Empire* (Yale
   University Press, 2004); and Jim Garrison's *America as Empire: Global Leader
   or Rogue Power?* (San Francisco: Berrett-Koehler, 2004).
4 Michael Cox discusses this application in 'Empire, Imperialism, and the
   Bush Doctrine,' *Review of International Studies* 30 (2004): 585–608. Paul
   Kennedy describes overextension in terms of 'imperial overstretch' in *The
   Rise and Fall of the Great Powers* (New York: Random House, 1989). Niall
   Ferguson considers the growing danger of American economic collapse
   owing to its international overcommitments in *Colossus: The Price of
   America's Empire* (New York: Penguin, 2004). Chalmers Johnson presents a
   similar argument in *The Sorrows of Empire: Militarism, Secrecy and the End of
   the Republic* (New York: Metropolitan, 2004).
5 Cox puts it bluntly: 'The tale of imperial denial is a familiar one. The
   United States, it has been routinely argued (by Americans) waged a war of
   national liberation against those brutal British red-coats. It then went on to
   build a democratic country like no other. And as their leaders repeated *ad
   nauseam* thereafter, the new republic formed part of an ideologically
   progressive New World which stood in sharp contrast to that reactionary
   Old one with its penchant for taking over other people's land.' 'Empire,'
   588.
6 Michael Doyle, *Empires* (Ithaca: Cornell University Press, 1986), 45.
7 See Johnson, *The Sorrows of Empire,* for a discussion of the relationship
   between foreign U.S. military bases and imperialism.
8 Canada, for example, is economically dependent on its southern neigh-
   bour yet remains an independent country. For example, it refused to
   participate in the Vietnam War and the invasion of Iraq and has a healthy
   trade relationship with Cuba, all to the consternation of the United States.
9 The United States' failure to convince most of its allies (including Mexico and
   Canada) to participate in the invasion of Iraq seems a clear example; another
   is Turkey's refusal to allow the U.S. military to launch operations from its
   territory. The United States demobilized troops in South Korea and evacu-
   ated its military bases in Saudi Arabia, against its interest and at the behest of
   those governments. Likewise, despite the Americans' prolonged efforts to
   control their politics, the people of South and Central America have voted in
   a number of socialist and anti-American governments.
10 Michael Walzer considers the dominate economic position of the United
    State in relation to whether there is an American Empire: 'But empire is a
    form of *political* domination, and it's not at all clear that market domina-
    tion and the extraction of profits requires political domination. Perhaps
    they did in an earlier age – so the history of European empire and the

United States in Central America suggests. But the central claim of free marketers today is that political domination isn't necessary.' Walzer, 'Is There an American Empire?' *Dissent* 50, no. 4 (2003): 27–31 at 27.

11 Niall Ferguson, 'Hegemony or Empire,' *Foreign Affairs* 82, no. 5 (2003): 154. Walzer notes a similar distinction: '"Empire" needs extensive qualification if it is to describe anything like what exists, or what is possible, in the world today ... But perhaps there is a better way of thinking about contemporary global politics, drawing on the related idea of "hegemony." In common use today, "hegemonic" is simply a less vivid way of saying "imperialist," but it really points to something different: a looser form of rule, less authoritarian than empire is or was, more dependent on the agreement of others.' Walzer, 'Is There an American Empire?' 28.

12 Puerto Rico, for example, has had four plebiscites (1967, 1981, 1993, 1998), in which the people voted to remain part of the United States.

13 See Richard Ned Lebow and Robert Kelly's 'Thucydides and Hegemony: Athens and the United States,' *Review of International Studies* 27 (2001): 593–609.

14 He notes that 'the history of these years will show how the Athenian Empire came into being' (1.97).

15 *History*, 1.75.

16 The first step in this transformation was the aggressive expansion of the League into the independent city-state of Carystus. This was followed by a violent reaction to the withdrawal of the island of Naxos from the confederacy. He writes: 'Naxos left the league and the Athenians made war on the place. After a siege Naxos was forced back to allegiance. This was the first case when the original constitution of the League was broken and an allied city lost its independence, and the process was continued in the cases of the other allies as various circumstances arose' (1.98). Soon after, the island of Thasos was given similar treatment when it attempted to leave: its walls were destroyed and it was made to pay a large fine. No longer independent and sovereign states, Carystus, Naxos, Thasos, and the rest of league become beholden to Athens for their defence, indeed, their very existence.

17 See Geir Lundestad's 'Empire by Invitation? The United States and Western Europe, 1945–1952,' *Journal of Peace Research*, 23, no. 3 (1986).

18 *History*, 1.99.

19 According to Thucydides, 'the Melians are a colony from Sparta. They had refused to join the Athenian empire like the other islanders, and at first had remained neutral without helping either side; but afterwards when the Athenians had brought force to bear on them by laying waste their land, they became open enemies of Athens' (5.84).

20 *History*, 5.95.

21 *History*, 5.89.

22 A similar logic informed the American intervention in Cuba. In the late nineteenth century the United States assisted Cubans fighting for independence from Spain. They occupied the island until 1903 and thereafter retained a naval base at Guantánamo Bay supported by the Platt Amendment, which gave the United States 'the right to intervene for the preservation of Cuban independence, the maintenance of a government adequate for the protection of life, property, and individual liberty' (Article III).

23 *History*, 2.41.

24 From the 'Silent Majority' speech.

25 *History*, 2.63.

26 Bill Clinton described the United States as the 'indispensable nation' in his speech 'The Legacy of America's Leadership as We Enter the 21st Century.' In the same speech he observed: 'That is why I think, among other things, we have to resist those who believe that now that the Cold War is over, the United States can completely return to focusing on problems within our borders and basically ignore those beyond our borders. That escapism is not available to us because at the end of the Cold War, America truly is the world's indispensable nation. There are times when only America can make the difference between war and peace, between freedom and repression, between hope and fear. We cannot and should not try to be the world's policeman. But where our interests and values are clearly at stake, and where we can make a difference, we must act and lead.'

27 It has been argued that Presidential Decision Directive 25, signed by Clinton after the failure of Operation Restore Hope in Somalia, precluded American action in Rwanda to stop the genocide because it called for the American military to limit intervention to areas of 'national interest.'

28 Steven Smith, 'The End of the Unipolar Moment? September 11 and the Future of World Order,' *International Relations* 16, no. 2 (2002): 171–83 at 173.

29 *History*, 6.18.

30 *History*, 6.24.

4 The Freedom to Rule: Athenian Imperialism and Democratic Masculinity*

RYAN K. BALOT

In his ground-breaking work on empires and imperialism, Michael Doyle argues for a broad, flexible, and historically wide-ranging conception of empires. In this paper I follow Doyle and use the term 'imperialism' to mean, broadly, state-based exploitation of others, including the maintenance of control over other states' internal and external politics.[1] To put the matter into a more distinctively ancient idiom, imperialism exemplifies foreign policy in the tyrannical mode. For Doyle, the richly documented ancient empires of Classical Greece and Rome prove to be as illuminating for the study of imperial dispositions, centre–periphery relations, and systemic analyses as the extensively discussed modern exemplars of imperialism. This is as it should be: the ancient empires and imperialists – Doyle's list could be expanded to include those of Persia, Carthage, Macedon, the Sicilian tyrannies, and the Hellenistic Kingdoms – set into high relief the structural interrelations of states in the relatively cohesive, albeit anarchic, ancient Mediterranean world. And this is not to mention the potentially fruitful comparative investigation of ancient Mediterranean empires with the huge and successful ancient empires of the Far East.

Yet one could also argue that pre-modern interstate relations have by now been utterly transformed by technological innovation, nuclear weapons, the rise of Enlightenment liberalism, the dominance of democracy, the economic consequences of globalization, and many other critical and distinctively modern factors, so much so that any historical account of ancient imperialism would stand in need of substantial 'translation' should it purport to be relevant to modern political analysis.[2] This chapter undertakes such a project of 'translation' in order to clarify what is distinctive (and what is not) about our own ethical and pragmatic approaches to empire. I focus on the ancients' own reflections on the character of imperial regimes, the psychology of imperialism, the relationship between liberty and empire, and the constraints of empire. Examining the self-presentation of ancient imperialists and the challenges posed by their critics can improve the quality of our political conversations – and, indeed, lay bare ideas that, though typically obscure to us, have a considerable hold on our modes of waking thought.

Ancient Greek conversations are particularly relevant to us because the earliest Greek imperialists were democrats. At least until the fifth century BCE, Near Eastern monarchs had been the chief imperialists of the Eastern Mediterranean. After the Greek victories over Persia, however, democratic Athens began to exercise power over Greek states throughout the Aegean, taking foreign-policy decisions for its subject-states and intervening in their political, economic, social, and religious life as it saw fit. Athenian democracy was a novel experiment in the exercise of power; so too, within the Greek world, was Athenian imperialism.[3]

Athens was not the only imperialistic city-state in Mediterranean antiquity; nor was it the only democracy in Greece; nor was it alone among Mediterranean states in prizing pugnacity;[4] nor was it exceptional in valuing freedom from external control. Yet the Athenians were the only successful democratic imperialists in the ancient Mediterranean. In their empire's heyday they presented themselves as enjoying exceptional freedom and as exhibiting the virtue of *andreia*, or 'manly courage,' to the highest degree. Athenians often linked these attributes in an ideological framework that emphasized the superiority of democracy and the justice of Athenian imperialism. But Athens also produced thoughtful critics: Thucydides and Plato show that Athenian imperialism undermined the Athenians' democratic values.

To grasp the Athenians' development of an imperial ideology, it is useful to locate democratic courage and freedom in the post–Persian War period (i.e., the 470s BCE and onward). 'Manly courage' and freedom assumed a novel cultural significance then, because the Greeks believed that their 'manly courage' and their dedication to equality and freedom had been the deciding factors in their victory over Persia.[5] Courage (*aretê* or *andreia*) had always been the Greeks' manly virtue par excellence. Courage was the predominantly military virtue of heroes seeking glory; it consisted chiefly in overcoming fear on the killing fields. After Xerxes' invasion, however, the Greeks specifically prized courage as enabling them, as a group, to overcome fear in order to preserve their political freedom.[6] Courage became less the characteristic virtue of heroic individuals than a collective virtue produced within particular political systems. But this transformation did nothing to domesticate courage. 'Courage' is the standard translation of the Greek term *andreia*, an abstraction derived from the concrete noun *anêr* ('man' as opposed to 'woman'). *Andreia* is the name of a bellicose, aggressive, masculine virtue; it might properly be rendered 'machismo,' which brings out its connotations of pugnacity, hot-headedness, and readiness to fight.[7]

Freedom, too, was conceptually transformed after the Persian Wars. Though freedom had never been a central value in the aristocratic culture of archaic Greece, freedom took centre stage after the Persian Wars.[8] Greeks who had traditionally lived outside the Persian sphere of influence valued freedom, contrasting it with the 'slavery' of their Ionian cousins, who had long been Persian imperial subjects. They also contrasted the freedom of Greek citizens with the Persians' own 'enslavement' to their Great King. Finally, they envisioned freedom as a specifically masculine attribute, contrasting it with the reputedly weak and effeminate Persians. Only free Greek men – not women, slaves, or Persians – enjoyed the privilege of participating in politics and patriotically defending their own city-states. Obviously, such polarities were developed altogether in the shadow of pre-existing antitheses between free and slave, and man and woman. Remember well, though, that the general antitheses were capable of specific application and evolution, because our question is how, and with what effects, there emerged a distinctively Athenian or distinctively democratic conception of these values.

Distinctively Athenian conceptions of freedom and courage came about, at first, as the Athenians endeavoured to claim the bulk of the credit for victory over the Persians. Herodotus was reflecting Athenian ideology when he contended that it was Athenian courage, above all, that preserved Greek freedom.[9] As Herodotus indicates, this was a matter of dispute among Greek states. Athenians were anxious to develop a plausible 'national narrative' through which to tie the great victory to their own (sometimes) natural and (sometimes) democratic freedom and courage.[10] The Athenians' focus on competition against the other Greeks would later prove detrimental to their own long-term self-interests.

Athenians took a huge ideological step when they connected their freedom from Persia with their internal freedom from tyrants. In a patriotic distortion of history, they credited two 'tyrannicides' with founding their democracy through a unique act of civic courage. Early in the fifth century, in the central public space of the city, they erected larger-than-life statues of these quintessential democratic heroes.[11] Then, as Herodotus represents it, the Athenians stirred themselves against the Persians at Marathon (490 BCE) by recalling the glorious exploits of their heroic tyrannicides.[12] In this way, by making connections between internal politics and military exploits against the Persians, the Athenian democrats plausibly claimed for themselves the title of tyrant-slayers – both in the establishment of their own democracy at first, and then, partly as a result, in the repulse of the Persian king, who was figured as a tyrant in Athenian ideological representation. This nexus of ideas – internal liberty, external autonomy, and leadership of the Hellenic cause against invading 'barbarians' – helped crystallize for Athenians an image of Athens as the free and courageous Greek *polis* par excellence.

The Athenians developed this self-image over successive generations by contrasting themselves with the other Greeks. They maintained that their courage was an expression of the practical wisdom characteristic of democratic deliberation.[13] It was a staple of Athenian ideology that the democratic constitution produced a deeper, more thoughtful, and therefore superior form of courage compared to that of Athens' non-democratic rivals, particularly Sparta. This ideology was most vividly expressed, at least in surviving literature, in the Funeral Oration that Thucydides ascribed to Pericles.[14] As Thucydides would have it, Pericles emphasized that Athenian *andreia* resulted directly from the democratic constitution. Pericles envisioned an intellectualized form of manly courage that depended on free exchange in the assembly. He argued that democratic courage was thoughtful, deliberate, and wise, in that Athenians integrated the practical insights of all citizens into the use and deployment of their military courage. He maintained that, as a result, the Athenians' self-conscious *andreia* was superior to the rigidly conventional *andreia* exhibited by Spartans. This was yet another way in which courage and freedom (especially *qua* free speech) were closely linked in the Athenian political imagination. These self-proclaimed cultural *differentia* were central to the Athenians' ongoing competition with other Greeks.

In light of this compelling ideology, it is reductive to assert that Athens succeeded chiefly because of political unity or military power or extraordinary manpower.[15] No doubt these factors contributed to Athens' imperial success, but equally critical were psychological and emotional factors. Through their carefully reasoned ideology, the

Athenians explained to themselves both why they were more successful than other Greeks and why they deserved power and pre-eminence within the Greek world. Courage, freedom, and competitive success were closely intertwined in the Athenian self-image.

At first glance it is ironic that the Athenians claimed to be courageous freedom fighters just as they were beginning to project their power over other Greeks; but their competitiveness with the other Greeks fore-shadowed their pursuit of empire in the Greek world. Shortly after 479 BCE the Athenians began to use their unmatched naval forces to compel their 'allies' to pay tribute, to row in warships, to support their foreign policy, and to show tangible respect to their Athenian 'leaders.' By encouraging their allies to pay tribute instead of contributing ships to the Delian League, the Athenians both acquired control over extraordinary levels of fungible wealth and severely restricted the military capacity of their subordinates. The symbolism of empire tells much the same story: allies were required, for example, to offer a cow and a full suit of hoplite armour to be displayed at the Great Panathenaea in Athens.[16] The imperial Athenians ostentatiously displayed their power over their allies' wealth, and they symbolically subjected the allies' manhood to Athenian control.[17] By this point there could be no doubt about the Athenians' superiority to the other Greeks in freedom and manliness.

This is why, in fact, the other Greeks did not accept Athenian power easily. It was unprecedented for one Greek *polis* to assert effective and long-term control over the internal, as well as external, politics of another Greek *polis*.[18] The Athenians often chose to install democracies in their subject-states – a direct affront to the oligarchic, or timocratic, regimes that had hitherto governed most of the Greek world. Along with these facts on the ground, the polarized definitions of manhood and freedom canvassed previously placed the allies very much on the losing side of a crucial political, psychological, and cultural *agon* – as enslaved, as effeminized, as weak.

Accordingly, the Athenians' subjects described themselves as enslaved and Athens as a 'tyrant *polis*.'[19] Such terminology was common throughout contemporary literature – for example, in the anti-democratic 'Old Oligarch,'[20] in the democratically funded tragedies of Euripides,[21] and comedies of Aristophanes,[22] and in the critical history of Thucydides.[23] These accusations were not uncommon despite the widely acknowledged benefits of empire: safety from pirates, democratic politics, security from the Persian threat, and economic opportunities. Though the question of Athens' imperial popularity is a hotly contested one, it was meaningful and rhetorically powerful for Athens' subject-states to use the language of freedom and slavery to promote their own political and security interests in particular contexts. The underlying message was that, through an excessively free expression of virility, the Athenians had become as brutish and un-Greek as the Persians who had once marched west.

Corresponding to the allies' criticisms, there were significant ambiguities in the Athenians' public self-presentation. No doubt Athenians enjoyed wielding unaccountable power, and in highly restricted settings they happily acknowledged their self-satisfaction. In Aristophanes' *Knights*, Demos, the personification of the Athenian *demos*, is praised for his tyrannical authority over the Greeks[24] and admired as the monarch and king of all the Greeks.[25] We will see shortly why the carefree democratic virility of Demos could only remain fantastic. In Aristophanes' *Wasps*, moreover, the chorus declares that there is nothing manlier than an Attic wasp.[26] Tyranny had always found admirers in Greek culture, even after the Greeks' successful resistance against the Persians; for tyranny promised the successful few extraordinary freedom and exceptional opportunities to display their manliness. But the Athenians kept explicitly tyrannical aspirations at arm's length.

For outside comic and other settings with built-in 'distancing' mechanisms, the Athenians did not publicly embrace tyrannical masculinity.[27] More commonly, they were sensitive to critics who charged that, through their excessive ambition, they had transformed their *andreia* and their pursuit of freedom into vices characteristic of tyranny. Accordingly, self-justification was a central theme of their official rhetoric, which we glimpse primarily through nostalgic fourth-century speeches. In his funeral oration of the 390s, for example, Lysias argued that the Athenians had undertaken glorious risks in order to free the other Greeks, and that afterwards they calmed civic strife and granted equality to all.[28] Similarly, Isocrates argued that the Athenians had achieved success as imperialists by exporting their domestic benefits, such as democracy, to other Greeks and by ruling both sympathetically and impartially.[29] Employing a common ideological trope, and in order to reduce the appearance of blunt arrogance, the Athenians often presented their allies as tied to them through kinship and religion.[30]

In private, however, at least some Athenians were influenced by contemporary sophistic justifications of self-aggrandizement. Thucydides provides the basic ideas in speeches delivered by the Athenians at Sparta and at Melos, to the effect that imperialism is a necessary and natural consequence of human nature and of living in a hostile political world.[31] I strongly doubt that Athenian diplomats promoted the natural right of the stronger in speeches delivered to other Greeks. Instead, on my interpretation of the Thucydidean speeches, Thucydides was suggesting that, whatever the propaganda of the day, Athenians were, in reality, even if privately, driven by greed, self-interest, macho competitiveness, and a belief in the right of the stronger. Thucydides designed his speeches so as to enable his *readers* to understand accurately the Athenians' genuine (and typically deplorable, in his view) motives, insofar as he could discern them.[32] It is worth exploring the Thucydidean criticisms in more detail, because Thucydides was drawing attention to the Athenians' ideological and practical difficulties.

To ground his criticisms of Athens' democratic imperialism, Thucydides seized upon contradictions and tensions between the democrats' practices of imperialism and their claims to freedom and manly courage. In particular, he scrutinized the Athenian conception of freedom as the power to rule over the other Greeks.[33] The otherwise unknown Athenian speaker Diodotus, for example, explicitly connected freedom with the power to rule in general;[34] Euphemus, another Athenian speaking years later in Sicily, argued that the Athenians ruled over the other Greeks in order to avoid being subject to them.[35] Such ideas are also implicit in statements attributed to Pericles,[36] Cleon,[37] and Alcibiades,[38] to the effect that the Athenians held on to their tyrannical empire on pain of enslavement. The polarities that had informed early fifth-century Greek concepts of freedom now presented themselves to the Athenians as an immediate, frightening, and all-or-nothing necessity: freedom required the maintenance and even expansion of empire over the other Greeks, whether the Athenians wanted to rule them or not. In the Athenian mentality, which by that time was widespread, the only alternative was slavery.[39]

Fourth-century authors, particularly Isocrates, show why this zero-sum conception of Hellenic politics was not natural, necessary, or healthy. As Isocrates argues, Athens' proper role was that of leader, protector, and benefactor of the other Greeks. One might have supposed that fifth-century Athenian leadership, properly exercised, could have defused tensions within the Greek world, perhaps by focusing the Greeks' collective energies on the evident security risks posed by neighbouring empires, viz. Persia. Barry Strauss argues in this volume that Persian expansionism, not the intermittent and underwhelming resistance of other Greeks, was the real threat to Athenian political flourishing. Large questions loom here. But I agree that the Athenians would have been better off had they, *mutatis mutandis*, followed the Roman policy of integrating Italians and pushing their military frontiers ever farther away. And indeed, the Athenians arguably could have done so, had they been willing to extend citizenship to outsiders, in very un-Greek fashion, as the Romans did.[40]

To make the necessary policy moves, though, the Athenians would have been compelled to reconsider their grants of citizenship. They would also have had to imagine freedom differently – not as the freedom, won in competitions of manliness, to rule Greece, but rather as the freedom to lead the other Greeks in worthy causes. The Athenians could have acted as public-spirited leaders of the Greeks, if only they had understood their own enlightened self-interest. Instead, their competitiveness with other Greeks caused them to neglect the freedom to lead in order to exercise the only sort of freedom that was meaningful to them: the freedom to rule over the other Greeks. None of this was necessary, except that the Athenians, for lack of imagination, made it so.

If the Athenians subscribed to a narrow vision of the opportunities provided by 'super' power, then both serious military competitors and small agricultural villages throughout the Greek world came to understand that autonomy, neutrality, and indifference were impossible. Think of the small island of Melos: after the Athenians destroyed this non-threatening 'rival,' all other would-be neutrals knew that fence sitting would be interpreted as aggressive resistance. Perhaps, after considering the Athenians' easily provoked manliness, we can see more clearly why Machiavelli later maintained that neutrality, postponement of conflict, and purely defensive policies are chimerical.[41]

Be that as it may, through their unhealthy conceptions of freedom and courage, the Athenians consolidated an atmosphere of hostility throughout the Greek world – one that became obviously detrimental to Athens' own self-interest. As Thucydides shows, the late fifth-century Athenians' vaunted freedom to rule had become, towards the end of the Peloponnesian War, a bitter necessity.[42] Athenians had to fight wars continually, to destroy other cities for symbolic reasons, and to live in fear. In Thucydides' representation of the Sicilian debate, for example, Alcibiades argued successfully that the Athenians must, on pain of internal failure, be true to their traditions of aggressive imperialism; their *ethos* of pugnacity was their fate.[43] Pre-emptive attacks were necessary, said Alcibiades, because without them Athens would be enslaved by other Greeks. Thucydides had uncovered a hard political irony lurking beneath Athens' hypermasculine desires for untrammelled freedom and power.[44]

Thucydides utilized such insights when he examined Athenian imperialism as specifically democratic. The brittle, though anarchic, international environment had profoundly damaging effects on democratic politics, in that Athens' imperialistic behaviour abroad tended to erode the democratic ideals of freedom and equality at home.[45] For if the Athenians truly believed, as Thucydides would have it, that untrammelled, tyrannical freedom was (perhaps secretly) desirable, then they were poised once again to rear unjust tyrants in the city. For Thucydides, the key symbol of this ever-unfolding democratic tragedy was Alcibiades. During the Sicilian debate, Thucydides has Alcibiades candidly reject democratic equality and arrogantly praise himself for his outstanding contributions to the city.[46] The Athenians' blunt confidence in their superiority among Greek states tended to educate Athenian aristocrats to aspire to a similar superiority within the city. One is reminded of Aristotle's statement that imperialism is imprudent because it educates individual citizens, too, to want absolute power within the city.[47] Such aspirations conflict – in Alcibiades' case, manifestly – with the egalitarian ideals on which democracies, ancient or modern, depend.

On this point Thucydides and Plato were near allied as critics of imperial democracy. In his *Gorgias*, Plato drew together the foregoing constellation of Thucydidean insights in his portrait of the ambitious Callicles, who united admiration for *andreia* with contempt for egalitarian politics. Callicles the Athenian, the lover of Demos,[48] was a great admirer of Themistocles, Cimon, and Pericles, the architects of Athenian imperialism.[49] Callicles had been educated all too well by Athens' successful imperialists, for his ambitions far exceeded the capacities of the democratic polity to integrate them or to direct them meaningfully: 'This is the noble and just according to nature, and as I will tell you now openly: it is necessary for one who intends to live correctly to allow his desires to be as great as possible and not to control them, and to be ready and able to satisfy his enlarged appetites through manly courage (*andreia*) and intelligence, and to fill himself full of whatever he happens to desire.'[50]

Like Alcibiades, Callicles adamantly maintains that democratic equality is harmful and unjust, a tool employed by the weak to control the strong;[51] he envisions his 'strong man' as a tyrannical master ruling justifiably over slaves;[52] and he himself embodies many of the traits ascribed by the respective authors to the unrestrained, acquisitive, and pugnacious Athenian Empire.[53] In particular, as his own rhetoric shows, Callicles is dedicated to the ideal of *pleonexia* – the excessive desire to get more, regardless of prevailing standards of fairness, justice, and equality.[54] It is all too fitting that Callicles himself repeatedly envisions his ideal as an expression of the ultimate freedom and virility.[55]

However great the harm done to equality by such imperially educated figures, though, Thucydides teaches us that ambitious individuals like Alcibiades and Callicles also damaged the democratic ideal of free speech, in that their behaviour understandably gave rise to fear and suspicion among their fellow citizens. According to Thucydides, for example, the Athenian citizenry grew increasingly suspicious of Alcibiades because they feared he desired tyranny[56] – which, Thucydides says, ultimately deprived the Athenians of his good advice and led to the city's decline late in the war. As rulers of the other Greeks, the Athenians were not well positioned to teach their ambitious leaders that any aspiration to rule must be subordinated to the interests of the wider community of ordinary citizens. Perhaps if the Athenians had been better leaders of the Greeks, they could have educated their own aspiring leaders to act in more enlightened ways. Instead, as it was, ordinary Athenians could not trust their politicians; they had to keep their leaders under constant surveillance. They thereby made themselves susceptible to Diodotus' criticism that Athenian audiences were so suspicious of the ulterior motives of speakers that those speakers had to lie and deceive in order to be believed.[57] Imperial democracy is the source and inspiration for this iteration of the 'Cretan liar's paradox.' The practical wisdom that supposedly resulted from free exchange and open deliberation was threatened by the unhealthy relationship between ordinary citizens and their imperialistic leaders.

Free speech was also eroded, according to Thucydides, by the imperial democrats' tendency to embrace a hot-headed, militant conception of courage that presented obstacles to free exchange, favoured war hawks, and made the citizenry antagonistic towards anyone who counselled caution or delay.[58] During the Sicilian debate, for example, Alcibiades' rival Nicias urged the audience not to yield to a misguided sense of shame – that is, to the fear of being called a coward – during the ensuing vote.[59] During the eventual vote, however, Thucydides says, anyone opposed to the expedition kept quiet out of fear that he would appear disloyal or unpatriotic.[60] The constraints and demands of imperialism, which took on the aspect of necessity in the minds of classical Athenians, tended to erode both equality and liberty within the city.

None of this demonstrates, of course, that imperialism is intrinsically wrong. But Thucydides' critical examination suggests that imperialism, as the Athenians practised it, threatened the ideals of democracy. The Athenians could have done things differently. The Athenians could have – should have – utilized the cognitive resources of democratic deliberation to make a sustained and impartial inquiry into what freedom, courage, and military power were useful *for*, in the particular circumstances of the fifth-century Eastern Mediterranean. They had once been leaders of the Greeks against their aggressive neighbors to the East. In that role they had achieved extraordinary success and benefited themselves to an unfathomable degree. To remain in that role, instead of turning their power against the other Greeks, would have required the Athenians to think themselves out of long-standing cultural norms of competition over manliness. Their failure to muster the requisite level of imagination should be read as an opportunity lost, particularly in a direct, deliberative democracy. This opportunity lost should stand as a reminder to subsequent democracies of the advantages accruing from fidelity to the democratic ideals of open, transparent, and meaningful public dialogue about cultural values and military power. This is just the sort of dialogue that tends to be undermined when freedom is experienced as the bitter necessity of ruling.

NOTES

* In this paper I expand and develop ideas first explored in my *Greed and Injustice in Classical Athens* (Princeton: Princeton University Press, 2001); 'Pericles' Anatomy of Democratic Courage,' *American Journal of Philology* 122 (2001): 505–25; 'The Dark Side of Democratic Courage,' *Social Research* 71, no. 4 (2004) 73–106; 'Courage in the Democratic Polis,' *Classical Quarterly* 54, no. 2 (2004): 406–23; and *Greek Political Thought* (Oxford: Blackwell, 2006). I thank Josh Ober and Harvey Yunis for helpful discussions.

1 In accepting a broad view of imperialism, I follow Michael Doyle's *Empires* (Ithaca: Cornell University Press, 1986). Doyle relies on a popular definition of empire as 'effective control, whether formal or informal' (30). With Doyle I consider it unhelpful to confine the study of imperialism to modernity or to states that seek specifically to annex territory. For other reflections, see Giovanni Arrighi, *The Geometry of Imperialism* (London: NLB, 1978), and the classic essay, still well worth reading, of Joseph Schumpeter in his *Imperialism and Social Classes* (New York: Kelly; and Oxford: Blackwell, 1951).

2 Compare Strauss's contribution in this volume, which points to the differences between ancient and modern moral judgements concerning the treatment of foreign peoples.

3 One of the best discussions of the novelty of Athenian imperialism within the Greek world can be found in Kurt Raaflaub, *The Discovery of Freedom in Ancient Greece*, rev. ed. (Chicago: University of Chicago Press, 2004), 118–26. Raaflaub carefully distinguishes Athens' empire from Sparta's hegemony within the Peloponnesian League. On the connections between democracy and war, see the fine collection of essays in David McCann and Barry Strauss, eds., *War and Democracy: A Comparative Study of the Korean War and the Peloponnesian War* (London: East Gate, 2001).

4 On pugnacity as a general feature of the ancient Mediterranean world, see Eckstein's essay in this volume.

5 In his *Carnage and Culture: Landmark Battles in the Rise of Western Power* (New York: Doubleday, 2001), 27–59, Victor Hanson provides an interesting modern treatment of the postwar ideology, unusual in that it accepts the Greek ideological view as historical fact.

6 On the transformations from the heroic to the political conception of courage, see Karen Bassi, 'The Semantics of Manliness in Ancient Greece,' in Ralph.M. Rosen and Ineke Sluiter, eds., *Andreia: Studies in Manliness and Courage in Classical Antiquity* (Leiden: Brill, 2003), 25–58.

7 See my 'Courage in the Democratic Polis,' *Classical Quarterly* 54, no. 2 (2004): 406–23.

8 For a fuller discussion of the contrasts discussed in this paragraph, especially in connection with the Persian Wars, see the seminal study of Kurt Raaflaub, *Discovery of Freedom*; see also M.H. Hansen, *The Athenian Democracy in the Age of Demosthenes: Structure, Principles, and Ideology* (Oxford: Blackwell, 1991), 74–8; and M.H. Hansen, 'The Ancient Athenian and the Modern Liberal View of Liberty as a Democratic Ideal,' in Josiah Ober and Charles W. Hedrick, Jr, *Dēmokratia* (Princeton: Princeton University Press), 91–104.

9 Herodotus, *Histories*, 7.139.

10 On the concept of a national narrative, see the essays collected in Homi Bhabha, ed., *Nation and Narration* (London: Routledge, 1990), especially Bhabha's own introductory essay.

11 Ryan K. Balot, 'The Dark Side of Democratic Courage,' *Social Research* 71, no. 4 (2004): 73–106 at 82–3; M.W. Taylor, *The Tyrant Slayers: The Heroic Image in Fifth-Century Athenian Art and Politics* (Salem: Ayer, 1991), 1–15.

12 Herodotus, *Histories*, 6.109.

13 See my 'Pericles' Anatomy of Democratic Courage,' *American Journal of Philology* 122 (2001): 505–25.

14 Thucydides, *History of the Peloponnesian War*, 2.40.

15 Cf. Michael Doyle, *Empires* (Ithaca: Cornell University Press, 1986), 70–81.

16 See, for example, Meiggs and Lewis 46.41–42, 49.11–12, in Russell Meiggs and David Lewis, *A Selection of Greek Historical Inscriptions to the End of the Fifth Century BC* (Oxford: Clarendon, 1969).

17 Cf. Paul Cartledge, 'The *Machismo* of the Athenian Empire – or the Reign of the Phaulos?' in Lin Foxhall and John Salmon, eds., *When Men Were Men: Masculinity, Power, and Identity in Classical Antiquity* (London: Routledge, 1998), 54–67; Eva Keuls, *The Reign of the Phallus* (New York: Harper and Row, 1985); and my 'The Dark Side of Democratic Courage,' 85–6.

18 See Raaflaub's masterful discussion in *Discovery of Freedom* on the unprecedented nature of Athenian imperialism within the Greek world.

19 On Athens as a 'tyrant *polis*' (*polis tyrannos*), see the interesting conflict between three essays in *Popular Tyranny*, ed. Kathryn Morgan (Austin: University of Texas Press, 2003): Lisa Kallett, '*Dêmos Tyrannos*: Wealth, Power, and Economic Patronage,' 117–53; Kurt Raaflaub, 'Stick and Glue: The Function of Tyranny in Fifth-Century Athenian Democracy,' 59–94; and Josiah Ober, 'Tyrant Killing as Therapeutic *Stasis*: A Political Debate in Images and Texts,' 215–50. Though this paper takes a different tack, the seminal treatment remains that of W.K. Connor, '*Tyrannis Polis*,' in John D'Arms and John Eadie, eds., *Ancient and Modern: Essays in Honor of Gerald F. Else* (Ann Arbor: University of Michigan Press, 1977), 95–109. See also Strauss's essay in the present volume for interesting reflections on the 'tyranny' (or lack thereof) involved in Athens' imperial practices. I am inclined to view the issue of the popularity of empire as both highly contextual and dependent on the economic class and political outlook of the subjects in question. Certain subjects of Athens, or rather certain sectors of the subject populations, undoubtedly received benefits from Athens' imperialism – for example, proponents of democracy who summoned Athenians to help settle domestic political disputes. Others, such as members of the wealthy elite who probably shouldered much of the burden of tribute payments, came out on the opposite side. But opinions could change over time, depending on which superpower's ships were in the harbour and on the vicissitudes of warfare, economic surplus, and so on. On the thorny issues that are involved, see Geoffrey de Ste Croix, 'The Character of the Athenian Empire,' *Historia* 3 (1954): 1–41; de Ste Croix is properly critical of Thucydides; see also Charles Fornara, '*IG* I², 39.52-57, and the "Popularity" of the Athenian Empire,' *CSCA* 10 (1977): 39–55.

20 'Old Oligarch,' 1.18.

21 Euripides, *Suppliants*, 491–3.

22 Aristophanes, *Babylonians*, fr. 71 *Poetae Comici Graeci*.

23 Thucydides, *History of the Peloponnesian War*, 3.10–11. On the language of slavery in contemporary texts, see especially Raaflaub, *Discovery of Freedom*, 128–32, with notes and additional references.

24 Aristophanes, *Knights*, 1–1114.

25 Ibid., 1329–33. For discussion of the Aristophanic evidence, see especially Jeffrey Henderson, 'Demos, Demagogue, Tyrant in Attic Old Comedy,' in *Popular Tyranny*, ed. Kathryn Morgan (Austin: University of Texas Press, 2003), 155–80; and Raaflaub, 'Stick and Glue.'

26 Aristophanes, *Wasps*, 1071–90.

27 Here I side very strongly with Raaflaub and Ober, *contra* Kallet (above, n12). As Raaflaub and Ober point out, it is particularly important when discussing Athenian imperialism to distinguish between the private attitudes and public ideology of democratic Athenians.

28 Lysias, 2.55–6.

29 Isocrates, 4.104–6.

30 On many of these themes, see Balot, *Greek Political Thought*, 159–67; and Raaflaub, *Discovery of Freedom*, 166–81.

31 Thucydides, *History*, 1.76, 5.105.

32 On the status of the Thucydidean speeches, see Harvey Yunis, *Taming Democracy: Models of Political Rhetoric in Classical Athens* (Ithaca: Cornell University Press, 1996), 60–6; idem, 'Narrative, Rhetoric, and Ethical Instruction in Thucydides,' in *Papers on Rhetoric IV*, ed. Lucia Montefusco (Rome: 2002), 275–86; and idem, 'Writing for Reading: Thucydides, Plato, and the Emergence of the Critical Reader,' in *Written Texts and the Rise of Literate Culture in Ancient Greece*, ed. Yunis (Cambridge: Cambridge University Press, 2003), 189–212; *contra*, most recently, Thomas Garrity, 'Thucydides 1.22.1: Content and Form in the Speeches,' *American Journal of Philology* 119 (1998): 361–84.

33 Cf. Raaflaub, *Discovery of Freedom*, 187–93.

34 Thucydides, *History*, 3.45.

35 Ibid., 6.87.

36 Ibid., 2.63.

37 Ibid., 3.37.

38 Ibid., 6.18.

39 Cf. Strauss's essay; my suggestion is that the freedom/slavery dichotomy could be experienced as a psychological truth, even if it appears from a third-party perspective (such as ours) to exaggerate the facts on the ground.

40 Ian Morris, 'The Athenian Empire (478–404 BC)' at http://www.princeton.edu/~pswpc/pdfs/morris/120508.pdf.

41   Machiavelli, *The Prince*, 3.21; idem, *Discorsi*, 1.6, 2.19.

42   See my 'The Dark Side of Democratic Courage,' 87–90; Victoria Wohl, *Love Among the Ruins: The Erotics of Democracy in Classical Athens* (Princeton: Princeton University Press, 2002), 171–86.

43   See my *Greed and Injustice in Classical Athens* (Princeton: Princeton University Press, 2001), 166–72.

44   *History*, 6.18. On the ideology of freedom and its relation to power, see Raaflaub, *Discovery of Freedom*; on the subject of constraint and its attendant frustrations, see the helpful treatment of Wohl, *Love Among the Ruins*, 171–214; deeper reflections on compulsion and necessity in Thucydides can be found in Leo Strauss, *The City and Man* (Chicago: University of Chicago Press, 1964), 182–92.

45   See my 'Dark Side of Democratic Courage.'

46   Thucydides, *History*, 6.16.

47   Aristotle, *Politics*, 1333b29–36.

48   Plato, *Gorgias*, 481d.

49   Ibid., 517a7–b1.

50   Ibid., 491e6–492a3.

51   Ibid., 483b–c.

52   Ibid., 484a–b.

53   Cf. Arlene Saxonhouse, 'An Unspoken Theme in Plato's *Gorgias*: War,' *Interpretation* 11 (1983): 139–69.

54   Balot, *Greed and Injustice*, 1–14.

55   Plato, *Gorgias*, 483e–484c.

56   Thucydides, *History*, 6.15.

57   Ibid., 3.43.

58   See especially Balot, 'Dark Side of Democratic Courage,' 87–90.

59   Thucydides, *History*, 6.13.

60   Ibid., 6.24.

5 Liberty and Empire, with the Benefit of Limited Hindsight – or, What Herodotus of Halicarnassus Saw

CLIFFORD ORWIN

Liberty and Empire, with the Benefit of 2500 Years of Hindsight: that, or something like it, is what I would have titled this book. Certainly the other contributors have taken full advantage of this imposing parade of centuries, joining in looking back on antiquity from the vantage point of today. For all their differences in other respects, Ryan K. Balot, David Edward Tabachnick, Barry S. Strauss, David Hendrickson, Toivo Koivukoski, and Leah Bradshaw all bring the baggage of America's travail in Iraq to their analyses of the policies of ancient Athens. Such an exercise is not just pardonable but even mandatory. The spectacle of the United States, at once the freest country in the world and the most powerful, embroiled in a questionable war in the service of extending the sway of liberty, cannot but concentrate the mind on the paradox of liberal democratic empire.

My own approach will differ from theirs only in my extreme laziness. While I too will apply the benefit of hindsight to the relationship between freedom and empire, I'll dispense with the last 2,425 years of it. I'll expound not my own view of these matters, but that of the very first thinker to bring hindsight to his treatment of them – thus founding, in a manner of speaking, the genre in which the contributors to this volume persist. My hope is that this oldest such perspective on the problem of our volume, being the first and in that sense also the newest, will make up in freshness and thoughtfulness what it lacks in the way of scholarly citations.

The thinker that I mean was Herodotus, looking back on the Persian War and its consequences for the leading cities of Hellas from the vantage point of fifty-plus years. Such a span may seem paltry to us grazers on successive millennia of examples, but speaking actuarially, he could not reasonably have expected nature to grant him a longer one.

It is hardly surprising that a Hellenic thinker should have had the first word on the relationship of liberty to empire. The Hellenes were, by both their own and Herodotus' estimation, the first people to combine liberty with the benefits of what we would call civilized life. Unlike those dauntless rovers of the steppes, the Scythians, the Hellenes lived in cities like other peoples: they did not sacrifice all else to their liberty.[1] As a result they were vulnerable, as the Scythians were not, to encroachment by the great empires pressing upon them from the East, first the Lydian and then the Persian. This ongoing challenge favoured comparison of the way of life of free cities with that of despotic and imperial ones, and of this Herodotus has left us a document not to be surpassed. Several of his best known scenes pit a spokesman for liberty against an uncomprehending and therefore overconfident despot. Most famous of these is the running dialogue between Xerxes and Demaratos, the king of Sparta whom an unjust exile has driven to accompany the Persian host against his own city.[2] Surely, says Xerxes, the Hellenes will crumble before the vast conglomerate host of the Persians, even the Dorians who are the finest of them and the Spartans who are the finest of these. No, says Demaratos, for the Spartans fear their law, which bids them stand and fight, more than Xerxes' enslaved masses fear him.[3] Liberty thus emerges at the outset as erecting not a less but a more formidable master than the despot.

We today view liberty as inseparable from democracy, but the Hellenes were more open-minded. Indeed among the Hellenes not Athens but Sparta was widely admired as the very model of a free city. The despotism that Xerxes sought to impose was an offence to all who would deem themselves free, but this did not imply a greater attachment on their part to a regime of the few than to one of the many. It did imply a rejection of tyranny, the Hellenic counterpart to despotic monarchy in its lawlessness and tendency to excess. What the barbarian took for granted – that the relationship between master and slave pervaded every aspect of human life, to the exclusion therefore of any sphere that the Hellenes or we would recognize as political – the Hellene rejected as worthy only of barbarians.

Arguably, then, what oligarchs and democrats shared overshadowed the differences between them. The deepest fault line ran not between those who insisted on the rule of the majority and those who did not, but between those who would accept the rule of one and those who would not. Consider the great speech of Sokles the Corinthian at 5.92, the aim of which is to dissuade Sparta's allies from acquiescing in her plan to hamper the burgeoning power of newly democratic Athens by restoring her recently deposed tyrants. It's almost as if Sokles has read Montesquieu: the distinction that really matters is that between tyranny (what Montesquieu would call despotism) and all the others, those regimes that Montesquieu calls 'moderate' precisely in their rejection of absolutism. Sokles, the representative of an oligarchic city addressing an assembly of other such representatives of oligarchic cities, wholly abstracts from the difference between oligarchy and democracy: insofar as Athens abhors tyranny, her cause is equally that of every free city.

From the epic struggle between Persian and Hellene we might be tempted to conclude that empire is essentially an adjunct of despotism. Certainly Persia doubles in the work as both the despotic and the imperial power par excellence, and the Persians themselves see each as implying the other. But there is, as it turns out, a Persian notion of freedom. The Persians deem themselves free if they are ruled by despots of their own stock rather than by foreigners, and if they as a people rule other peoples rather than being ruled by them. They see freedom as a zero-sum game; one possesses it only insofar as one has extinguished it in others. The Persians had at one time been enslaved by the Medes; subsequently they turned the tables, and from there they went on to enslave others. The model of the one king wielding absolute power over his subjects seems to favour that of one people lording it over other peoples; just as the model of one Zeus ruling the whole vast expanse of heaven (by Zeus the naturalistic Persians mean the sky) justifies that of one monarch ruling the whole earth.[4]

There is yet another reason why the imperialism of Persia is in principle universal. The Persians suppose that they rank first among all peoples, followed by their nearest neighbours, followed by the first circle beyond these, and so on and so forth indefinitely, so that the farther away a people dwells the greater the Persians' title to rule it.[5] What might seem a harmless conceit of vanity implies the legitimacy of a policy of infinite imperial expansion.

On this point, however, the Persians prove to be misinformed. Their empire fares best closest to home, where their neighbours are suitable for despotizing over. It's when they stray too far afield, whether to the east (the Massagetae),[6] the north (the Scythians),[7] or the west (the Hellenes), that they find themselves overmatched. There are many reasons for this, but for our purposes we may as well stay with the most obvious: despotism at home proves incompatible with the cohesiveness, determination, and self-confidence required to defeat free men.

The event proves Demaratos right and Xerxes wrong: a handful of citizens strictly habituated to the defence of their freedom is a match for a slavish throng many times its size.

At the same time, we must note an irony of the world as Herodotus presents it. I earlier suggested that the success of the Hellenes in combining freedom with civilization left them vulnerable to imperial conquest in a way that the Scythians were not. That success also exposed them to another danger, one best described as a temptation – namely, that of coming to exercise empire themselves.

It is not just despotic, barbarous regimes that disclose an insatiable thirst to dominate others; so too do free Hellenic ones. If we could grow tired of anything in the hands of a master storyteller like Herodotus, it would be the endless petty, vicious wars that rage among all his Hellenic cities, often waged with great cruelty in the name of pretexts that barely qualify as flimsy.[8] You might expect these cities themselves to grow tired of these wars, but you would be mistaken. Only when one of them has fared so badly (as have the Argives at the hands of the Spartans)[9] that its very survival as an autonomous city is threatened, does it grasp the necessity of taking a breather for a decade or two.

Except for some tribes so remote as to preclude first-hand knowledge of them,[10] Herodotus knows of only two peoples whose ways can be described as peace loving. The first of these are the Egyptians, whose servility and unmanliness no healthy people would envy. The others are the Lydians, a once fierce people reduced to effeminacy as a matter of policy by their Persian conquerors.[11] Simply stated, Herodotus presents no civilized people that combines a resolve to preserve its own liberty with an equal respect for the liberty of others.

Which is to say that in the absence of a common enemy – such as the Persians supply for the Hellenes – the free cities known to Herodotus pursue foreign policies no less predatory than those of despotic monarchies. Divested of its dubious theological trappings, Herodotus' view of the world seems every bit as harsh as that of the spokesmen in Thucydides for what Leo Strauss has called the Athenian thesis.[12] It is only to be expected that every state, be it free or unfree, will strive to expand its power at the expense of other states. Outside the Hellenic world this leads to an endless ebb and flow of empires. Even tame Egypt and the wild Scythians have each managed one kick at the can of dominion over others, however incongruous with their respective histories otherwise.[13] While their laws may differ widely, all non-Hellenic civilized peoples of which Herodotus knows are despotisms – a family resemblance that smooths any wrinkles between the domestic and the foreign. One despotism may or may not be as well adapted to empire as another (in this, Persia far outshines the others), but a king accustomed to keeping his own people in subjection is unlikely to lose any sleep over subduing foreign ones. Nor will his original subjects smart at the injustice of reducing others to a state yet lower than their own. Rather they will understand liberty as the Persians do: as the status of the people that while despotically governed itself delights in dwelling near the apex of a vaster pyramid of subjugation.

A free people will understand its liberty very differently, as it will that of other peoples. As we have seen, however, this offers no guarantee that it will limit its exercise of its own liberty out of deference for that of others. The peoples we encounter in Herodotus remain largely oblivious to any tension between the practice of self-government at home and that of subjection abroad. As free peoples vary, however, so does the inter-face between liberty and empire. Of the Spartans it might be said that they are too attached to the freedom of their city to risk it in the pursuit of empire. This sounds better (or at any rate nobler) than it proves to be in practice. Republican scruples play no part in this reticence: we recall how willing the Spartans were to reimpose tyranny on Athens after the expulsion of the Peisistratids in order to maintain their sphere of influence.[14] The Spartans eschew empire because they are cautious and for no loftier reason; comparing the poverty of Hellas with the opulence of Asia, they think the Persians mad for having risked so much for so lit-tle.[15] They retire from the fray as soon as Europe and therefore their own city is no longer in danger;[16] for the same reason that they eschew em-pire, they leave their allies in the lurch.

With Athens the problem is the obverse. No one could accuse her of a lack of zeal for the common Hellenic cause. Determined to see the struggle through, by the end of Herodotus' narrative they have already pushed the Persians out of Europe and have begun to encroach on them in Asia. Even more worrisome, however, is that with Sparta – her only peer among the allies – temporarily out of the picture, she has already begun the natural slide from hegemony towards empire.

This last development of course implies an eventual conflict be-tween Athens and Sparta. Herodotus ends his work with a cautionary parable against imperialism.[17] Clearly, this admonition is aimed at the Hellenic reader, and it is just as clearly a *vaticinium post eventum*.[18] Earlier, at 6.98, Herodotus suggests a possible interpretation of the unprecedented earthquake that shook the sacred island of Delos on the eve of the Battle of Marathon. It might have augured the three generations of unprecedented misfortunes about to engulf the Hellenes, 'more than befell [them] in the twenty generations before Darius.' 'Some of these came about through the Persians, and some by the actions of the chief peoples of Hellas warring against each other.' Herodotus knows of two kinds of calamity: the presence of a foe so powerful and destructive as to unite the chief cities of Hellas against him, and the absence of such a foe. We don't know the precise date of the publication of Herodotus' work, but if we count three generations beginning from this earthquake on Delos, that would bring us into the Peloponnesian War.[19]

Modern democracy is inimical to empire in principle, for it rests from the outset on the inalienable right of every people to self-government. That may or may not preclude non-democratic experiments in self-government, but it does bar the extended sway of one people over another. Where would we look in classical democracy for a similar regulative principle? In the Herodotean text, perhaps to the speech of Sokles aforementioned.

If it is wrong for one Hellenic city to impose a tyrannical regime on another, should it not be equally so for one such city to rule another by whatever means? If it is unthinkable for any city not subject to arbitrary and unlimited power to subject another city to it, doesn't this imply a policy of non-intervention in the affairs of other cities – except perhaps to rescue them from the clutches of arbitrary power, whether that power be home-grown or foreign? We can't presume that Sokles himself subscribes to either of these positions, for he represents an oligarchic city; and despite or because of his deliberate abstraction from the distinction between democracy and oligarchy, he might not have objected to a decision to foist the latter on Athens.

Still, Sokles does underline the inconsistency of any city depriving others of the freedom that it cherishes for itself. Such statements are rare in ancient texts, but this one at least enjoys exceptional prominence in the text in which it appears. And it can't simply be said that Herodotus knows of no city that has honoured this principle in practice, for on this one occasion (if on no other), not just Corinth (for which Sokles speaks), but *all* of the allies whom Sparta has summoned to assist it in reimposing the yoke of tyranny on Athens, decline to collaborate in so doing.[20]

One swallow does not make a summer, but might a universal and systematic statement of Sokles' position command general and permanent assent among human beings? Might the enjoyment of liberty at home be forever recognized as incompatible with the exercise of empire abroad? Does not the liberal-democratic argument consist precisely in an attempt to generalize and systematize Sokles' position?

From the very beginning, this liberal-democratic argument has entailed a seismic shift away from the principles of political thought bequeathed to the West by Plato and Aristotle. (If they were chary of imperialism, it was for quite different reasons.) Still, Sokles, as a character in Herodotus, is as innocent of those Platonic/Aristotelian principles as his author. Indifferent to the interests of philosophy, remaining on the plane of politics and therefore accepting the primacy of liberty among the human goods, he first propounds the liberty of other cities as the limit on that of one's own.[21]

NOTES

1 *Histories,* 4.46. I cite Herodotus by book and chapter; translations are my own. I recommend the translation of David Grene: Herodotus, *The Histories* (Chicago: University of Chicago Press, 1987). For my general approach to Herodotus I am most indebted to the following: Seth Benardete, *Herodotean Inquiries* [1969], 2nd ed. (South Bend: St Augustine's Press, 2004); Stanley Rosen, 'Herodotus Reconsidered,' *Giornale di Metafisica* 18 (1963): 194–218, reprinted (minus most of its footnotes and with one elision) in Herodotus, *The Histories,* Norton Critical Edition, ed. Walter Blanco and Jennifer Tolbert Roberts (New York: Norton, 1992), 332–56, and reworked in Rosen, *The Quarrel between Philosophy and Poetry: Studies in Ancient Thought* (New York and London: Routledge, Chapman, and Hall, 1988), 33–47; and Norma Thompson, *Herodotus and the Origins of Political Community: Arion's Leap* (New Haven: Yale University Press, 1996). For a recent select bibliography, see Herodotus, *The Histories*, trans. Robin Waterfield (Oxford: Oxford University Press, 1998), xliii–xlv.
2 On Demaratos see Deborah Boedeker, 'The Two Faces of Demaratus,' *Arethusa* 20, nos. 1 and 2 (1987): 185–201.
3 *Histories,* 7.101–4; cf. 209.
4 Ibid., 7.8.
5 Ibid., 1.134, cf. 1.4 and 7.8–9.
6 Ibid., 1.201–16.
7 Ibid., 4.1–142.
8 Ibid., 3.44–59.
9 Ibid., 6.75–83, 7.148–52.
10 Ibid., 4.23–7.
11 Ibid., 1.154–6.

12 Leo Strauss, *The City and Man* (Chicago: Rand McNally, 1964), esp. 183–5.
13 *Histories*, 2.104–10; 1.103–6.
14 Ibid., 5.90–1.
15 Ibid., 9.82.
16 Ibid., 9.106, 114.
17 Ibid., 9.122.
18 The *locus classicus* for the view that the past serves Herodotus as a vehicle
    for admonishing the present is Charles Fornara, *Herodotus: An Interpretive
    Essay* (Oxford: Oxford University Press, 1971). Cf. Christian Meier,
    'Historical Answers to Historical Questions: The Origin of History in
    Ancient Greece,' *Arethusa* 20, nos. 1 and 2 (1987): 41–57; Kurt Raaflaub,
    'Herodotus, Political Thought, and the Meaning of History,' *Arethusa* 20,
    nos. 1 and 2 (1987): 221–48; and James Redfield, 'Herodotus the Tourist,'
    Classical Philology 80 (1985): 114–15.
19 J.A.S. Evans goes so far as to speak of an 'iron law of imperialism' in
    Herodotus, but proves to mean this only in a qualified sense: 'Herodotus
    did not treat imperialism as an expression of human nature, as Thucydi-
    des did, but rather as a *nomos* that is elected freely, but once chosen, cannot
    be abandoned without cost.' Evans, *Herodotus: Explorer of the Past: Three
    Essays* (Princeton: Princeton University Press, 1991), 26–9, 66. So too
    Raaflaub (see note 18) as well as Rosaria Vignolo Munson, '*Ananke* in
    Herodotus,' *Journal of Hellenic Studies* 121 (2001): 30–50. If Evans and
    these others are right, the problem for the reader would lie in identifying
    the fatal moment of free election.
20 For this Sokles deserves much of the credit. For a review of recent inter-
    pretations of the speech, and a ringing defence of it against charges of its
    inaptitude to its situation, see David M. Johnson, 'Herodotus' Storytelling
    Speeches: Socles (5.92) and Leotychides (6.86),' *Classical Journal* 97, no. 1
    (2001): 1–26.
21 For a further elaboration of Herodotus' position on the relationship
    between democracy and imperialism, see my 'Democracy in Motion: Some
    Reflections on Herodotean Politics,' in *Logos and Eros: Essays Honoring
    Stanley Rosen*, ed. Nalin Ranasinghe (South Bend: St Augustine's Press,
    2006), 118-33.

6 Empire and the Eclipse of Politics

LEAH BRADSHAW

In Western political thought, the organization of political communities has been conceived principally between two poles, *polis* and empire. The Greek *polis*, as we know, was a small entity, characterized by a strong sense of citizenship and participatory assembly, and encapsulating what Hannah Arendt called the *res publica*. Public display, common deliberation, and friendship (according to Aristotle) were core elements of political life in this classical Greek model. In contrast to this, the ancient world also offers us the legacy of empire. Empires aim for growth, not self-sufficiency; they breed bureaucracy rather than deliberative assembly; and they eschew the slow and comradely process of public debate for the efficiency of rules and orders. Though ancient Greece certainly had the experience of empire, we usually associate classical empire with Rome, which was famous for disseminating the rule of law over disparate territories and peoples and for its remarkable feats of engineering, such as the aqueduct system that spread throughout Europe.

John Pocock outlines clear and distinct models of citizenship that have shaped the West, one descending from the ancient Greek model of the *polis*, the other from the Roman model of jurisprudence. For Aristotle, 'what makes the citizen the highest order of being is his capacity to rule, and it follows that rule over one's equal is possible only where one's equal rules over one. Therefore the citizen rules and is ruled; citizens join each other in making decisions where each respects the authority of the others, and all join in obeying the decisions.'[1] Such a concept of citizenship cannot be extended into empire without destroying the political community, and this, arguably, is what happened to Athens. Empire was antithetical to the structure of the *polis*, and when Athens became swollen with luxury, licentiousness, and ambition, it imploded.

The second great Western definition of the 'political universe' according to Pocock comes to us from the Romans – specifically, from the Roman jurist Gaius, for whom 'the citizen [is] a legal being, existing in a world of persons, actions and things regulated by law.'[2] 'A "citizen" came to mean someone free to act by law, free to ask and expect the law's protection, a citizen of such and such a legal community of such and such a legal standing in the community.'[3] The shift is dramatic, because the deliberative and *active* participatory element of citizenship is no longer central to this Roman conception. If citizens are no longer conceived as equal partners in the shaping of their political life, but as subjects who are protected by a uniform law, the boundaries of political territory are opened to expansion. Citizenship as equal access to jurisprudence lends itself to empire in a way that the ancient Greek understanding of citizenship does not. According to Pocock, 'it was the notion of law that profoundly affected the meaning of the political. As Paul and Gaius both knew, law denoted something imperial, universal, and multiform.'[4] The Gaian formula works its way through the Western tradition and morphs into something even grander than the legal empire imagined by the Romans, when it is coupled with the modern understanding of individual right. In the contemporary world it is possible to imagine citizenship in a 'global universe.'

The legacies of these two patterns of political organization persist. In some quarters we value 'deliberative democracy,' we worry about representation, we lament the decay of 'communitarian' senses of belonging. Much more predominant, however, is the language of 'globalization,' the emphasis on integrated markets, the mobility of populations through education and technology, and the expansion of human-rights discourse as a universal doctrine. Globalization is an imperial strategy insofar as it is unquestionably the expansion of the political and economic triumph of Western accomplishments throughout the entire world. In this chapter I closely examine the connection between these two models of political organization and their epistemological underpinnings. When we look at patterns of imperialism in the modern world, we may see that they conform to an understanding of the individual that really makes the restitution of *politics*, in the classical Greek sense of human being belonging to a *polis*, impossible. Empire may be triumphant in modernity. Politics may be over.

Empires have always been an integral part of politics in the West, and they are always expansionist, though what they are interested in promoting may vary. A big question is whether modern empire is consistent with earlier forms of empire, or whether there is something unique about the modern experience. In Laura Johnson Bagby's contribution to this volume, the author argues that the imperial expansion of ancient Athens was categorically different from the kind of imperialism we see now. Drawing on the examples of the demagogues Pericles and Alcibiades, and the accounts of Thucydides, she makes the case that the principal motivation for empire in ancient Athens was the desire for honour and glory. Emboldened by leaders like Alcibiades, Athens sought to expand its territories and its reputation. Bagby draws a clear line between this ancient, democratic, honour-driven imperialism and the expansionism of modern *liberal democracy*. She argues that 'for modern ·advocates of liberal democracy, democracy and empire are incompatible. They are often even supremely sensitive to charges of economic or cultural imperialism, because the liberal democratic ideal of individual right has become, at the international level, the right to self-determination. Democratic peace theory now points to liberal democracy as the answer to world conflict.' She further contends that if any American president were to announce boldly that he was advancing military action in another part of the world so as to increase the honour and glory of his homeland, he or she would be considered a pariah both in America and overseas.

It is not absolutely clear to me, as it seems to be to Bagby, that modern empire is without an 'honour' motive. Waller Newell, also in this volume, makes a persuasive case that Machiavelli formulated a new and distinctly modern vision of a *'liberal empire,* an empire in which republican virtue is the basis for the liberty of the individual.' Newell argues that given the choice between the archetype of Sparta and that of Rome (small, vigorous city-state versus splendid empire), Machiavelli opted for empire. Drawing on Machiavelli to illuminate American imperial ambitions, Newell points to the American expansion of economic and military power throughout the world in the nineteenth and twentieth centuries, 'accompanied by the crusade to extend the individual's liberty to achieve a better life to all peoples on earth.' As Newell sees it, the American project has been one of harnessing 'the democratic energies of the people [as the] vehicle for a republic's expansion into empire in which all classes would benefit.'

Modern empire may be honour driven, as in Newell's understanding of republican expansionism, but it may be driven also by those very things – a universal commitment to the liberal idea of right – that Bagby regards as antithetical to empire. Jennifer Pitts in her recent book *A Turn to Empire* tries to show how, by the mid-nineteenth century, Europeans had embarked fully on an imperial mission to assert the superiority of European culture throughout the world. We know that these ambitions resulted in decades of colonization, brutal exploitation of less developed parts of the world, and the trafficking in human beings; yet Pitts argues that nonetheless, imperial ambition was fuelled by a commitment to universal values that the imperial powers truly believed should be exported to all of humanity. Examining the work of Burke, Tocqueville, and John Stuart Mill, Pitts shows that despite their differences, these thinkers shared a belief in the values of 'human dignity, freedom, the rule of law, and representative government.' They were all universalists in the sense that they 'adhered to the principles that all human beings are naturally equals and that certain moral principles are universally valid.'[5] Imperialism in the mid-nineteenth century had a proselytizing agenda and a mission to admit all of humanity into a progressive economic and moral universe.

Pitts identifies something in the cast of modern empire that may be significantly different from classical notions of the same, in that underscoring imperial ambition is the professed belief in universal values that are potentially extendable to all human beings. The universal reach of Enlightenment commitments continues with a powerful voice in the contemporary world, though the inspiration for those commitments tends to rely less on the republican vigour of Machiavelli and his heirs, and more on the rights-based theory of the German philosopher Immanuel Kant. Kant defends the universal expansion of right on the grounds that the protection of individual autonomy is the first priority of a moral agent. For Kant, our purpose as human beings is to act in accordance with a categorical imperative, something that we can know through reason, independent of any divine infusion. Reason leads us to the dictum that we ought to respect the autonomy and rights of others as we respect our own. The end of the state, for Kant, 'which is indeed the highest formal condition (*conditio sine qua non*) of all other external duties is the *right* of men *under coercive public laws* by which each can be given what is due to him and secured from any attack by others.' '*Right* is the restriction of each's individual freedom so that it harmonizes with the freedom of everyone else (insofar as this is possible within the terms of a general law). And *public right* is the distinctive quality of the *external laws* which make this constant harmony possible.'[6] In the Kantian world, politics is about framing the right sort of laws to guarantee the maximum amount of individual liberty. Kant predicted that there would be less violence in the modern world, more charity, less quarrel, more 'reliability in keeping one's word,' and so on, but he thought that these measures would come about almost inadvertently, 'partly from a love of honour, partly from a lively awareness of where one's advantage lies.' The integration of economic markets Kant thought to be one of the principal catalysts for what we now term 'globalization.' The expansion of human rights (i.e., the right to autonomy) Kant thought inevitably attendant on these developments. Though Kant did not recommend the abandonment of the sovereign state as the guarantor of individual freedoms, this was more of a pragmatic measure than a principled one. In theory, all sovereign states could be collapsed into a 'cosmopolitan humanity,' since the goals of individuals are universally the same everywhere. We have now reached the stage, Kant announced in the eighteenth century, where a violation of right in any part of the world is considered an affront to our sense of right at home. Kant's 'imperialism' is duty-based, not honour-based, and while it does not inspire the warrior or freedom fighter, it may encourage deference to international courts and war-crimes tribunals. If we think back to John Pocock's distinction between *polis* citizenship and Roman citizenship, we may see that the Kantian moral universe is the full working out of the latter strain.

Even though, as Bagby remarked, liberal democrats are 'sensitive to charges of economic and cultural imperialism,' the process of global modernization has continued unabated throughout the last century, as has the push for international human rights. There are critics in the West who praise the imperial quest of liberal democracies, but who also see that quest as a matter of material expediency rather than a moral mission or even a mission of 'honour.' Deepak Lal argues that 'globalization is not new. It has been a cyclical phenomenon of history for millennia, being associated with the rise and fall of empires.'[7] Lal's book, *In Praise of Empires*, boldly argues that imperial expansion is the norm in the West; furthermore, periods of imperial hegemony are the most stable and prosperous, and the empire we are living under now is the United States. 'The United States is undoubtedly an empire', Lal declares, and 'it is more than a hegemon, as it seeks control over not only foreign but also aspects of domestic policy in other countries.' Lal thinks that this is a good thing, with one proviso: the United States should back off any residue of moral proselytizing on human rights and should stick to the imperial project of advancing the institutions of civil society in unstable parts of the world. 'The most serious problem facing a new

U.S. imperium,' he writes, 'is the self-image of the United States as the only moral nation pursuing universal values.'[8] Lal distinguishes between the *cosmological* and *material* aspects of empire, the former being the export of ideas, beliefs, and values, the latter being the export of the bases for economic stability and security. If the United States wants to continue to succeed in its imperial strategy, Lal advises it to abandon its moral aspirations for human rights and embrace coldly the materialist base of expansion. Drawing on Hedley Bull's analysis of the anarchical society, he asserts that there *are* elementary and universal goods which all societies want and that it is to these universals that the American empire ought to turn its attention. These goods are (1) security against death and violent bodily harm, (2) the keeping of promises and contracts, and (3) stabilization of possession through rules of property.[9] In fact, Lal says, empires can secure these universal goods better than independent sovereign states, because they are more powerful.

Lal's list of universal goods – security, contract, and stabilization of possession – conform almost perfectly to those things which Thomas Hobbes in the seventeenth century identified as the sole concern of men united into a commonwealth. According to Hannah Arendt, Hobbes is the real genius of modern imperialism because it is through Hobbes that we can understand that 'what imperialists wanted was expansion of political power without the foundation of a body politic.'[10] Hobbes starts with the assumption that human beings are by nature solitary, atomistic, and apolitical, and that any political arrangements they live inside are legitimate only by contract. The principal object of political community is the security of the individual in body and possession, and it is political authority that makes this possible. The state is purely instrumental for securing the goods of the individual. For Hobbes, 'the final cause, end or design of men (who naturally love liberty, and dominion over others) in the introduction of that restraint upon themselves (in which we see them live in commonwealths) is the foresight of their own preservation and of a more contented life thereby, that is to say, of getting themselves out of that miserable condition of war which is necessarily consequent upon the natural passions of man.'[11] All justice and morality follows from the contract into government, and the terms of justice and morality refer back to the primary purpose of securing the individual against aggression and impediment from his fellow citizens. Given Hobbes's assumptions about the natural state of war, the only means whereby we can secure ourselves is by pursuing power after power. As Arendt says, it follows from Hobbes's logic that the goal of modern expansion is neither pillage nor conquest (typical of ancient empire), nor the project to extend some categorical imperative of rights, but rather, 'business speculation, where expansion meant the permanent broadening of industrial production and economic transactions characteristic of the 19th century.'[12] Hobbes provides the theoretical foundations of this novel form of expansion in his conception of the individual as an interest-driven, fearful, and solitary creature. The Hobbesian man does not seek the glory of political conquest, or the good opinion of mankind, but the means of a secure and contented life, and there is no assurance of the latter without the relentless quest for power.

Membership in any political community is for Hobbes 'a temporary and limited affair which essentially does not change the solitary and private character of the individual (who has "no pleasure, but on the contrary, a great deale of griefe in keeping company, where there is no power to overwhelm them all"), or create permanent bonds between him and his fellow men.'[13] Hobbes's subjects are chronically irascible and restless and always in pursuit of power, which they understand as the only means whereby they can secure any peace for themselves. '[Hobbes] realized that acquisition of wealth conceived as a never-ending process that can be guaranteed only by the seizure of political power for the accumulating process must sooner or later force open all existing territorial limits. He foresaw that a society which had entered the path of never-ending acquisition had to engineer a dynamic political organization capable of a corresponding never-ending process of power-generation.'[14]

Hobbes in his account offers no reason why any political community should restrict its size, nor indeed does he offer any reason why one would maintain allegiance to a political sovereign who cannot guarantee stability and security. Political loyalties are fluid and calculated and are always seen in relation to the individually pursued goods they can advance. If economic empire can secure security and prosperity more assuredly than a walled-in state, then empire is the more reasonable course. The issue is not an evaluative one – the moral stance of state versus empire – but merely a strategic one.

The Hobbesian world view, with its drive for security and its corresponding impetus for power, may seem a long stretch from the Kantian promotion of universal right, or even from the Machiavellian extension of republican honour, but in certain respects the differences may be trivial. The state in all cases is instrumental in the advancement of individual goods. Those individual goods are universally defined as either security and commodious living or the autonomy of right, but as Arendt says, politics is conceived as an apparatus for advancing an essentially *private* good. Francis Fukuyama points out why these nuanced differences between 'moral' imperialism and 'material' imperialism may not be all that important in the current climate. He tells us that since the Cold War the real problem on the international scene has been the failed state: 'Weak or failing states commit human rights abuse, provoke humanitarian disaster, drive massive waves of immigration, and attack their neighbours. Since September 11, they shelter international terrorists who can do significant damage to the United States and other developed countries.'[15] The failed state, as Fukuyama says, is both a humanitarian and a security issue. The failed state violates the covenant of modern politics, whether we see that covenant in lofty terms of guaranteeing human rights, or in more materialist terms of securing people against violence. Humanitarian interventions in the 1990s had already led to a 'de facto international imperial power' in which the United Nations and other aid agencies and non-governmental organizations had taken over in cases of failed sovereignty. 'This international imperium may be a well-meaning one based on human rights and democracy, but it was an imperium nonetheless.' The United States may deny that it is an empire, but as Fukuyama points out, the *2002 National Security Strategy of the United States* is a 'doctrine of pre-emption or more properly, preventative war that in effect will put the U.S. in a position of governing potentially hostile populations in countries that threaten it with terrorism.'[16]

Fukuyama discusses at length the differences between Europe and America in their aspirations for empire. Americans tend to be more sovereigntist, in that they see the state as a constitutional contract by citizens; thus 'international law and organization has no existence independent of voluntary agreement between sovereign nation-states.'[17] Because international agencies do not have the authority of law, backed up by force and the consent of the governed, they are not binding in their mandate. Europeans, by and large, have a more 'Kantian' view of international law, believing that it has a higher morality than the law of the state because it rests on the claim of the dignity of each and every person. According to Fukuyama, 'many countries, particularly in continental Europe, have always had a concept of the state as the guardian of the public interest, standing above the particular interests of the state's citizens.' These differences lead, of course, to strong disagreements over foreign policy. Americans tend to think that the only way to guarantee order is to impose sovereignty through force (invasion and occupation in the case of Iraq). Europeans, especially continental Europeans, tend to favour deference to international agencies of cooperation. This is also a position adopted by Robert Kagan, who declares that '[Europe] is entering a post-historical paradise of peace and relative prosperity, the realization of Kant's "perpetual peace." Meanwhile, the United States remains mired in history, exercising power in an anarchic Hobbesian world where international laws and rules are unreliable, and where true security and the defense and promotion of a liberal order still depend on the possession and use of military might.'[18]

In Fukuyama's account, both the United States and Europe are engaged in imperial design, a project that he ultimately traces back to his Hegelian thesis about the 'end of history.'[19] There is only one version of reality at this historical end point, and it is the reality of the triumph of the goals of the French Revolution, with its related imperative of the autonomous individual asserting his or her will. Fukuyama has very recently gone public with his denunciation of the neoconservative agenda in the United States, but it has to be pointed out that he does not disagree with the imperialism of rights, security, and contract. He disagrees only with the misjudgement of America regarding how best to accomplish these goals. The Europeans are *better* at the end of history than the Americans. That is Fukuyama's complaint. In his analysis of failed states and what to do about them, he writes: 'The Europeans are the ones who actually believe they are living at the end of history – that is, in a largely peaceful world that in increasing degree can be governed by laws, norms and international agreements ... Americans, by contrast, think they are still living in history, and need to use traditional power-political means to deal with threats.'[20] Failed and weak states are a problem for us all, he asserts, and what we have to do is 'insist that we are promoting democracy, self-government and human rights, and that any effort to rule other people is merely transitional rather than imperial in ambition.'[21] The United States is not interested in annexing territory. It is, however, interested in securing an international scene in which its values and interests are universally triumphant. In the *2002 National Security Strategy*, it is affirmed that 'the great struggles of the twentieth century between liberty and totalitarianism ended with a decisive victory for the forces of freedom – and a single sustainable model for national success: freedom, democracy and free enterprise.' Furthermore, the document proclaims that 'these values of freedom are right and true for every person, in every society – and the duty of protecting these values against their enemies is the common calling of freedom-loving people across the globe and across all ages.' The United States then declares its intention 'to bring the hope of democracy, development, free markets and free trade to every corner of the world.'

To sum up the argument so far: modern Western politics is by definition imperialistic, insofar as our conception of what we are fitted for as human beings is something we take to be extendable to all human beings. Imperial ambition may have originally been understood in the West as an aberration from the truly *political*. This certainly seems to have been the case for ancient Greece. If John Pocock is right, there occurred a fundamental shift in the very conception of the *political* under the authority of Roman jurisprudence, in which the universality of the law made it possible to extend the reach of political authority over vast territories and peoples. The Roman shift meant a justification of empire, something we cannot find in the wisdom of the Greeks. The justification of empire becomes even more far-reaching in the modern world, because of the ontological shifts in how we understand human beings and what they are fitted for by nature. The major philosophical premise that informs modern empire is the assertion that we are by nature fundamentally alone, singular, individualistic, and free. We live under political authority because we have to, in order to guarantee ourselves some modicum of security and prosperity, and perhaps because we recognize – being the rational creatures we are – that we ought to acknowledge similar ends in others. The 'high ground' of Western empire is the language of universal human dignity and autonomy (Pitts, Kant), envisaging a world in which all political institutions protect the same rights. The cruder ground (Lal, Hobbes) is the language of acquisition and power, fuelled by fear. It may make some difference which story we take to be the truer account of ourselves (see Fukuyama's and Kagan's comments on Europe and the United States), but for the purposes of this paper, I want to emphasize the universalizing implications of both. Modern conceptions of the self in the West lend themselves to empire in a way more forcefully than any previous conceptions in our tradition. Empire is in fact the logical political incarnation of our deepest understanding of ourselves.

Now we turn to examine the *polis* – which is the root of the word 'political' – and what it means in the classical sense to be a citizen, a political being, to show just how far removed we are today from this original formulation. The classical moral theorists, who saw government as necessarily tied to a comprehensive understanding of human functioning, are dismissed by Hobbes as irrelevant, as men who accomplished nothing but the description of their own passions.[22] 'I believe that scarce anything can be more absurdly said in natural philosophy than that which is now called Aristotle's *Metaphysics*, nor more repugnant to government than much of what he hath said in his *Politics*, nor more ignorantly, than a great part of his *Ethics*.'[23] Hobbes explicitly abandons classical political science for his 'new' political science based on what he claims to be a truly novel and absolute universal doctrine.

The most marked difference between the classical idea of politics, and modern Western politics, is the absence of a universal good that is attributed to all human beings regardless of race, place of origin, sex, or culture. The classical Greeks had no notion of universal right, or even of the good for the individual, outside of his or her particular community of belonging. There is certainly in the classical texts of ancient political science an understanding of human *happiness*, but it is not formulaic and it has little connection with, say, the Kantian notion of autonomy and freedom. Happiness, for Aristotle, is bound up with the practice of virtue, and even that is variable. In his discussion of the difference between the good man and the good citizen, Aristotle says that the virtue of the good man is of a 'ruling sort,'[24] whereas the virtue of a good citizen consists both 'of a ruling and a ruled sort.' The kind of virtue that is required for ruling in the *polis* seems to be an attention to those things that are the object of contemplation (wisdom, possibly the gods) in combination with an astute comprehension of the particular configurations of one's political community. It is impossible for a city to be composed entirely of *good men*. 'If each performs his own work well, and this [means] out of virtue, there would still not be a single virtue of the citizen and the good man, since it is impossible for all the citizens to be similar.'[25] Even though the citizens are not all similar in the tasks they perform, and therefore in the specific kinds of virtue they may practise, the 'preservation of the partnership [of the *polis*] is their task, and the regime is [this] partnership; hence the virtue of the citizen must necessarily be with a view to the regime.'[26] The virtue of the citizen, then, is always measured with a view to preserving the common purpose of the *polis* in which he shares. We know also that for Aristotle, famously, the *polis* is prior in genus to any of its inclusive elements, including the household, the family, and discrete individuals. This is the most important and fundamental premise of the ancient *polis* – a formulation, I suggest, that it is almost impossible for us in the modern world to fathom. For Aristotle, a human being really is not *thinkable* outside the parameters of political life. Aristotle says (again, famously) that to imagine what it would be like to live outside a political community is to imagine that one is either a beast or a God, neither of which is appropriate for human beings.

Aristotle has much to say about different kinds of political organiza-tion, but his general precepts are very few. Nonetheless, they are worth noting, because though few, they directly contradict the imperatives of empire. Most political quarrels, says Aristotle, are about property and honour, so generally, in political communities, we need a minimum of property and work, so that no one is in desperate need, and we need the virtue of moderation, to prevent us from pursuing excess.[27] We also need military strength – not so much that we antagonize and threaten our neighbours, but sufficient to ward off attack. The more people there are within the state who share in this common project, the better, so citizenship seems to accord best with democratic sorts of regimes.[28] The city, or *polis*, is defined simply by Aristotle as 'the multitude of such persons that is adequate with a view to a self-sufficient life.'[29] When we consider these things, we see clearly that those regimes which look to the common advantage are 'correct regimes according to what is un-qualifiedly just.'[30]

Aristotle was aware that one could abandon the political way of life for other ways of life, but for him, these other ways were deviant and corrupt. 'The city is prior by nature to the household and each of us. For the whole must of necessity be prior to the part; for if the whole [body] is destroyed, there will be not a foot or a hand, unless in the sense that the term is similar (as when one speaks of a hand made of stone), but the thing itself will be defective.'[31] I think it is important to emphasize that Aristotle is not just giving us a version of political organization that he prefers. He is *defining* politics. The characteristic features he lists – a modicum of property and honour, the right sort of military defence, the object of self-sufficiency, the common advantage as definitive of the as-sociations that exist in the polis – *are* politics. For Aristotle, peoples who do not live in accordance with these plans are barbarians. They are *non-political*. Aristotle actually addresses the kinds of precepts that underscore a theory like Hobbes's and tries to explain why these are subversions of politics. If we do not understand the virtue for which political association strives, then 'the partnership becomes [nothing but] an alliance which differs from others – from [alliances] of remote allies – only by location. And law becomes a compact and as the sophist Lycophron says, a guarantee among one another of the just things, but not the sort of thing to make citizens good and just.'[32] It is possible to adjudicate just relations among people based on reciprocity, exchange, and distribution (Aristotle enumerates all of these carefully in the *Nicomachean Ethics*), but this is not *political* justice.

Remarkably, Aristotle addresses just the sort of justice that is defended by Hobbes and Kant as the basis of modern constitutional law, and he rejects it as profoundly *unpolitical*. 'Even if they joined together while participating in this way [by contract], but each nevertheless treated his household as a city and each other as if they were a defensive alliance merely for assistance against those committing injustice, it would not by this fact be held a city by those studying the matter precisely ... if, that is, they participated in a similar way when joined together, as they had when separated. It is evident therefore that the city is not a partnership in a location for the sake of not committing injustice against each other and of transacting business.'[33]

Friendship is indispensable to Aristotle's understanding of politics, and citizenship ought to be modelled in some manner on the sharing in virtue that defines friendship. True friends, Aristotle says, have no need of justice between them, because a friend cares for another as if he were the self. Though political communities can never approximate the bonds of friends, one ought to bear friendship in mind as the ideal against which all ties of the *polis* are measured. Political communities, for Aristotle, cannot survive without a true sense of concord among the citizens that leads them to care in some way for one another in a way that they would not care for strangers. The friendship of politics is not merely a 'sharing of belief,' because strangers can share common beliefs, or principles. Rather, 'a city is said to be in concord when [the citizens] agree about what is advantageous, make the same decisions, and act on their common resolution.'[34]

There are no universal moral principles – there is not even a universal caution of expediency – in Aristotle's political science. The political community, for Aristotle, embodies an understanding of a good life that is profoundly alien to us and that includes some harsh elements which are antithetical to the modern sensibility. Political belonging entails hierarchy of individuals and of relationships: some people are equals as citizens (male Athenians), some are equals in the household (husband and wife), and some are not equal at all (master and slave). From the point of view of the modern individual, whose principal aim in assenting to government is the equal protection of body and property and the advancement of individual autonomy, some of Aristotle's notions of equality are strange and disconcerting; nonetheless, his attention to the participatory and deliberative aspects of rule have appeal in some quarters. There have been many efforts in contemporary political theory to wed some of the more attractive elements of classical politics to the modern understanding. One can argue that communitarian theory, deliberative-democracy theory, and identity theory have all been inspired by the classical model of politics, insofar as they promote vague feelings of belonging, solidarity, and attachment to one's place and to one's laws, as well as obligations on the part of the self-interested and atomized individual to her fellow citizens.

Perhaps, though, the gulf between classical politics and modern empire cannot be bridged. If we start with the assumption that all political arrangements are legitimate, but only if they are consented to by individuals who are seeking the protection of the state for the advancement of their own interests, whether those be property or some more elevated notion of achieving autonomy, and even if we add on to that primary motive the moral imperative that we ought to have the reason to recognize and protect those same ambitions in others, we are still, in Aristotle's words, looking to state structures to regulate business transactions, or to prevent us from committing injustices against one another. This is not a political community. In this understanding of things, there is no reason why we should treat those who live beside us on the same street any differently from those who, as Aristotle says, we may have loose alliances with in foreign relations. There is no reason why we would limit the size of the state. There is no reason why we would truly recognize the commonly shared conceptions of virtue and good that challenge our individual interests and freedoms. There is no reason to practise moderation with regard to either honour or wealth. There is no reason why any right-thinking and well-educated individual, with ample opportunities for self-advancement, would have loyalties to the country in which he was habituated. There is no reason for politics. If empire is more efficient in realizing these individual ends, then it is the more reasonable course.

But at the much more concrete political level, we may see evidence that even the 'high ground' of Western imperialism – the doctrine of universal human rights – fails us badly. The advancement of human rights as an agent of universal justice has at times been dismally ineffective. Romeo Dallaire, the Canadian general in charge of the disastrous UN Mission in Rwanda, impresses on us the dispassionate response he received from the world's leading enforcers of rights, as he saw the impending genocide approaching in this small African country. Dallaire implores the world 'community' to act more conscientiously to advance human rights internationally. He asks this question: 'Are we all human or are some more human than others? ... The only conclusion I can reach is that we are in a desperate need of a transfusion of humanity. If we believe that all humans are human, how are we going to prove it?'[35] Dallaire's question is a good one. What makes us human? For Aristotle, to be human is to live according to reason in a *polis*. We in the modern West reject this account of being human and instead hold to the idea that we are human because we have rights. This idea has universal appeal, but it has no universal enforcement. Almost fifty years ago, Hannah Arendt wrote that 'the right to have rights or the right of every human being to belong to humanity should be guaranteed by humanity itself. It is by no means certain that this is possible ... If a human being loses his political status, he should, according to the inborn and inalienable rights of man, come under exactly the situation for which the declaration of such general rights provides. Actually the opposite is the case. It seems that a man who is nothing but a man loses the very qualities which make it possible for people to treat him as a fellow man.'[36]

If we take our bearings from Aristotle, and understand with him that man is by nature a political being, that means that human *nature*, insofar as it inclines towards friendship, concord, and justice, requires that people live in self-sufficient communities, with a common purpose that is defined by law and institution and that can provide for the common advantage of those who belong to that community. Without a *polis*, Aristotle says, men descend into beasts and incline towards war. If Aristotle is right, then no amount of human-rights declarations are going to protect us from barbarism. Here is Arendt again: 'Not the loss of specific rights, but the loss of a community willing and able to guarantee any rights whatsoever, has been the calamity that has befallen ever increasing numbers of people. Man, as it turns out, can lose all the so-called rights of man without losing his essential quality as a man, his human dignity. Only the loss of a polity itself expels him from humanity.'[37] Modern rights-based imperialism, with its ontology of the individual and its emphasis on the universal goals of security and freedom, would seem to be an all-inclusive doctrine, one in which no person is excluded theoretically on the grounds of race, or ethnicity, or gender. The reality, as Arendt warned, may be that we are creating whole populations of human beings who have no state protection and who are living, metaphorically, in Hobbes's 'natural condition.' In Hobbes's version of the social contract, 'those who are excluded from society – the unsuccessful, the unfortunate, the criminal – [are liberated] from every obligation toward society and state if the state does not take care of them. They may give free reign to their desire for power and are told to take advantage of their elemental ability to kill, thus restoring that natural equality which society conceals only for the sake of expediency. Hobbes foresees and justifies the social outcasts' 'organization into a gang of murderers.'[38] In Hobbes's singular commonwealth, the outcasts are contained within national borders, but in a globalized world, the outcasts are everywhere. They are on the peripheries of Paris, and in the middle of Amsterdam, they are in New Orleans, they are in Iraq and Afghanistan, they are in the massive refugee camps of Africa and Asia. Arendt foretold that a 'global, universally interrelated civilization may produce barbarians from our own midst, by forcing millions of people into conditions which, despite all appearances, are the conditions of savages.'[39] A savage is one who is living, or who is forced to live, outside the limits of what we are fitted for, which is a *political* existence.

What is the outlook for contemporary rights expansion and empire? David Hendrickson, another contributor to this volume, looks at the foibles of American empire through the lens of Thucydides and draws from the example of Athens' great democrat Pericles. Pericles' judgement of Athens' ambition was that 'though it may have been wrong to take the empire, it would be dangerous to let it go.' Pericles cautioned restraint. Athens did not exercise the restraint that Pericles advised, and we know the outcome, and Hendrickson hopes that the United States will learn from this lesson.

Ancient empire was occasioned by greed for honour, reputation, and wealth; and as Newell says, 'all the classical thinkers are at one in downplaying and severely criticizing the kind of dynamic and expansionist foreign policy that is needed to establish the path to imperial rule.' Perhaps it was impossible, though, for Athens to restrain itself. Newell takes this line when he sharpens the tensions between the strategic goals of a small city-state (self-preservation, discipline, closed borders, exemplified in Sparta) and the citizenship goals of open discussion and freedom (Athens). 'There is no middle way,' Newell says, between the two disparate paths. This was the genius that Newell identifies in Machiavelli – that he saw that freedom and openness lead beyond the *polis*. You can have a small and hardy state with ferocious and ethnocentric defenders, or you can have an open and expansive state that will inevitably spiral into luxury, lassitude, and decay. If anything, modern empire, with its strong foundations not merely in the familiar pursuit of honour and riches, but *philosophically justified* foundations in the notion of right, building on the Roman legacy of law, may have even less, or no, resistance to the perils of expansion. I am not optimistic that Aristotle's alternative understanding of human beings and their political life can save us, and I consider seriously Newell's suggestion that the actuality of the Aristotelian 'middle way' may never have existed. Still, with John Pocock, I consider too the possibility that the universal goals of right and law can never satisfy a fundamental hunger 'to be free of the world of things, free to interact with other persons as free in themselves in a community of pure action and personal freedom, in a community good in itself and an end in itself.'[40] Having been once articulated as a hope and a fitting end for human beings, the Aristotelian ideal 'simply cannot be eradicated from the ideals of a Greek-derived civilization.'[41] Politics on the Aristotelian model may be eclipsed in the modern world, but the idea of politics remains a powerful basis within the civilization for understanding what we are really doing when we marry right to might.

NOTES

I would like to thank Travis Smith for his helpful comments on an earlier draft of this paper presented at the New York State Political Science Association Annual Meeting in New York City, April, 2006.

1 John Pocock, 'The Ideal of Citizenship Since Classical Times,' *Queen's Quarterly* 99, no. 1 (1992): 966–85. Reprinted in Ronald Beiner, *Theorizing Citizenship* (Albany: SUNY Press, 1995), 32.
2 Ibid., in Beiner, 34.
3 Ibid., 35–6.
4 Ibid., 37.
5 Jennifer Pitts, *A Turn to Empire* (Princeton: Princeton University Press, 2005), 3.
6 Immanuel Kant, 'Theory and Practice,' in *Kant's Political Writings,* ed. Hans S. Reiss, trans. Hugh Nisbet (Cambridge: Cambridge University Press, 1970), 73.
7 Deepak Lal, *In Praise of Empires: Globalization and Order* (New York: Palgrave Macmillan, 2004), xix.
8 Ibid., xxv.
9 Ibid., xxi.

10   Hannah Arendt, *The Origins of Totalitarianism* (New York: Harcourt Brace and World, 1978 [1948]), 139.
11   Thomas Hobbes, *Leviathan*, ed. Aloysius P. Martinich, (Peterborough: Broadview, 2002), 85.
12   Arendt, *Origins*, 125.
13   Ibid., 140.
14   Ibid., 146.
15   Francis Fukuyama, *State-Building: Governance and World Order in the 21st Century* (Ithaca: Cornell University Press, 2004), 92–3.
16   Ibid., 94–5.
17   Ibid., 109–10.
18   Robert Kagan, *On Paradise and Power: America and Europe in the New World Order* (New York: Knopf, 2003), 3.
19   Fukuyama draws on Alexandre Kojève's analysis of the end of history. Kojève writes in an exchange with Leo Strauss that 'it is exclusively the *philosophical* idea going all the way back to Socrates that acts *politically* on earth, and that continues in our time to guide the political actions and entities striving to actualize the *universal* State or Empire. But the political goal humanity is pursuing (or fighting) at present is not only that of the politically universal state; it is just as much that of the socially *homogeneous* State or of 'the classless society." Alexandre Kojève, 'Tyranny and Wisdom,' in Victor Gourevitch and Michael Roth, eds., *Leo Strauss on Tyranny* (New York: Free Press, 1973), 173.
20   Fukuyama, *State-Building*, 116–17.
21   Ibid., 121.
22   Hobbes, *Leviathan*, 370.
23   Ibid., 370.
24   Aristotle, *The Politics*, trans. Carnes Lord (Chicago: University of Chicago Press, 1984),1277a25
25   Ibid., 1277a1.
26   Ibid., 1276b1.
27   Ibid., 1267a10.
28   Ibid., 1275a25.
29   Ibid., 1275b19.
30   Ibid., 1279a15.
31   Ibid., 1253a20.
32   Ibid., 1280b1.
33   Ibid., 1280b1,20–30.
34   Aristotle, *Nicomachean Ethics*, trans. Terence Irwin (Indianapolis: Harcourt, 1985), 1167a25.

35 Romeo Dallaire, *Shake Hands With the Devil* (Toronto: Random House, 2002), 522.
36 Arendt, *Origins*, 298–300. Romeo Dallaire reports of his mission in Rwanda: 'Engraved still in my brain is the judgment of a small group of bureaucrats who came to 'assess' the situation in the first weeks of the genocide: 'We will recommend to our government not to intervene as the risks are high and all that is here are humans.' Dallaire, *Shake Hands*, 6.
37 Arendt, *Origins*, 297.
38 Ibid., 142.
39 Ibid., 302.
40 Pocock, *The Ideal of Citizenship*, 41.
41 Ibid., 41.

7 Imperial Compulsions

TOIVO KOIVUKOSKI

The attitude that changing times, and especially moments of crisis, require new modes of thinking and acting, is a recurrent theme in the
history of political thought, and one that represents a moment of opportunity for reflection and recollection. Consider, for example, an
argument made by the Corinthians to the Spartans in the fifth century
BCE, during the ramp-up to the Peloponnesian War, urging the land-
based city to quit its conservative, inward habits and engage more
forcefully with the dynamic Athenian empire, 'always an innovator,
quick to form a resolution and quick at carrying it out.'[1] The Corinthian
ambassadors continue (if a long quotation may be indulged in our own
quick-tempered times) on the matter of a proper response to Athens'
aggressive imperial foreign policy,

> that the likeliest way of securing peace is this: not only to use one's power
> in the cause of justice, but to make it perfectly plain that one is resolved
> not to tolerate aggression. On the contrary, your idea of proper behaviour
> is firstly to avoid harming others and then to avoid being harmed your-
> selves, even if it is a matter of defending your own interests. Even if you
> had on your frontiers a power holding to the same principles as you do, it
> is hard to see how such a policy could have been a success. But at the
> present time, as we have just pointed out to you, your whole way of life is
> out of date compared with theirs. And it is just as true in politics as it is in
> any art or craft: new methods must drive out old ones.[2]

I would like to consider the sense of compulsiveness expressed here –
experienced in an inner dimension via the drive towards novel political
methods and formations, and outwardly in response to exigent threats

– that urges on empire building. Here the Corinthians are making three distinct though related basic arguments that are worth considering in order to understand the motives for what we might call reactionary imperialism. [3] In general terms, the Corinthians are insisting that non-interference with the affairs of other powers is no guarantee of pacific relations – very simply, that a state can be attacked regardless of its good intentions. This leads to the argument that sovereign power need not be considered as a purely defensive instrument limited to protecting territorial borders, but can also be used as an activist tool in the cause of justice. This argument issues forth in an expansive conception of justice, one that transcends the territorial boundaries of a given political community. Here we can see at least an outward likeness between this ancient endorsement of empire and the rationale that informs the remarkably unabashed current debate on the benefits and even necessity of an empire for America and the world. [4]

In the particular entreaty of the Corinthians, the military force of Sparta is being called on to break the Athenian siege of the colony of Potidea and to lift its blockade of a free port, a blockade prohibited by treaty. [5] Mobility to trade and travel was the real boon of empire to the ancient Greek society of travellers, seafarers, and island dwellers, who in the aftermath of the Persian Wars and in the time before the fateful end of the Peloponnesian War were experiencing what we might call a scaled-down version of globalization on the Mediterranean – a situation we see recorded in the opening lines of the *Republic*, for example, where Socrates bears witness to an Athens whose citizens and aliens appear indistinguishable and where native religions and customs have blended together with foreign gods, practices, and outlooks – pregnant novelties in combination for a philosopher, though worrisome for those imperial helmsmen trying to square the circle of securing the imperial centre while expanding trade, influence, and power abroad.

The activist dimension of the Corinthians' endorsement of empire is complemented by a third, even more fluid conception of the limits of statecraft and the justifiable uses of political power, in their presentation of politics as a craft or technique like any other, and, therefore, as susceptible to technological development. This raises an enduring question about empires and development: If the means or instruments at the statesperson's disposal change, and if the potential effective range of their sphere of influence thereby increases, do the rules and limits of political order change also? Or put more speculatively, does technological development in the political sphere necessarily translate into an imperial dynamic, with available techniques of domination, transportation, and communication setting the limits of empires?[6]

Though the fact that the Corinthians would have to make their entreaties to the tradition-based and landlocked Spartans suggests that powerful states do have choices to make about the legitimate uses of power, Thucydides' narrative illustrates the compulsiveness that attends the expansion of empires – in terms of outcomes, at least. There is a sense in which empires get on rails as their development unfolds in reaction to the exigencies of enemies, circumstances, and 'the vast influence of accident in war.'[7] But at a more fundamental level, in terms of their intrinsic motivations, I would argue that empires expand out of a perceived necessity based in a particularly unstable political psychology, moved by a terror of civilizational collapse – a state of being that paradoxically produces a profound level of anxiety regarding potential future threats, while providing a commonsense basis for social cohesion within such large organizations as are empires. Security is an agreed-upon end for all forms of political association, but in an empire the political psychology underlying the security imperative is twisted into a death fixation even more obsessive than that seen in Hobbes's image of a 'war of all against all.' The impulse that animates empires and that holds them together internally goes beyond a discrete, self-interested fear of violent death to a general paranoia that includes the fear not only of the end of one's own life, but also of the extinction of one's own social order and, at the extreme reaches of the terrorized imagination, of the possibility of the end of civilized life as such. In the minds of those who view themselves as the guardians of civilization, this translates into volatile and immoderate reactions to their own declining powers. The thinking is that if their empire weren't to exist, then existence could hardly be called worthwhile. Better, then, to have the world burn than to witness the fall of their empire.

The subtle arguments for a reactionary form of imperialism given by the Corinthians – who are saying in effect that the only working response to an expanding empire is to counterbalance its power with another – to a tradition-bound Spartan audience are echoed even more explicitly by the Athenians in their justification of the expansion of their perimeter defences and naval powers.[8] They suggest that theirs was also an empire not by choice, but rather by necessity, at first forced upon the autonomous city by the Persian Empire, against which Athens served as hegemon within an alliance of Greek cities, and then later against what became the subjects of Athens' continued hegemony after

the Persian wars when its colonies and erstwhile allies threatened revolt and insurgency. Yet if Athens was an empire by default at first, its
influence over other Greek cities offered it opportunities and advantages that it could not easily refuse once they had been gained. For what
incentives could there be for giving up such a superlative sphere of influence? Thus the Athenians argue against the cautious Spartans: 'We
have done nothing extraordinary, nothing contrary to human nature in
accepting an empire when it was offered to us and then in refusing to
give it up. Three very powerful motives prevent us from doing so – fear,
honour, and self-interest.'[9]

I will consider each of these three justifications of imperial wars
– self-interest, honour, and fear – one by one later in this essay, but
it is worth remarking in general that each of these motives can be
understood as a species of erotic desire not easily satisfied in an imperial context. During the Athenians' war debate over the proposed
invasion of Sicily, the elder statesman and general Nicias, speaking
against Alcibiades, calls the desire for far-off things and the impression of unlimited power δύσερως[10] as in a kind of adolescent love
sickness, like Plato's image of desires flowing from leaky jars.[11] Yet
this is exactly the aspect of desire that most inspires Socrates' failed
student and the most vigorous proponent for Athens' imperial wars,
Alcibiades: the desire for one thing after the next; the desire for
power and the reputation of power; or, more fundamentally perhaps, as Nietzsche indulges, the desire for desire itself.[12] It is in this
spirit of self-overcoming driven by internalized conflict that
Alcibiades encourages a new war and conquest as a test of will,
arguing that, if Athens were to endeavour to merely keep the peace,
'by sinking into inaction, the city, like everything else, will wear itself out, and its skill in everything decay; while each fresh struggle
will give it fresh experience, and make it more used to defend itself
not in word but in deed.'[13]

Alcibiades' own paean to self-overcoming power as the restless ani-
mus behind imperial adventurism bears a striking resemblance to the
early modern conception of human nature, according to which human
beings are erotic automatons driven by 'a perpetuall and restlesse desire of Power after power'[14] on trajectories of spiralling acquisitions
leading predictably to war. Similarly, Machiavelli argues that 'it is perfectly natural that men should want to acquire things,'[15] the only limit
to acquisition being the means, or the powers available to secure some
future apparent good, and of course the resistances that the will butts

up against in others and in nature. It is interesting, though, that Machiavelli's account of human nature distinguishes between the war-like noble classes with their personal political projects and the limited desires of political subjects, citizens, or (in antiquated language) the masses – that is, those who 'simply want not to be oppressed.'[16] While Machiavelli is brutally honest in speaking power to power – and what else are realist theories of power politics but this? – this passage from *The Prince* hints at his republican sensibilities in a general expression of affinity for the people. Yet wherever one's sympathies may lie – whether for anarchic rule by the strong, or for honour-bound aristocracy, or for law-bound egalitarianism, or for anarchic libertarianism – what is curious is how those who value their freedoms so much would subjugate others in order to subsidize their own security and prosperity. This raises questions – and here the relevance to contemporary global politics should be obvious – concerning how a democracy based on the free consent of the governed can act out as an empire in its foreign affairs, what undemocratic influences may accompany the exigencies of an imperial project, and what sort of social psychology underlies, animates, and offers self-rationalization to an imperial trajectory.

Intermezzo – between Empire and the Hobbesian State

In ballistics there is a point of apparent stillness at the apex of the arc, which from the perspective of the projectile itself considered as a local system seems to possess a sense of weightlessness, as if neither the initial explosion nor the immanent force of gravity were at play – like Wile E. Coyote at that moment of shocked apprehension in his transformation from predator to prey. This sense of stillness in motion can easily incline an observer within such a local system to think in terms of the sorts of imagined teleologies and ultimate purposes assumed by pre-Newtonian physics – in effect, to think that the projectile is somehow realizing its end – whereas really that high pertains not to a metaphysical kingdom of final causes but rather to a sensation abstracted from its circumstances – to a stomach that rises into the chest while the rest of the body is already falling. This feeling of a culminating high point should be understood rather as an existential impasse before the fall, with two vectors of motion held together in a precarious balance at the limit condition of an ascent: that is a crisis, which is also a turning point, and an opening for unprecedented futures and unanticipated recoveries of the past.

So it appeared in the moment of relative peace following the end of the Cold War, which ushered in a new albeit short-lived age of apparent weightlessness, of politics supposedly sublimated into peaceful contests for prosperity, what we could call the decade of economic and cultural globalization, now taken over by a new era of militant globalization via imperial integration. Compared to present living conditions in the global village,[17] those early days of globalization are beginning to appear more and more like a golden age of humankind, in which the 'sweet dreams' of cosmopolitanism[18] – unfettered global communications and universal mobility rights – seemed like technological possibilities for the first time in human history. As consequences of the democratic freedom of people to 'vote with their feet,' and under new conditions of transparency, relations between states were to have transcended the specific gravity of power politics; the pull of the desire to subjugate others was to have been forgotten as a backward, subrational component of the human psyche; and, with the end of that irrationally compulsive desire, the two most unstable kinds of power units – tyrannies and empires – were to have been made extinct. The desire for power after power that 'ceaseth only in death'[19] was to have been redirected (so as to avoid the catastrophic death potential of modern militaries) into economic competitiveness and technological innovations of supposedly universal benefit. The walls and fences and demilitarized zones between states were to have become porous – as the scholarly saying goes – through increased trade, communications, and human traffic: the Berlin Wall broken down by the hands of free men and women, with relatives, friends, and lovers carrying blue jeans and flowers back and forth across those imagined borders between fenced-in states, now no more than memories of some dark age of humankind. There was to have been something called a global community, moved by complex, roiling cultural exchanges and enlivened by the novelties found in combination. Yet that moment of humankind's weightless aspiration has turned out to be a quick hope; and curiously now, the state that was supposed to have withered away under the influences of free trade, communications, and travel – the 'globalization makes us free' argument – has had its renaissance, and in a distinctly unenlightened form of empire patterned after the Hobbesian state: a retrofitted machine for the provision of security, with a sword in one hand and a mace in the other and ready to use them. It is as if the social responsibilities that have been demanded of the state over its five-hundred-year development since *Leviathan* lumbered off the printing press are being stripped away, exposing the bare substructure of the state as security mechanism. Yet whereas the Hobbesian state was to have been limited in the actual use of its monopoly on the means of organized violence beyond its borders by the basic self-interestedness of citizen-subjects – who should have no incentive to risk their own lives to go to war for anything but purely defensive reasons – and by a subsequently limited conception of security as the defence of national borders, the new, stripped-down version of the imperial security state in our new era of militant globalization is not so territorially limited. Understanding the imperial behaviours of modern states requires going back behind the mechanistic Hobbesian state, based as it is on the calculation of discrete interests and forces, in order to understand the weightless imaginations and anxious paranoia that compelled the Athenian Empire.

On Terror and the End of Empire

The Athenians loved their own freedoms so much that they were willing to subjugate other cities by siege, invasion, and the slaughter of resistant populations in order to buttress their own sweet exceptionalism. How can one make sense of the paradoxical relation between the political and personal freedoms enjoyed at the centre of the Athenian Empire and the patterns of invasion and subjugation that were seen as necessary to both subsidize and preserve those privileged lifestyles? Or in terms that are perhaps more palatable to today's neoliberal spirit and sensibilities and less burdened by genuflection, how can a people be forced to be free through submission to imperial ordering? The sort of racial antipathy that sneers from Aristotle's often quoted quotation of an indignant Achilles ...

> 'it is fitting for Greeks to rule barbarians'[20]

... has often stood in as a self-legitimation of various Western imperialisms, but even as Aristotle presents it, the notion is more of an assumption underlying imperialism than a reason justifying it. For considered in the context of Aristotle's discussion of natural slavery, the rational basis for the argument is little more than this: if a people do not possess the necessary means and powers of collective defence – the most basic and necessary end of political association – then they cannot be called autonomous (or in contemporary jargon, they constitute a 'failed state'), in that they are incapable of exercising their autonomy by defending their borders; and so, for their own safety and for the security and well-being of their neighbours, they are probably better off being invaded, occupied, and civilized lest they fritter away their lives and resources in a tenuous tribal existence. [21] According to that train of thought, a people who cannot maintain their sovereignty have effectively proven themselves to be slavish barbarians who require the protection of a superior civilization. Imperial expansion thus acts as its own legitimization – at least when it succeeds – with peoples losing their autonomy as if by self-fulfilling prophecy. Yet this kind of circular argument acts more as a window into the imperial psychology than as a rationale for imperial wars, which are considered to be justified if they succeed and are seen to be manifestly destabilizing if they do not, with legitimacy conditional upon outcomes. Within the circle of such rationalizations, political theories and ethical considerations are crowded out by strategic studies pertaining to who won and how.[22] To frame a theory of empire capable of penetrating through the facade of circular logic thus requires that we understand the driving motives that give rise to such delusions of self-importance.

In this regard, Aristotle points to the *demos* and the demagogues who provoked boundless desires, sensitive conceits, and anxious fears among the masses as 'the cause of the acquisition of a maritime empire during the Persian wars.'[23] Note that Aristotle was identifying demagoguery – with all its classical connotations of irrationality and instability – as a cause of imperialism at a time when the justifications for Athenian hegemony seem to have had the most legitimacy, just as Athens was leading a federation of Greek cities against an invading empire. The reasons for the expansion of Athens' sphere of influence would of course become even more contested later on in the history of its rise and fall.

At the apex of Athens' power trajectory, just prior to the Sicilian expedition that would prove to be the tipping point in its imperial overreach, the Athenian people found themselves embroiled in a bizarre set of conspiracy theories centring on Alcibiades and his cronies, who were suspected of defacing public statues (or worse), profaning the Eleusinian mysteries in their own secret cults, and plotting to overthrow the democracy for some sort of oligarchy. Yet, though Alcibiades was eventually assassinated, all that the riled distraction of the masses did at the time was to sap their critical faculties by turning them into puppets of the same manipulative demagogue they trusted least. One can do little but speculate on the already speculative reports of the unsolved crimes of an ancient vandal; that said, the manifest effect of the public crimes, whoever committed them, was to distract the

Athenians from Alcibiades' explicit imperial and personal projects that were bringing Athens to ruin.

Alcibiades seems to have had the ability to enrage, excite, and baffle audiences with his audacity. As a celebrity politician, he was an expert at the outrageous sound bite, as in this offhand indignity to the Athenians: 'Let them seem how much we care for the peace we are now enjoying.'[24] Here's another: Plutarch reports that when asked whether he trusted his countrymen, Alcibiades replied, 'Yes, in other things, if you like. But when my life is at stake, I wouldn't trust my own mother not to mistake a black pebble for a white one when she casts her vote.'[25] And yet another: he once told Socrates, 'What need is there for me to practice and have the trouble of learning? For I am sure that my natural powers alone will give me an easy victory.'[26]

Yet whatever his personal faults, poor judgement, and crimes against Athenian democracy, Alcibiades' arrogance lends a certain transparency to his ambition for unlimited power and to the underlying causes of Athens' imperial dynamic. I now return to the three naked compulsions offered as Athens' motivations for expanding its empire: fear, honour, and interest.[27] Though fear of civilizational collapse may be the most urgent psychological drive at the root of imperialism, I will first, and briefly, consider the other two root causes, because they are simpler to understand than fear, especially the total albeit amorphous sort of fear that is terror.

The unique honour of empire consists in universal recognition, or as near to it as can be technically accomplished, whether what is placed on a pedestal for recognition are civilizational principles, a set of laws, the bare military power of a state, or the person of the emperor himself. However, though the aim of any empire may be to have its particular instantiation of a universal good recognized, the honours thereby attributed are not necessarily distributed homogenously; rather, they vary according to the locale of each particular spectator within the imperial territories being inhabited. So, for example, an emperor may be admired by his close advisers, respected among friends and allies, and held in awe by citizens within the imperial capital, even while being regarded with quivering fear and hatred by subjected peoples at the bloody margins of empire. But in any case, the imperial centre, however abstractly considered – as code, god, or man – serves as monolith, spectacle, and centre of attention. In terms of human motivations this is a fairly obvious attraction of empires – that it is sweet to feel as if one lives at the centre of the world, however one's actions are regarded.

If a universal spectacle is the public honour unique to imperial power, then the interests of empire are its booty, won through the expansion of spheres of influence. These interests are the productive 'stuff' that the imperial helmsmen hope to gain and that they worry most about losing – that is, after power itself – for it is those interests that supply the riches needed to fund the extensive militaries and bureaucracies and political and personal allies that make empires operational, as well as to subsidize levels of consumption in the imperial heartland in order to keep domestic populations compliant with obnoxious violence abroad. Forcefully expanding the influence of a state beyond its borders is an expensive task; and beyond the desire for power after power, in practical terms it helps to keep the imperial momentum up if the empire can find external funding, with occupations on the cheap helping to shore up political capital among domestic audiences and citizen voters. The only truly discrete political rationale for Athens to invade Sicily – beyond what Thucydides calls the 'specious pretext' of taking a stand to defend Hellenic civilization on the island against barbarians,[28] or the supposed need to depose the tyrant of Syracuse,[29] or the possible need to prevent a future attack by the Siceliots[30] – consisted of the treasuries of Syracuse. It was this perennial promise of imperial spoils that sparked the interest of the Athenian voter, though as it turned out, the promised booty happened to be a vulgar exaggeration based on bad intelligence – which, mind, was willingly accepted in order to commit the Athenians to a speculative and ruinous war in the far west.[31]

In this context the drum call to war did not have the tone of dumb obedience; rather, it worked by enflaming the passions of the Athenian *demos*, who were entranced by the promise of increasing the honour and influence of their city and so enjoying the benefits of its empire for themselves. Yet while some of those interests are easy to measure – as in promises of rich treasuries to loot – the overarching imperative to expand Athens' influence was distinctly open-ended. As Alcibiades insisted to the Athenians when he endorsed launching a war for the purpose of preventative defence: 'Men do not rest content with parrying the attacks of a superior, but often strike the first blow to prevent the attack being made. And we cannot fix the exact point at which our empire shall stop; we have reached a position in which we must not be content with retaining but must scheme to extend it, for, if we cease to rule others, we are in danger of being ruled ourselves.'[32]

The perceived need to grow an empire to address an open-ended security imperative is even more bluntly stated by an Athenian embassy to the islanders of Melos before their conquest by siege, invasion, slaughter, and enslavement – actions also justified by the Athenians in terms of preventative defence. In response to a request to respect Melian autonomy, the Athenians argue that this would create a perception of weakness: 'If any maintain their independence it is because they are strong, and … if we do not molest them it is because we are afraid.'[33]

Imperial powers are afraid to look afraid. Embedded in the imperial dynamic is a psychological instability according to which all are seen as potential enemies. From this follows the noisy demonstration of force, intended to subdue; though as the Melians note, this anxiety-ridden policy can work as a self-fulfilling prophecy, with neutral states transforming themselves into enemies, each fearing they will be next and so adopting pre-emptive defences of their own.[34]

Here the insurgencies provoked by imperial invasions and occupations act reciprocally to confirm the paranoid logic that compels empires to expand; in this way, means and ends are blended in a cycle of expanding influence and retributive violence. Once this dynamic is entered into, imperial expansion itself begins to serve as a self-referential civilizational cause, over and above the particular security dilemmas or interests that seemed to make expansion necessary in the first place. It is this kind of circular logic that Pericles employs when he exhorts the Athenians to accept the death of citizens as a necessity bound up with the privileges of life at the centre of an empire: 'And not contented with ideas derived only from words of the advantages that are bound up with the defence of your country, though these would furnish a valuable text to a speaker even before an audience so alive to them as the present, you must yourselves realize the power of Athens, and feed your eyes upon her from day to day, till love of her fills your hearts.'[35]

There is a sense expressed in that passage from Pericles' Funeral Oration that the calculation of advantages and interests and even security is epiphenomenal to the core imperial drive, which is simply the desire for power as such. This open-ended drive is compacted into an apparent textual ambiguity, in that it is unclear whether the Athenians are being asked to love their city or the *power* of their city (τῆσ πόλεωσ δύναμιν). In this conflation of ends and means, Athenian civic spiritedness was uprooted from the city itself and became a cipher for a broader civilizational project of potentially boundless expansion. Within the deterritorialized presentation of civic identity given by both Pericles and Alcibiades, it would seem that the common object of desire called on to bind Athenians together as subjects and soldiers was not a love of home and country, but rather the fluid, extensive power of Athens' maritime empire as such. This 'as such' is difficult to define precisely because it does not refer to a definite category of things; it is a power as amorphous as the liquid element on which it depends. One could point to what Pericles calls the 'memory of this greatness'[36] as a fixed motive: acting for the future; and indeed we still do remember the civilizational accoutrements of Athens' hegemony – its schools of philosophy, architectural ruins, preserved dramas, poems, and histories – as highwater marks of a culture made possible by collecting and concentrating a cacophony of foreign gods, practices, and new perceptions at the shores of empire. But though the remains of a once living culture may attest to perennial capacities of the human spirit, like broken bits of shells and corals on a beach they endure as traces of deeper, hidden processes, such that interpreting the patterned beauty found in such artefacts gives one only indirect clues as to the nature of the forces that delivered them. Yet, to the end of understanding the veneration of the power of Athens in and of itself and for its own sake – even if it is the power of a homeless people without a country of their own and set out to sea – one would perhaps find better clues as to the nature of imperial striving in Nietzsche than in either Plato or Aristotle, those most polished remains of the Hellenes. Put this other shell to your ear and hear how 'one would have to know precisely how great the plastic power of a man, a people or a culture is. I mean the power distinctively to grow out of itself, transforming and assimilating everything that is past and alien.'[37]

Nietzsche, like Pericles, takes as his audience living, desiring human beings who are 'alive' to the present, rather than the objectively self-interested or rationally longing ciphers of desire – men on paper only – those who speak to 'life alone, that dark, driving, insatiably self-desiring power.'[38]

And Nietzsche, too, saw the imperial potential in this view of human life, if desire were relieved of the idea of an enduring object, and if peoples were cured of the petty delusions of territorially bound nationalities, and if – as in the dominant interpretation of a prophecy according to which the Athenians were to have exchanged the stone and masonry walls of their city for the wooden walls of ships,[39] 'dismissing all thoughts of our land and houses'[40] – peoples were defined not by their homelands and origins but by where they might go. Based on a such a fluid criterion for civilizational identity, Nietzsche presaged the imperial politics of the twentieth century with remarkable clarity when he wrote that 'the time for petty politics is over: the very next century will bring the fight for the dominion of the earth – the compulsion to large-scale politics.'[41]

For beyond technical constraints on the projection of power – from triremes to steamships to nuclear submarines to satellites – if self-overcoming power is considered to be an end in itself, then a global empire starts to seem less like a statesman's dream and more like a necessity that unfolds as a self-fulfilling prophecy working to transform the world and its peoples into a moving image of empire. The self-justifications of imperialism, past and present, are the echoes of this will to power. So the Athenians say: 'We are not the first to act in this way. Far from it. It has always been a rule that the weak should be subject to the strong; and besides, we think that we are worthy of our power.'[42]

Putting self-conceptions of worthiness aside, in this classical realist formulation of the legitimacy of the rule of the strong over the weak – toned in tradition-bound terms for a conservative Spartan audience – rule is divorced from universal codes or laws, in that the rule itself assumes a heterogeneous arrangement of power among states. As is their custom, the Athenians are brutally honest and immoderately explicit about their power politics. According to their apologetics for empire, and in a twist on a question fundamental to statecraft, concerning the necessary means of security and prosperity, the Athenians argue in effect that the only truly strong and vital state is an empire – one, moreover, that is motivated by selfishness, fear, and the sorts of honours that go along with a civilization that claims to be universal. The Athenian ambassadors present these objectives of imperial statecraft as self-evident goods that require no further rational justification beyond the possession of the necessary means to satisfy such desires. That is, the ends of an empire are constituted by its means, while its limits are technological.

As an endnote, and in an illuminating mirror image to the Athenians' position, the twentieth-century thinker and European Union bureaucrat Alexandre Kojève rephrases the ancient notion that the only truly sovereign state is an empire when he writes that 'the modern state, the current political reality, requires larger bases than those represented by Nations properly so-called. To be *politically* viable, the modern state must rest on a vast "imperial" union of related nations. The modern State is only truly a State if it is an Empire.'[43]

From this it would seem that, aside from the issue of relative stages of technological development, the key difference between, on the one hand, Kojève's idealist conflation of the necessary and the good in some form of imperial union driving towards global integration, and on the other hand, the classical realist argument for the naturalness of empires ruling over weaker peoples, consists in the order of things – that is, in a realization of the ideal versus an idealization of the real. Yet in either formulation, and in the absence of a distinction between what is perceived as necessary and what is considered good, the imperial dynamic is animated by an overwhelming compulsiveness, such that even the most discrete motives – as in interests, honour, and security – spin off into apparently boundless acquisitions, global spectacles, and endless episodes of war.

NOTES

1 Thucydides, *History of the Peloponnesian War,* trans. Richard Crawley (London: Everyman, 1993), 1.70.
2 Ibid., 1.71.
3 Much of the current academic discourse around empires has hinged on the qualifiers that distinguish current versions of empire, yet between a prefix like French foreign minister Hubert Védrine's *'hyperpuissance'* and a predicate such as 'empire lite' (Michael Ignatieff, *Empire Lite*, [Toronto: Penguin, 2004]), a general consensus is that empires today are distinguished by their deterritorialized character, in that they are not necessarily dependent on the possession of colonies and the direct political administration of outlying territories.
      Yet the political administration of conquered countries does appear to be a function of empires still, though perhaps temporarily and not by choice; and as we can see from the Corinthians' advice and from the example of Athens, even in the ancient world power was exerted by empires from centre to peripheries through a range of means that extended beyond direct political control of territories: from depopulation and colonization; to the taxation of tributaries; to punitive naval blockades, hit-and-run raids, and other threatening military gestures; to rough trade negotiations; to the bullying of allies and the arming of proxies.
      Though empires today may not colour the map the way that, for example, the Roman Empire did, with an empire in white coming up against dark, cross-hatched Goth and Arabian territories, empires still display a characteristic dynamism, with barbed-wire frontiers and bloody hinterlands in the place of discrete boundaries, such that, as with earlier

empires, their limits are determined by their moment of decline. Edward Gibbon captures this precarious sense of imperial limits in his record of the last words of the Emperor Augustus, who advised the Senate and his successors to confine their empire 'within those limits which nature seemed to have placed on its permanent bulwarks and boundaries: on the west the Atlantic Ocean; the Rhine and Danube on the north; the Euphrates on the east; and towards the south the sandy deserts of Arabia and Africa' (cited in Gibbon, *The Decline and Fall of the Roman Empire*, ed. Anthony Lenton and Brian Norman [Herts.: Wordsworth, 1998], 4).

A dying emperor, perceiving his own end, reminds his successors of their own finite limits. But this is easier advice for a dying emperor to give than for a young emperor to take. And it is even harder advice for us to take as moderns, for what are the natural boundaries of an empire armed with intercontinental missiles, aircraft carriers, and satellites? It would seem that the dynamic character of empires is not fundamentally modified but rather illuminated by the effects of such deterritorializing technologies.

4 The many outspoken advocates of an empire for America represent a startling cross-section of academic opinion. Dimitri K. Simes, co-publisher of the *National Interest*, writes in *Foreign Affairs* that American policy makers should get over their 'negative imperial stereotypes' so that they can do their business of managing their imperial role, though he limits the function of an American empire to mere military domination rather than direct political control of the globe, social services in developing countries apparently not having a high place on his neoconservative agenda of principles (Simes, 'America's Imperial Dilemma,' *Foreign Affairs*, November–December 2003). The liberal political theorist Jean Bethke Elshtain makes a case for an imperial foreign policy from just-war theory, arguing that fighting ongoing wars against 'apocalyptic nihilists' is 'the burden of empire and it is time Americans faced up to it' (Elshtain, 'How to Fight a Just War,' in *Worlds in Collision: Terror and the Future of Global Order*, ed. Ken Booth and Tim Dunne [New York: Macmillan, 2002]). In a similar spirit though from a different ideological perspective and drawing from historical comparisons to legacies of the British Empire, Niall Ferguson expresses a sentimental, 'chin-up' attitude towards America's new imperial status in his advocacy of empires as perennial necessities for maintaining a semblance of global order by backing up free trade, property ownership, and contract rights with effective force. See his 'An Empire in Denial: The Limits of US Imperialism,' *Harvard International Review* (Fall 2003); his widely read *Empire: The Rise and Demise of the British World Order and Its Lessons for Global Power* (New York: Basic Books, 2003);

and his somewhat more moderate reconsideration of the limits of America's empire, *Colossus: The Price of America's Empire* (New York: Penguin, 2004).

5 Thucydides, *History*, 1.67.
6 The Canadian economic historian Harold Innis proposes a thesis along these lines, explaining the rise and decline of empires in terms of the realization of and overextension beyond the technological limits of various communication and transportation media. See Innis, *Empire and Communications*, ed. David Godfrey (Vancouver: Beach Holme, 1986).
7 Thucydides, *History*, 1.78.
8 As the Spartans intuited, perimeter fortifications such as Athens' long wall to the Piraeus had complementary offensive and defensive purposes, freeing up the empire to wage wars overseas while lessening the danger of counter-attacks (Thucydides, *History*, 1.90). A similar overlap of offence and defence can be seen in the contemporary strategic value of theatre missile-defence systems, as well as in the conscious confusion of opposites expressed as foreign policy in the *National Security Strategy of the United States (2002)*, which states that 'the best defence is a good offence' – a distinctly imperial stratagem for a superpower to assume.
9 Thucydides, *History*, 1.76.
10 Ibid. 6.13.1.
11 Plato, *Gorgias*, trans. W.R.M. Lamb (Cambridge: Loeb Classical Library, 1925), 493e.
12 Nietzsche, *Beyond Good and Evil*, trans. Walter Kaufmann (New York: Random House, 1989), §175.
13 Thucydides, *History*, 6.18.
14 Hobbes, *Leviathan*, ed. C.B. Macpherson (London: Penguin, 1985), XI:161.
15 Machiavelli, *The Prince*, ed. Robert M. Adams (London: Norton, 1992), III:10.
16 Ibid., 28.
17 This often misunderstood term is explained in Marshall McLuhan and Bruce Powers's book *The Global Village: Transformations in World Life and Media in the 21st Century* (Oxford: Oxford University Press, 1989), in which the authors cogently suggest that 'the satellite will body forth new tribal separatists who will make Yasser Arafat seem tame by comparison' (115). According to McLuhan's analysis of the retribalizing effects of electronic media, the concrete conditions of possibility for globalization are also the grounds of global war (suggested by the title of another book of his – *War and Peace in the Global Village*), a condition of violent antimonies within which tribal empires and cosmopolitan barbarians are forced to live together.

18 Immanuel Kant, 'To Perpetual Peace: A Philosophical Sketch,' trans. Lewis White Beck (New York: Macmillan, 1957).
19 Hobbes, *Leviathan*, XI:161.
20 Aristotle, *Politics*, trans. Carnes Lord (Chicago: University of Chicago Press, 1985), 1252b8; Euripides, *Iphigenia in Aulis*, 1400–1.
21 Aristotle, *Politics*, 1252b.
22 The replacement of political theory by journalistic reportage is evident in the works of such contemporary commentators as Robert Kaplan (see for example 'Supremacy by Stealth,' *Atlantic Monthly*, http://www.theatlantic.com/doc/prem/200307/kaplan) and Michael Ignatieff, who interpret a press pass as an epistemological privilege. It is worth noting the distinction between their situation embedded with armed forces in the thick of the fight and the perspective suggested in the original sense of *theoria* to describe an official embassy to the Olympic Games (Liddell and Scott), where the perspective of the theorist is privileged by an elevation above the field of play, seeing both goals, uncommitted to either side, and witnessing the unfolding of a game as seen all in one view, so to speak. This concrete, original sense of theory could also apply to a delegation sent to observe a religious procession, again without a decided commitment to the local gods worshipped. Socrates provides an example of this basic sense of theory as elevated observance when he compares native Athenian worshippers with foreign devotees of a Thracian goddess in the opening lines of the *Republic*, reporting back from the port that both processions were equally fine.
23 Aristotle, *Politics*, 1274a.
24 Thucydides, *History*, 6.18.
25 Plutarch, *Lives*, 'Alcibiades,' trans. Ian Scott-Kilvert (London: Penguin, 1960), 22.
26 Plato, *Alcibiades I*, trans. W.R.M. Lamb (Cambridge: Loeb Classical Library, 1927), 119c.
27 Thucydides, *History*, 1.76.
28 Ibid., 6.6.
29 Ibid., 6.20.
30 Ibid., 6.18.
31 Ibid., 6.8.
32 Ibid., 6.18.
33 Ibid., 5.97.
34 Ibid., 5.98.
35 Ibid., 2.43.
36 Ibid., 2.64.

37 *On the Advantage and Disadvantage of History for Life,* trans. Peter Preuss (Indianapolis: Hackett, 1991), para. 1.
38 Ibid., para. 4.
39 Herodotus, *Histories,* trans. David Grene (Chicago: University of Chicago Press, 1987), 7.141.
40 Thucydides, *History,* 1.143.
41 Nietzsche, *Beyond Good and Evil,* trans. Walter Kaufman, para. 208.
42 Thucydides, *History,* 1.76.
43 Alexandre Kojève, 'Outline of a Doctrine of French Policy,' trans. Erik de Vries, *Policy Review* (August–September 2004).

8 Rome and the Hellenistic World: Masculinity and Militarism, Monarchy and Republic

ARTHUR M. ECKSTEIN

In January of 49 BCE, the army of C. Julius Caesar stood on the banks of the Rubicon, the boundary between Caesar's legally assigned province and Italy proper. Caesar faced a decision. The Senate in Rome had demanded that he step down from his governorship of Gaul, which he had held for ten years; it had, indeed, already named a successor to the post; and when Caesar failed to respond, it had declared him a public enemy of Rome. We are told that the recalled governor hesitated at the Rubicon about what to do. To submit to the Senate meant political disaster for himself; but to cross the river meant disaster for the entire world – the beginning of a civil war. Caesar pondered these two fatal alternatives – but (our sources say) not for long. Within a day, he launched his forces down the Italian peninsula towards Rome.[1]

Whatever else Caesar's decision at the Rubicon was, it was an act of monumental egotism. This egotism stands out starkly in a statement Caesar made a year-and-a-half later as he surveyed the battlefield at Pharsalus in Greece, which was littered with thousands of Roman dead. According to an eyewitness, he remarked: 'This is what they wanted [*hoc voluerunt*]. I, Gaius Caesar, after so many great deeds, would have been condemned in the *law-courts*, unless I turned to my army to help me.'[2] Speaking to friends, he thus adduces no great issues behind the civil war, only the outrageous possibility that he, the doer of many great deeds, the conqueror of so many Gallic peoples, might have had to undergo a civic procedure that ordinary Romans faced every day.

This essay has two purposes. I want to suggest what experiences as a long-term ruler out in Rome's provinces might have led Caesar towards overthrowing the Republic in the name merely of his *sacro egoism*. He certainly seems an example of how empires can create an authoritarian 'counterculture' on the periphery that runs against a republican culture of political give and take, ups and downs, at the centre. I also want to explore whether the crossing of the Rubicon was the final expression of a predatory masculinity that made Roman aristocratic culture exceptionally ferocious among ancient Mediterranean states. I will answer this second question first, for it is important that the answer here is: 'No.' Roman aristocratic culture, while militaristic, was not exceptional in its ancient Mediterranean context. On the contrary: precisely because Rome was a republic, the opportunities for developing and expressing an exceptionally predatory and militaristic individual masculinity were less available to most Roman aristocrats than they were to Rome's great competitors for empire, the Hellenistic kings. This is because in a republic, power and opportunity are more diffuse. *All* ancient Mediterranean states were militarized, militaristic, bellicose, and ruled by a hypermasculine ideology of achievement in war. This was a natural result of their anarchic environment and their need to survive within that environment. Nevertheless, the difference here in the scale of individual *sacro egoismo* between monarchy and republic is important.

The Militaristic Culture of the Roman Republic versus the Militaristic Culture of the Hellenistic Monarchies

So: there is no doubt that the Roman Republic in the third and second centuries BCE was a heavily militarized, bellicose, and very assertive state. And there is no doubt that the Roman aristocracy and to some extent the Roman populace were characterized by a militarized concept of masculinity, in which the prime requisite for honour was military valour: 'glory got by courage of manhood.'[3] Thus the Roman senatorial aristocracy was schooled in war from adolescence. Since no one could run for even the lowest public office in Rome in this period without having served ten campaigns in the army,[4] and since election to public office was the only honorable career for the son of a senatorial family, it follows that long exposure to war and the army was the central experience of every Roman aristocratic male between seventeen and twenty-seven. The psychological and social impact must have been profound. Similarly, the highest elected public offices – including the consulship (the highest regular office) – were essentially army commands. And after the consulship, senior men still went out to serve on the staffs – or to command the legions – of their kinsmen. Achievement in war was the primary road to an individual's power and influence within the

Senate and before the assemblies of the people – and ultimately it was the primary road to a glorious memory. Moreover, a significant portion of the *general* male population was itself enrolled in the fighting forces every year (a stunning average of about 13 percent annually between 203 and 133 BCE).[5] Everyone, high and low, benefited from successful war, and meanwhile Roman courage, as the third-century poet Ennius says, 'reached to the skies.' Livy in fact records many cases of the opposite – of shaky Roman morale and panic – but such at least was the self-concept. Senatorial elders expressed disgust when, in the 150s, they saw the younger generation of aristocrats seeking ways to avoid military service by claiming physical defects.[6]

William V. Harris, whose work on Roman militarism and imperialism is central to modern views on the expansion of the Roman Republic, in fact argues that the Roman aristocracy and populace, in its obsession with the male military virtues, represented a polity with 'a pathological character,' one that had 'dark and irrational roots.'[7] He argues further that the predatory and bullying character of Roman aristocratic culture (and the exceptional militarism of Roman male culture in general) was the key to Roman success in imperial expansion. Roman society was a war machine, and by the third and second centuries it was creating at others' expense the wars on which the war machine – aristocracy and populace alike – depended for honour, prestige, military glory, and individual wealth. Thus the story of Rome is a story of continual aggression against relatively blameless neighbours by a state that had become an insatiable predator in the system of Mediterranean states.[8] From this perspective, Caesar's overthrowing of the republic was the last savage recompense for the culture of exceptional and pathological hypermasculinity that had brought Rome to world power.

Widespread as this view is, I think it is misguided. It is the product of an introverted historiography that only looks at Rome and that does not carefully examine the ideology and behaviour of Rome's competitors. If one raises one's eyes from Rome itself to look at the broader geopolitical field, one sees that Rome's main rivals were all like Rome: highly aggressive, expansionist, and imperialistic states. The savage competition of the world they faced helps explain why the Romans suffered *ninety* severe defeats on the battlefield under the Republic, and the deaths in battle (mostly in defeat) of some forty commanding generals.[9] And when one look at Rome's major competitors, the Hellenistic kings, one sees that the pathological hypermasculinity supposedly characteristic of Rome is displayed in a far more blatant manner among the kings than within the Roman aristocracy.

To be sure, the Roman Republic went to war almost every year. But so did the Hellenistic monarchs. So did Hannibal. Men such as Seleucus II, Antiochus III, and Philip V spent every year of their reigns on campaign, spent every year in the camps of their armies and leading those troops into battle. Many kings were famous generals, and all tried to be. They took titles indicating their ferocity and their success: 'The Eagle,' 'The Hawk,' 'The Invincible Victor,' 'The Beautiful Victor,' 'The Great.' When they appeared in public, they usually wore armour and surrounded themselves with military insignia: that was their official regalia. Indeed, we have no statues of Hellenistic kings in civilian attire.[10] The very definition of Hellenistic kingship was, as one source says, 'management of the army' (the Suda). And, like Roman aristocrats, they led from the front: this was true of Ptolemy I of Egypt (who single-handedly slew enemy war elephants with his eighteen-foot spear), as it was true 150 years later of his descendant Ptolemy VI (who died leading a cavalry charge while attempting to conquer Syria). Like Roman generals of the Republic, too, kings engaged in triumphal processions – but unlike the Romans of the Republic, *every* triumphal procession was that of the king himself and no one else; glory was not shared. As for masculinity, one need only note that the great military parade of Ptolemy II at Alexandria in 279, with more than 80,000 troops, was led by a float consisting of a penis 150 feet long, with a twenty-foot star coming out of its tip.[11] No Roman aristocrat could match that.

Hellenistic kings were not simply full-time generals: they were also warriors on the front line of battle – as Caesar was. Some scholars have pointed out that Rome gave special rewards to aristocrats for acts of valour in battle, including the *spolia opima* for personally killing an enemy commander in single combat. Supposedly, this indicates the exceptional bloodthirstiness of Roman Republican culture.[12] The Romans certainly did have an elaborate system of honouring military bravery.[13] But single combat between commanders and/or the honouring of commanders fighting on the battle line was *usual* in the warlike cultures of the ancient Mediterranean. It was a powerful tradition among the Persians: Shah Darius I on the Behestun Inscription describes at length his sterling qualities in personal combat; Shah Artaxerxes II in 401 personally slew in battle the pretender to his throne – his own brother Cyrus.[14] Among the Greeks the tradition went back to Homer: the *Iliad* is one long tale of aristocratic man-to-man combat, occasionally actually in front of the assembled armies, but mostly on the battle line (yet still in the form of aristocratic duels).[15] In the Classical period it was usual for Greek generals to fight in the infantry ranks, especially on the front line, and at the centre of battle. We have the names of thirty Classical Greek commanding generals who died fighting in combat. Such men were viewed as heroes.[16]

This Greek tradition was very much alive in the Hellenistic age. Alexander fought hand to hand with Persian governors and sought single combat with Shah Darius III; Pyrrhus the king of Epirus in the 280s and 270s was a famous lover of single combat even when in the role of commander-in-chief; Acrotatus the prince of Sparta returned from battle in 274 literally soaked in the blood of his victims – to huge approbation from Sparta's old men and Sparta's women;[17] King Hiero II of Syracuse (fl. 250) was famous as the victorious veteran of many single combats.[18] Hannibal, too, fought in the front line (and was wounded). Both King Antiochus III and King Philip V, ca. 200, were renowned for their courage – and feared for their skill and ferocity in man-to-man combat. When Antiochus was wounded in the mouth while leading a cavalry charge in Afghanistan in 208 – he had to eat mush for the rest of his life – Polybius heartily commended his bravery. His wounds did not stop him from seeking to conquer the rest of the world, or from dancing war dances after banquets well into his fifties.[19] Indeed, the historian Polybius himself was not averse to combat on the battle line, even at the age of fifty-five: a lesson to us all.[20]

Rome honoured bravery in combat, especially by aristocratic commanders; so did everyone else. It was a natural consequence of the almost constant warfare among ancient states. 'Battle,' Homer said, 'is where men win glory.'[21]

A monarch got to demonstrate his courageous manliness every single year. Antiochus III – 'the Great' – went personally to war for thirty-four straight years (223 to 189 BCE); he rebuilt Alexander's empire in the East, and eventually his realm stretched from Iran to the Adriatic. Polybius remarks that as Antiochus got older and older, he proved a disappointment because his energy no longer seemed to match his world-conquering project;[22] the statement amply demonstrates Antiochus' longevity as a predator. By contrast, an aristocrat of the Roman Republic normally held office and command for only one year, with perhaps a one-year extension. That is, his power in command had a time limit (much more severe than that of an American president): power had to be shared among the three hundred other men in the Senate. A Roman aristocrat was tied to militarism and predatory manliness, but he was not tied to militarism and predatory manliness with the intensity and long duration we see among monarchs. Because we are talking about three hundred or so senators, not one king, the militarism and predatory masculinity, though intense, was more 'diffuse' in the Republic than in a monarchy; and for each individual the exhilaration of command was much less lasting.

Furthermore, every senator was bound to the rules of the Senate, and bound to proper behaviour as his fellow senators as a collective saw it. A king was a law unto himself: when Philip V of Macedon sold innocent populations into slavery, or looted sanctuaries and temples sacred to the gods in order to get money, or killed his own son, there was no institution in Macedon to reprove him. By contrast, when Popilius Laenas attacked innocent foreigners in 172, and when Sulpicius Galba did so in 150, both were called to account by the institutions of the Senate and the Republic. So: just as republican institutions set limits on the duration of power, so too they set limits on personal behaviour.

Moreover, continual war as the dominant feature of Roman life began to disappear after the first half of the second century BCE.[23] Though the textbook dates for the *Pax Romana* – the famous 'Roman Peace' in the Mediterranean – are 31 BCE to AD 250, the fact is that the Roman Peace emerged in large regions of the Mediterranean under the Republic, and at a much earlier date: in Sicily after 210 BCE; in Peninsular Italy after 200; in the Po Valley after 190; in Spain after 133; in North Africa after 100; and for ever longer stretches in the Greek East.[24] This suggests that Republican Rome, far from being a war machine mechanically grinding out the wars it needed, diminished its militarism when the serious threats to its existence had finally all been dealt with, when control was finally established where the Romans needed it or simply desired it.[25] More and more officials went out to govern provinces as garrison commanders, not fighting generals. The fact is that as the strategic environment from the Roman point of view improved, the Roman aristocracy – and Roman society in general – became less and less militarized. Here the emblematic figure is M. Tullius Cicero: lawyer, orator, politician, philosopher, also consul and saviour of the Republic from internal treason, but not a general.[26]

Caesar

And it is here that Caesar stands at the transition point in Rome between Republic and dictatorship (the emperors). Aristotle, three hundred years earlier, had already warned that imperial expansion was dangerous for a free polity, because the imperial experience of absolute power might educate individual citizens to want absolute power within the city itself.[27] In Caesar's case the experience of continual command for more than a decade, the experience of exercising sole authority over large regions and huge numbers of people, the experience of total independence and power and control, the *taste* for it (and for the great wealth that could accrue from it) – a very unusual experience for most Romans, one must stress – this indeed appears a case of what one may call an 'imperial counterculture' to the law-ruled and increasingly pacific state existing at the centre. The contrast between the conduct of politics in the imperial metropole and the situation on the imperial peripheries was very sharp. In the centre, under the Republic, politicians had to deal with many differing foci of power: it was a world where no single individual exercised overwhelming and long-lasting predominance, where to a great extent men had to cooperate, to be *dependent* on one another, in order to get things done. Out in the provinces it was different: one person, one superior person, made all major decisions. It was a royal power. Out of this difference, conflict and tragedy might arise.

We often find in later republican empires fears expressed about the politically corrupting impact on individual governors of long-term personal control over large regions of the imperial periphery. The classic case for the American Republic is the fear expressed in the 1940s and 1950s concerning General Douglas MacArthur. None of those later fears ever materialized into the imposition of tyranny upon the centre – and again, MacArthur is a good American example of that. But then, MacArthur was seventy years old to Caesar's fifty, and he was not overwhelmingly rich – which Caesar had become. Those fears of the imperial commander do, however, constitute the recognition of a reality of imperial political life: the counterculture of potentially unlimited personal exercise of military and political power on the imperial periphery, the breaking of republican *limits* on behaviour. Caesar is the best historical example of it, and all subsequent fears exist under his shadow.

What, then, was the cause of the conflict between Caesar and the Senate that led to the civil war that destroyed the Roman Republic? In legal terms, it was a dispute over the termination date of Caesar's special provincial command in Gaul. This vast special command, over all of what is now northern Italy, the northern coasts of the Adriatic Sea, and modern France, had been gained by Caesar as consul in 59, as his payoff in a complex deal with the politicians Crassus and Pompeius. It seems that after ten years of exercising unlimited personal power far from Rome, and far from the constraints of republican political life, Caesar was reluctant to make the transition back to being an ordinary senator, even a highly prominent and protected one. True, he did not want to be prosecuted for his actions back in 59, when he illegally pushed through the People's Assembly various legislative measures that the other two men had wanted; but the issue went deeper than Caesar's disdain for appearing in the law courts like an ordinary Roman. Pompey's help would have prevented prosecution, or at any rate conviction: but that would have required Caesar to cooperate with him, to be to some extent *dependent* on him. Such dependence, which was typical of republican politics at the centre, had become inimical to the conqueror of Gaul.

So even after Pompey in 52 had procured special legislation for Caesar that permitted Caesar to run for a second consulship in absentia, so that he would not have to lay down his status as an official and thus become legally vulnerable to prosecution – even that was not enough. By late 50 there was still no sign of Caesar giving up his Gallic armies. This made Pompey, now in command of relatively small forces in Italy by special assignment, increasingly suspicious. Cato the Younger and the leaders of other senatorial factions hostile to Caesar worked on those suspicions. And knowledge that Pompey was increasingly associating with his enemies in turn alienated Caesar. But though their intervention was harmful, the ultimate cause of the cleavage did not lie with Caesar's senatorial enemies. It lay with Caesar – his obvious hesitation to lay down the Gallic command and come home, even under special conditions.

Where did that reluctance come from? The problem here runs deeper than a mere legal dispute over the termination date of a provincial command, deeper even than a struggle for political superiority between Caesar and Pompey. If all that was involved in the crisis of late 50 and early 49 had been these issues, then some manner of compromise could have been found – after all, the Romans were the ancient world's greatest diplomats, and not least among themselves. That was the way the Republic had always worked. That the problem went deeper than the particular issues of late 50 and early 49 was the judgement of the ancients themselves: Caesar's biographer Suetonius, in explaining how the civil war originated, emphasizes that while Caesar's special command in the North had a reasonable origin in the threats to Rome from among the Celtic tribes, his 'habit of command' (*imperii consuetudo*), growing over time, gave him a love of power for its own sake; he added that this was Cicero's opinion as well.[28] Appian is similar: Caesar simply did not wish to give up his command, period.[29]

Imperii consuetudo: the deep point that these ancient writers were making was this. To stand successfully for a second consulship in absentia, to have that second consulship carried through with honour and dignity, preceded no doubt by a senatorially approved magnificent

triumph for the victories in Gaul, to avoid prosecution (or at least conviction) for his actions in 59 and later, to proceed thence to an honoured
and secure place in the Senate, or perhaps to another great command,
this time against the Parthians – all of this would have required Caesar
entering once more, after a long absence, into the hurly-burly of normal
Republican politics. At the least, it would have required him to cooperate with Pompey. That is: it would have required Caesar's dependence
on another man. Caesar in 50 BCE, it is true, was suspicious of Pompey
because of his increasing association with his political enemies; but the
ancient writers indicate that this was not the basic problem: Caesar disliked the general situation, not just the specific man. To the point, he
disliked any situation where his independent will would not automatically reign supreme.

The extraordinary fact is that Caesar in 50 had not been without possession of the power of *imperium* since his praetorship in 62 – that is, for
twelve full years. First he was praetor; then governor of the province of
Further Spain; then consul in 59; and then governor of the huge special
province created for him in the North, from 58 to 50. Part of his time in
Further Spain and Gaul was spent as a judge giving rulings that could
not be appealed. Most of it was spent in absolute command of an army,
in a camp where everyone obeyed his orders instantly – and had to. In
the end, Caesar preferred to plunge the world into civil war rather than
give all this up.

Caesar was brilliant and charming: so says Cicero. But he was also
arrogant and self-willed – and had always been supremely aware of his
superiority in intellect and character over so many of his contemporaries. Republics, however, run best on mediocrity. His consulship in 59
had been followed by a decade of essentially monarchical power in
Gaul, the achievement of unprecedented military glory, and the obtaining of enormous wealth; this had not softened him. In Gaul he created his own policies, aggressive and warlike, without consulting the
Senate. He dictated the fates of entire peoples by a wave of his hand. He
had experiences we can only dimly imagine: What was it *like* to sell
53,000 people into slavery at a single stroke, as Caesar did in 57?[30] His
slave trading was in fact a major source of his fortune, which by 50 BCE
rivalled that of the Roman State Treasury itself.

Roman commanders traditionally enjoyed wide freedom of action in
their provinces: this was a function of their distance from the centre and
the primitive state of ancient communications; partly, in the Republic, it
was also an aspect of mutual trust among aristocrats.[31] But no one in the
history of the Republic had ever ruled such a vast territory for such a

long time as Caesar. The best parallel is Scipio Africanus during the crisis of the Second Punic War: he conquered eastern Spain in 210–206 BCE, was consul in 205, and then commanded in Africa in 204–201, defeating Hannibal. It is significant that Polybius, who details Scipio's conquests, thought that Scipio could have become a king – except that he was unthinkingly loyal to the Republic.[32]

Caesar was different. The power and above all the independence that went with his huge and long-lasting special command might well have become addictive. By 49 he had spent close to one-fifth of his life as the absolute monarch of Gaul. Could he ever become an ordinary senator again, even if he had wished it? Here we may note his later actions. The civil war with Pompey and his supporters, which Caesar started in 49 BCE, lasted four full years, with fighting on a massive scale all over the Mediterranean. Caesar was always in the thick of it: in Italy; Spain; Greece; Egypt; Asia Minor; North Africa; and then in Spain again. In Egypt he took a Ptolemaic queen less than half his age as his mistress and the mother of his son (Caesar was fifty-two, Cleopatra twenty). This is militaristic predatory manliness at its height; but then, Hellenistic kings were praised not only as fountains of military energy but for their sexual energy as well.[33] Not surprisingly, their statuary depicted them to their publics as young and vigorous no matter how old they actually were.[34]

It is also striking that on his return to Rome in late 45, Caesar could not settle down to life in the city, even as supreme ruler. True, he rapidly enacted a hodgepodge of administrative reforms, but his eyes turned immediately to more warfare: a vast campaign of conquest against the Parthians that would take at least three years – perhaps a lot longer. He was setting off for this campaign when he was assassinated in March of 44.

From a modern perspective, Caesar's plans for undertaking a huge new war in the East look irresponsible: he was now well into middle age; he had many capable generals to deal with the Parthian problem; his place was at Rome, attempting to construct a system to replace the republic he had shattered. But evidently he found the work of imperial administration a bore. And his dealings even with an overawed Senate were complicated and tense: he kept ex-consuls waiting for hours to see him; once he explained his failure to rise upon a visit by the Senate on grounds that he had diarrhea. Caesar had many virtues, but patience was not one of them. War promised excitement – even exaltation. In the camp he would be surrounded by adulation, there would be no attempts to limit his conduct, everyone would obey him instantly. The fact is that essentially he made his home there for the entire last fifteen years of his life. Caesar, in short, had transformed himself from a republican public official into a typical Hellenistic king.[35]

According to Roman estimates, Caesar initiated wars during his lifetime that cost the lives of more than one million human beings – many of them Romans. What is striking is that at the end of his life he was happily planning for more.[36] How could such a man, not a modern man but an archaic and titanic war machine, habituated to absolute power after many years in Gaul, ever have returned to normal republican politics in 49? Thus, when the writers, intellectuals, and statesmen of later republican empires worried about 'Caesarism' in the sense of imperial administrators who had developed a habit of command in the provinces that was dangerous to the central state (*imperii consuetudo*), they were looking back at a real phenomenon. The best way to preserve the republic – and so far, in the American case, this has been quite easily done – is to recognize, appreciate, and impose strict limits on the behaviour of the commanders on our imperial peripheries.

NOTES

1 Caesar at the Rubicon: see Suetonius, *Jul.*, 29–30; Plutarch, *Caes.*, 32; Appian, *BC*, 2.35. The central modern study remains Hermann Strassburger, 'Caesar im Urteil des Zeitgenossen,' *Historische Zeitschrift* 175 (1953): 225–64. See also Zvi Yavetz, *Julius Caesar and His Public Image* (Ithaca: Cornell University Pres, 1983), ch. 1.
2 Suet., *Jul.*, 30.
3 Cf. Bertram Wyatt-Brown, *Southern Honor: Ethics and Behavior in the Old South* (Oxford: Oxford University Press, 1982), 28.
4 Polybius, 3.19.4.
5 See the chart in Keith Hopkins, *Conquerors and Slaves: Sociological Studies in Roman History* (Cambridge: Cambridge University Press, 1978), 33. This 'average' figure is a bit misleading, since in the crisis in the last part of the third century the army was taking over 25 percent annually, whereas after 170 BCE it was well below 10 percent annually. Ibid.
6 Polyb., 35.4.
7 William V. Harris, *War and Imperialism in Republican Rome* (Oxford: Oxford University Press, 1979), 53.
8 See Harris, *War and Imperialism*, chs. 2 and 3 and ch. 5 passim; cf. also idem, 'New Directions in the Study of Roman Imperialism,' in *The Imperialism of Mid-Republican Rome* (Ann Arbor: University of Michigan

Press, 1984), ed. Harris, esp. 13–15 and 21–2; and idem, 'Roman Warfare in the Economic and Social Context of the Fourth Century,' in *Staat und Stattlichkeit in der frühen römischen Republik*, ed. Walter (Stuttgart: Steiner, 1990), 494–510, esp. 495.

9 See the startlingly long list of Roman disasters at the end of Nathan Rosenstein, *Imperatores Victi: Military Defeat and Aristocratic Competition in the Middle and Late Republic* (Berkeley: University of California Press, 1990).

10 See Jim Roy, 'The Masculinity of the Hellenistic King,' in Lin Foxhall and John Salmon, eds., *When Men Were Men: Masculinity, Power, and Identity in Classical Antiquity* (London: Routledge , 1998), 114.

11 Athenaeus, 196A–203B.

12 Harris, *War and Imperialism*, 38–9; Stephen P. Oakley, 'Single Combat in the Roman Republic,' *Classical Quarterly* 35 (1985): 392–410, cf. Oakley, 'The Roman Conquest of Italy,' in John Rich and Graham Shipley, eds., *War and Society in the Roman World* (London: Routledge, 1993), 30.

13 See Polybius, 6.39, with Arthur M. Eckstein, '*Physis* and *Nomos*: Polybius, the Romans, and Cato the Elder,' in *Hellenistic Constructs: Essays in Culture, History, and Historiography*, ed. Paul Cartledge, Peter Garnsey, and Erich Gruen (Berkeley: University of California Press, 1997), 184–5.

14 Shah Darius' military skills as depicted on the Behestun Inscription: Pierre Briant, 'The Achaemenid Empire,' in *War and Society in the Ancient and Medieval Worlds*, ed. Kurt Raaflaub and Nathan Rosenstein (Cambridge, MA: Harvard University Press, 1999), 111; and Artaxerxes II and Cyrus II: Plutonius, *Artax.*, 14.1–10 and 15–16.

15 See Hans van Wees, 'Kings in Battle,' *Classical Quarterly* 38 (1986). The Homeric model is noted by Oakley, 'Single Combat in the Roman Republic,' 402.

16 See Victor Hanson, *The Western Way of War: Infantry Battle in Classical Greece* (Berkeley: University of California Press, 2000), ch. 9, esp. the list at 113–14; cf. Ronald Ridley, 'The Hoplite as Citizen: Athenian Military Institutions in their Social Context,' *Antiquité Classique* 48 (1979): 513–14.

17 Plutarch, *Pyrrhus*, 28.2–3.

18 Justin, 23.4.12.

19 Pyrrhus of Epirus: Plutarch, *Pyrrhus*, 7.5 (with spears, then swords, against the opposing commander), 28.4, 34.1–2. Antiochus III: Polyb. 10.49 (to Polybius' great approval). Philip V: Livy, 27.32–3, 31.24.10–16, and 37.9.

20 Polybius in the battle line: Ammianus Marcellinus 24.2.16–17. Note Polybius' warm approval of the courageous deaths in battle of the Greek generals Epaminondas, Pelopidas, Brasidas, and Cleombrotus: frg. 139 B–W, with Arthur M. Eckstein, *Moral Vision in the Histories of Polybius* (Berkeley: University of California Press, 1995), 36.

21 *Iliad*, 4.225. The generally approving tone of our Greek sources: Paul Beston, 'Hellenistic Military Leadership,' in Hans van Wees, ed., *War and Violence in Ancient Greece* (Swansea: Classical Press of Wales, 2000), 325–8, esp. n70. The widespread impact of Homeric ideals of conduct, virtues that were 'largely related to success in war and battle': see Jon. E. Lendon, 'Homeric Vengeance and the Outbreak of Greek Wars,' in van Wees, ed., *War and Violence in Ancient Greece*, 3–4. On Polybius' Homeric values, see already Eckstein, *Moral Vision in the Histories of Polybius*, esp. 28, 55, 110–11.

22 Polyb., 15.37.1–2.

23 See Timothy Cornell, 'The End of Roman Imperialism,' in John Rich and Graham Shipley, eds., *War and Society in the Roman World* (London: Routledge, 1993), 155.

24 Ibid., 157–60.

25 Ibid., 144–55.

26 Which does not mean completely unmilitarized; even Cicero had seen a bit of army service as a young man in 89 BCE during the Social War: see Thomas Mitchell, *Cicero: The Ascending Years* (New Haven: Yale University Press, 1979): 8–9.

27 Aristotle, *Politics*, 1333b29–36.

28 See Suet., *Jul.*, 30.

29 Appian, *Bellum Civile*, 2.28.

30 See Caesar, *BG*, 2.33.

31 See Arthur M. Eckstein, *Senate and General: Individual Decision Making and Roman Foreign Relations, 264–194 BC* (Berkeley: University of California Press, 1987).

32 Polyb., 10.40.

33 Theocritus, 14.57–68.

34 See Roy, 'The Masculinity of the Hellenistic King,' 120. Hence, alongside the usual public image of Hellenistic kings as fiercely armoured for war, we often find kings depicted in a condition of (young and vigorous) 'heroic nudity': ibid., 114.

35 The parallel would be with the isolated, arrogant, archaic, 'Titanic' figure of Alexander the Great as presented by Fritz Schachermeyer, *Alexander der Grosse: Ingenium und Macht* (Stuttgart: Anton Pustet, 1949). Caesar as a governor of western Spain in 61 – that is, a republican public official – is said to have bitterly proclaimed himself inferior in status and achievement to Alexander; see Yavetz, *Julius Caesar and His Public Image*, 18, 26, 28, 36.

36 Pliny, *Natural History*, 7.91–2.

9 Imperial Power in the Roman Republic

SUSAN MATTERN

The Roman army was not a perfect machine, easily overcoming all opposition in a relentless drive towards world conquest. I have long argued[1] that the Romans acquired and maintained their empire only at great cost to themselves, and that any explanation of what drove them to do this must address values and culture – the Romans' perception of what was at stake and their priorities that dictated victory at all costs. In particular, they perceived foreign policy as a zero-sum game of honour in which one's perceived ability to inflict violence was the essential, irreducible item on which everything depended. (It was perceived ability, not actual ability, that counted in this system, as the Romans themselves well understood.)

However, the question of Roman motives is not the one that I shall address here, but rather the problem of how imperial power actually worked – how the Romans made their subjects do what they wanted them to do, if in fact that is what occurred; and what means were available and what means they used, and with what degree of effectiveness. This question is a practical rather than a moral or theoretical one, and it yields a different answer. In particular, this answer cannot be supplied by looking only at what the Romans themselves thought they were doing, even though that is what the surviving evidence mainly allows. Rather, it must look at how the Romans interacted with their subjects, at the give and take of power.

Most Roman historians agree[2] that to conceive of the Roman Empire, especially in the period of the Republic but arguably at any time, mainly in terms of territory is to misunderstand its nature;[3] the essence of *imperium* was power. Not only is it impossible to say when most of the areas subject to Rome were made 'provinces,' but it is not clear that the word *provincia* itself had any territorial meaning before the later first century BCE. The examples I discuss below come from the late Republican period and involve two regions – Sicily and Transalpine Gaul – long under the direct administration of Rome and customarily referred to as provinces in the later sense; but even here, as I will argue, it was a question not of holding territory but of negotiating power.

Throughout most of the history of the Republic, the Romans appointed magistrates to oversee certain parts of the world, defined vaguely ('Africa'), or in some cases, certain functions and responsibilities; these were 'provinces.' Some regions, particularly Spain, required the deployment of magistrates and armies every year; that is, the Romans occupied them. Brunt's chart[4] shows the distribution of the army between 167 and 91 BCE: two legions were posted in Spain almost permanently; Cisalpine Gaul and Sardinia also required long-term military commitments, and the Romans kept one legion in Macedonia after 149. Periodically the army in those provinces had to be reinforced because of some disturbance, or troops had to be sent elsewhere. But Rome had no limitless well of manpower from which to recruit the armies that helped it control subject populations; it exercised most of this control by other means. In the second century BCE, Rome claimed dominion over a far wider area than those regions to which it sent magistrates and armies – those that we usually call 'provinces.' As the historian Polybius remarked, by 167 BCE Rome held sway over the whole world;[5] by which this Greek writer meant mainly the world once conquered by Alexander and ruled by Greco-Macedonian dynasties. But at the time he wrote, all of those kingdoms except Macedonia were still intact under their traditional rulers. In fact, the Romans lacked the military capability to rule more than a small territory by main force; and the horrific ways in which they sometimes retaliated for disobedience were paradoxically an acknowledgment of this limitation.[6] The Romans relied partly on their reputation for brutality to scare subjects into doing what they wanted.

The Romans did not dominate their subjects by pure military might – arguably, an impossible scenario in any time or place. They also did not export an extensive bureaucracy or large populations of settlers.[7] This has implications for how the day-to-day mechanics of imperial power might be approached or interpreted. The interactions that formed the *normal* mechanisms of imperialism contrast with the brief and relatively infrequent episodes of terror and brutality that were also important policy tools for the Romans. In what follows I propose a view of imperialism as a complex negotiation of power among many parties; one in which the subjects' agenda was as important as that of the conqueror, and in which simple distinctions between conqueror and subject are difficult to make. I also argue that Roman imperialism should not be understood only or mainly as a military phenomenon, but rather as a diplomatic and even social one. None of this is meant to imply that imperialism does not involve – usually as a fundamental feature – exploitation, brutality, and violence, especially warfare. But perceiving it only in those terms will not explain how it works.

For the remainder of this paper I will focus on two specific examples: one illustrates how the Romans became involved in a new region, and the other shows how they administered an area long under their control. For the first point I will use the case of Gallia Comata, or 'Long-Haired Gaul' – that is, the part of Gaul conquered by Julius Caesar. I choose this example for the sake of convenience only, because a good account of the conquest survives in Caesar's *Commentaries on the Gallic War*. This source is by no means unproblematic – Caesar is not an impartial witness of his own actions, and the *Commentaries* are very tendentious despite their plain literary style. It will be important to bear in mind that Caesar's portrayal of the relationships among and within Gallic tribes, for example – as well as the very concept of Gaul itself – reflects his own agenda and not some objective reality, a point I shall return to later. Nevertheless it is significant that the imperial process as he, a Roman general, describes it is less a series of victorious campaigns against hapless rivals than a complex social and diplomatic negotiation among many parties. Caesar's account is so complicated from this point of view that I will confine my discussion to book 1 only, which describes conflicts with the Helvetians (Gauls, according to his ethnographic system) and the ('German') Suebi. All the events described in book 1 took place in the year 58 BCE, Caesar's first year in his provinces.

In both conflicts the essential elements drawing Caesar in, as he tells it, are a network of past relationships between Rome and certain Gallic tribes and a tense and changing political landscape in Gaul.[8] When the Helvetians seek to migrate westward from their home across the Rhône (in what today is Switzerland), Caesar explains this as a result of a triangular conspiracy. As chief players he identifies Orgetorix, an ambitious Helvetian nobleman; Casticus, son of the former king of the Sequani, whose father had held the title of 'Friend of the Roman People';

and Dumnorix, brother of the pro-Roman chief of the Aedui.[9] The Aedui, as Caesar writes later and repeatedly, are 'Brothers and Kinsmen' of the Romans,[10] with whom they enjoy ties of 'hospitality and friendship.'[11] The title 'Brothers and Kinsmen,' like 'Friend,' was the gift of the Roman Senate, and the Aedui in particular have been honoured with many senatorial resolutions.[12] As far as we know today, this relationship began in 121 BCE when the Aedui appealed to the Romans for intervention against the Arverni – events Caesar himself refers to later when negotiating with the Germans.[13] These conspirators, writes Caesar, aimed at supremacy over all of Gaul.[14] Thus he portrays the migration as a dangerous threat to Rome's interests, involving subversive manoeuvres among two of Rome's allies that would align them with the Helvetians in the future. In particular, he describes at length the treachery of Dumnorix and his plot to overthrow his pro-Roman brother Diviciacus.[15]

Thus when Caesar complains that the Helvetians' migration plans will threaten or impinge on peoples loyal to the Romans or subject to them – the Allobroges,[16] the Tolosates,[17] and especially the Aedui and also their kinsmen the Ambarri, who send embassies to Caesar begging for protection from the pillaging invaders and reminding Caesar of their long-standing loyalty to Rome[18] – that is only part of the story. The Helvetians, as Caesar tells it, are encouraged and invited by subversive elements within tribes allied with the Romans; just as loyal elements of those same tribes call in the Romans against the Helvetians. Tribal politics, relations among tribes, and tribal relations with Rome and the Helvetians – two polarizing powers that tend to draw networks of alliances to themselves – all entangle to form a dense web of power negotiations in this story.

There is one further element in Caesar's account of the Helvetians to which I would like to draw attention before moving on. In this case Caesar identifies all of the participants as Gallic tribes; but the Helvetians are marginal Gauls, living near the Germans and, as Caesar says, surpassing other Gauls in *virtus* (here, military prowess) as a result.[19] In its broadest strokes, Caesar describes his defeat of the Helvetians not as the conquest of Gaul but as an alliance with Gallic tribes against an invader. When the Gauls later revolt under Vercingetorix and betray the alliance, he suppresses the revolt brutally; but he had acquired Gaul in the first place not by conquest but by alliance. This theme is even more important in the story of Ariovistus and the 'German' Suebi, which follows that of the Helvetians. This story begins with an assembly of Gallic tribes, at which Diviciacus and others petition Caesar to intervene for them against the depredations of Ariovistus. They explain Ariovistus' arrival in Gaul as the result of a long-standing conflict between rival alliances of Gallic tribes, centred on the Aedui and the Arverni; it was the Arverni, with their allies the Sequani, who invited Ariovistus' Suebi to aid them against the Aedui. As a result of this alliance the Sequani became the dominant power in the area and the Aedui were obliged to surrender hostages to them and, moreover, to promise not to solicit help from Rome.[20] In time, Ariovistus and his Suebi occupied the territory of the Sequani and reduced them to a servile condition, exacting hostages and torturing them, and demanding tribute from a wide territory around.[21] Caesar considers it an insupportable insult to himself and to Rome that the Aedui in particular have been forced to hand over hostages; but Ariovistus replies that he will not return the hostages or free the Aedui from tribute regardless of their status as 'Brothers of the Roman People.'[22] Thus two tribes, the Aedui and the Sequani – former rivals of each other, but both with past diplomatic ties to Rome – have surrendered power in the region to the newcomer Ariovistus. Furthermore, it is these tribes, according to Caesar, that inform him of the situation and solicit his aid. (Caesar adds that Diviciacus has already approached the Roman Senate.)[23] As in the case of the Helvetians, Caesar takes great trouble to describe the local rivalries and circumstances that have brought about his decision to intervene.

There is another wrinkle. Ariovistus is himself a recipient of the titles 'King' and 'Friend' from the Roman senate, which he obtained during Caesar's consulship and with his support.[24] This item – to which Caesar repeatedly refers – offers the best illustration of the principle of obedience in Roman imperialism. Ariovistus' main obligation as a Roman ally is to obey Rome's wishes in certain respects, and Caesar goes to great lengths to portray him as arrogant and out of control.[25] That is why Caesar places so much emphasis on hostages; in his commentaries, they are mainly guarantees of obedience.[26]

But what kind of obedience is expected from allies? What exactly are they supposed to do? In his negotiations with Ariovistus, Caesar mentions several items that also surface in other sources: the German must restore the hostages he has taken; he must refrain from taxing and otherwise oppressing Rome's allies; he must refrain from military aggression against Rome's allies; and he must bring no more of his people across the Rhine.[27] It is interesting that Caesar insists less on Ariovistus' own obedience to Rome (he demands no hostages or tribute himself) than on the principle that Ariovistus should not himself command obedience from Rome's allies or interfere with their obligations to Rome.

Besides the items I have mentioned, obedience also commonly involved military and logistical support for Rome during a campaign – a point I will return to in a moment. But it is important to realize that no legalistic formula spelled out the rights and obligations of Rome's 'friends' or even 'brothers.'[28] There are general areas in which Caesar expects and demands compliance, but there are many things which he does not mention and in which he does not bother to interfere, as well as large grey areas open to interpretation. Even in foreign policy, allies and subjects could operate quite independently, taking a calculated risk that the Romans would not notice or care what they were doing.[29] Always in the background was the idea that if the Romans did take offence at something, they would retaliate with extreme brutality, even wiping the perpetrators off the map, as in the case of Corinth in 146 BCE. Such events did not have to be frequent to be powerful deterrents. But a potential ally might easily calculate that the burdens of a relationship with the Romans were outweighed by Rome's utility to his own agenda.

According to Caesar, allies expected the Romans to support and enhance their influence in their own spheres.[30] This explains the constant influx of embassies to the Roman senate and of individual generals seeking diplomatic ties,[31] as well as the surprising complexity of Rome's pre-existing commitments in an area in which it had had little previous military involvement. Once established, a diplomatic relationship could be called on by either side as circumstances suggested, and acknowledged or ignored also as circumstances suggested, in a prolonged and open-ended negotiation of power.

This negotiation was not only between peoples and states but also between individuals. Caesar's story amply attests to the importance of personal relationships in foreign affairs. Diviciacus, the pro-Roman chief of the Aedui, has always displayed 'the greatest zeal for the Roman people and the greatest goodwill toward himself'[32] – his ties of loyalty are to Caesar, not just to Rome. Caesar defers subjecting Diviciacus' hostile brother Dumnorix to harsh punishment while he consults Diviciacus; not through the 'usual interpreters' but with the help of another 'close friend' (familiaris) of his, an enfranchised Gaul from Transalpina called C. Valerius Troucillus. Another enfranchised Gaul whom Caesar describes as his 'close friend and host' (familiaris et hospes), C. Valerius Procillus, plays an important role when Caesar sends him to negotiate with Ariovistus, along with M. Metius, who has a relationship of *hospitium* or hospitality with the German chief; and Caesar personally rescues him when he is taken prisoner.[33] Caesar thus has social connections with individuals among the leading classes within his province and outside of it. Ariovistus himself, as I have mentioned, is one of these; Caesar reminds him repeatedly of 'the great favor done for him by himself and the Roman people.'[34] He construes Ariovistus' affronts as insults not just to Rome but to himself personally, as Ariovistus turns from friend to enemy: '[Ariovistus said that] he would deal with him [Caesar] not as a friend but as an enemy; and that if he killed him, many of the nobles and leaders of the Roman people would be grateful to him (and he knew this from them, through their envoys).'[35]

Ariovistus' comment raises an important point: because personal power ran parallel to state power (and the Romans separated these two concepts with difficulty), the rivalries in which the Roman aristocracy was constantly entangled were part of the network of power I am describing; thus, for example, subject peoples or individuals might align themselves with one Roman commander against another. (The story of King Herod of Judaea, who played two generations of triumvirs against one another in the civil wars that ended the Roman Republic, is the most famous example.) Caesar avoids bringing his rivalry with Pompey into his account of the Gallic campaigns except in the passage I have quoted, but his desire to equal Pompey's military achievements played a large role in his decisions, at least according to the hostile tradition that survives in some historiography. Later, in 49 BCE, he and Pompey divided the loyalties and manpower of the entire Mediterranean world between them when they went to war.[36]

It is fair to say that part of what guaranteed Caesar's influence in Gaul was the army he commanded and his willingness to use it. The *Commentaries* are about war, after all; Caesar's pitched battles against the Helvetians[37] and Ariovistus[38] are the climactic events of book 1. But once again, a close examination of Caesar's own account complicates this point. For the sake of brevity I will leave aside the question of the composition of Caesar's 'Roman' legionary army (one legion was already stationed in Transalpine Gaul when he arrived; by the end of the campaigns of 58 he had recruited or transferred four more legions for a total of six).[39] But Caesar is militarily helpless without his Gallic allies and subjects. In the first place, it is clear from one incident – where Caesar mounts legionaries on Gallic horses to serve as a bodyguard[40] – that he has no legionary cavalry at all. As he writes, 'all his cavalry, numbering four thousand … he had raised from throughout the

[Transalpine] province and from the Aedui and their allies.'[41] Cavalry was of course essential against an enemy whose main strength was in cavalry, and all of Caesar's horses were Gallic.

Perhaps even more important, Caesar depends on his allies to supply his troops, especially with grain.[42] He calls a special congress of Aeduan chiefs to berate them for their failure to provide sufficient grain for his campaign against the Helvetians;[43] and other passages confirm that he relies on the logistical support of all his allies.[44] Grain could of course be procured by foraging and pillaging, but this creates new tactical problems; in fact Caesar perceives the supply of his army as one of the primary obligations of his allies.[45] Rather than a simple victory-narrative of a 'Roman' army conquering 'native' subjects, Caesar's work actually portrays, even in the military sphere, an array of power relationships at work.

I have mentioned that despite their simple rhetorical style, Caesar's commentaries are highly tendentious and ideological,[46] and I would like to confront this point directly before leaving him behind. Perhaps the most obvious and most often noticed element of self-serving propaganda is Caesar's distinction between 'Gauls' and 'Germans,' with the Rhine as notional boundary between the two. This distinction is a complex theme throughout the work that I cannot address fully here; only, scholars find no support for Caesar's ethnographic scheme using archaeology, linguistic analysis, or any other method.[47] It is unlikely that the tribes he describes as Gallic had a sense of cultural or national identity at that time.[48] But Caesar presents his intervention against Ariovistus as a response to a pan-Gallic plea for help against a German invader.[49] By constructing the Rhine as the notional boundary between Gaul and Germany, Caesar arguably extended his own province or authorized sphere of action, 'Transalpine Gaul,' as far as that river and created an automatic justification for war against any perceived 'Germans' found west of its banks. Just as Caesar presented his war against the Helvetians as an intervention on behalf of allies against an invader, here he aids all Gallic tribes against a German enemy; it is by this mechanism that Caesar 'conquers' Gaul.

There are other obviously tendentious elements in the way Caesar describes his diplomatic negotiations with Gauls and Germans, and I have mentioned some of them already. The theme of an allied people led by two brothers, one pro-Roman and one hostile and subversive, is common in Roman historiography.[50] Dumnorix panders to the Gallic masses and aims at kingship.[51] Ariovistus is cruel, tyrannical, and bigamous.[52] Caesar's allies weep, prostrate themselves, and beg for his intervention.[53] Should we not then dismiss Caesar's entire account and conclude that local politics and power networks did not matter, that in reality he simply stampeded into Gaul in quest of money and glory, plundering and pillaging whatever he could get? I would like to propose a different and perhaps more useful approach. Using Caesar's own narrative, one could set Roman interests aside and retell the story of Gaul as a tale of local tribal and dynastic conflict in which the Romans and other parties are brought in as allies. This perspective is constantly in the background, constantly alluded to, because Caesar had virtually no way of finding out what the political situation in Gaul was except from current or potential allies seeking his intervention.[54] What they told him would be some amalgam of their interpretation of the situation and whatever they thought was most likely to secure his support. The point is that no description of the network of differing interests and power relationships in which imperialism operates can be objective; it is all interpreted and negotiated all the time; and this process of interpretation and negotiation is in fact how it operates. To understand imperialism properly it is more useful to collect as many perspectives on the situation as possible, however biased these might be, than to reduce it to a simple story of battles won and lost.

Caesar's commentaries provide the most convenient example illustrating the mechanics of how imperial power expands. I would also like to examine how administration works in areas that have long been subject to the ruling power. The most detailed source of evidence for administration in the Republican period is the two long speeches that Cicero gave (rather, he gave one of them; the other was never delivered but was published along with the first) in 70 BCE when he prosecuted Gaius Verres, former pro-praetorian governor of Sicily, for extortion. Verres had ruled Sicily for three years, from 73 to 71 BCE. Once again, the text I have chosen is very tendentious. Cicero is doing whatever he can to paint Verres as a bad governor. But in the process he reveals a great deal of information about how power worked in the province.

Cicero's speech is full of the rhetoric of paternalism. The Sicilians (whom he construes as Greeks,[55] like good children, are obedient and tolerant of Rome's rule and even of its abuses.[56] Rome's allies are in awe of the power of the imperial magistrates, and afraid that any insult to that authority will result in violent retaliation;[57] Rome, in turn, has a moral duty to protect the interests of her loyal subjects. A careful reading of the speeches, however, does not entirely support this paternalistic image of Roman rule; the real power relationship is much more complicated.

In the first place, Cicero's simple distinction between Sicilians and Romans oversimplifies the situation. Rome had not one relationship with 'Sicily,' but a range of relationships with individual communities that partly reflected the degree of their support for Rome in the First Punic War and subsequent conflicts, as well as their relationships with individual Roman patrons. For example, in one passage Cicero outlines the complex system of taxation to which the province is subject, one that is neither similar to that imposed on any other territory nor uniform throughout it. For some cities, tax contracts are sold by the censors at Rome to corporations of *publicani;* two cities pay on their own without contracts; five cities are exempt from taxation. The rest pay one-tenth of the crop according to the same system that prevailed under Hiero II, the king of Syracuse, who controlled a wide region after the First Punic War and whose kingdom the Romans allowed to stand until 211, when they sacked the city during the Second Punic War.[58] The contracts for that tithe were supposed to be sold in Sicily – that is, to local corporations.[59] Cities might also have special relationships with Roman aristocrats and their descendants.[60] A typical way for subjects to negotiate with rulers was to send a delegation of their most prominent and eloquent citizens to plead their case to the Roman senate or to an aristocratic patron. Such delegations normally came from individual cities,[61] though some represented the entire province.[62] Some aristocrats, including the family of the Claudii Marcelli – whose most famous ancestor captured Syracuse in 211 BCE – or Cicero himself, who served his quaestorship in Sicily, considered themselves patrons of Sicily as a whole.[63] As in the case of Caesar, personal relationships were inextricable from diplomatic ones. Thus Cicero writes that the Sicilians are 'allies and friends of the Roman people and close connections of myself.'[64]

It is quite difficult to identify and define the Roman presence in Sicily. Verres, as was customary, brought an entourage with him from Italy, which Cicero calls his *cohors*.[65] This included members of his household (his slaves and freedmen),[66] an assortment of his friends (called *comites* or companions),[67] his two quaestors,[68] his six lictors,[69] and a small number of deputies or legates whom he appointed himself.[70] There was no 'Roman' army in Sicily; there was a small Sicilian army and navy,[71] but it plays almost no role in the case. When Verres uses shock troops to force provincials to comply with his rapacious demands, the personnel

Cicero always mentions are slaves of the temple of Aphrodite/Venus at Eryx, which had a small contingent of guards to protect the treasury.[72] This was apparently the only public labour force under his control.

So much for the apparatus of the Roman state. What about the other Romans in Sicily? In one lofty rhetorical passage, Cicero speaks as though large numbers of Italians have settled there as farmers and businessmen (negotiatores).[73] The latter category, to which Cicero refers frequently, was a very broad and indefinite one and could include representatives of the Roman corporations that collected some Sicilian taxes – the customs duties, for example, and some of the grain tax, as I have noted. Cicero mentions Carpinatius, especially, as a representative of the company that collects the pasture tax.[74] However, nothing in the speeches suggests that Roman corporations exported a substantial apparatus to collect the tax rather then enlisting the cooperation of locals. In fact, most taxes in Sicily were farmed to local corporations. Cicero normally refers to these local tax collectors as decumani,[75] so called because they collected the 10 per cent grain tax of Hiero; he also calls them publicani.[76] Some have Roman-sounding names and some have Greek-sounding names; beyond that it is impossible to distinguish their ethnic identity as 'Romans' or 'Sicilians,' if that is a meaningful question.

As for the landowners in Sicily, Verres' main victims: some land was owned by absentee landlords, Roman senators living in Italy.[77] But for the most part Verres' Roman citizen victims were men, including some of equestrian status, who farmed and paid taxes in Sicily.[78] These citizens could be emigrants from Italy or their descendants (or those of their freedmen), or enfranchised provincials or their descendants (or freedmen);[79] 'knights,' by this time, were simply citizens of substantial wealth. Roman citizens and knights had legal privileges that others did not have and more claim on the support of the Roman state and individual patrons, and could wield extra influence if they were organized into separate communities called conventus, which were prominent in Sicily's largest cities of Syracuse, Agrigentum, and Lilybaeum.[80] Overall it is likely that they were wealthier than the average Sicilian, though this is impossible to measure.

However, the 'Roman' population of Sicily did not amount to a ruling class even if it was ethnically (as opposed to legally) distinguishable from the class of subjects, which is very debatable. In fact, it is the consensus that the 'Roman' population by any definition was very small in the provinces, at least before the massive colonization efforts of Caesar and Augustus, and arguably after that as well.[81] The group that most accurately fit the description of a ruling class in late Republican Sicily was still its local municipal senators and civic officials, the Hellenic or Hellenized urban aristocracy whose negotiations and interactions with Verres and his friends and enemies, in Sicily and in Rome, play a role at every stage of Cicero's long indictment. As I have mentioned, this is the class whose most eloquent members represented their cities to the Roman government and to individual Roman patrons. They had close personal ties with Roman aristocrats; the social bond Cicero describes most frequently is *hospitium*,[82] something I have also mentioned in my discussion of Caesar. Roman senators travelled with a large entourage; housing, feeding, and entertaining them was no small responsibility, and *hospitium* was a relationship on a plane with, and often associated with, friendship and patronage.[83] That is, people with this relationship were expected to support one another in other ways, for example, in legal proceedings. It is an especially damning sign that evidence against Verres can be extracted, on cross-examination, from his own *hospes*, Heius of Messana;[84] and that he presided over the unjust conviction of another of his *hospites*, Sthenius of Thermae.[85]

Based on the Verrine orations, it is safe to say that the two main tasks of the governor in Sicily were collecting taxes and resolving legal disputes. I have spoken briefly about the first of these and would like to focus on the second for a moment. A law of Publius Rupilius in 131 BCE laid down rules for appointing panels of judges according to the status of plaintiff and defendant and stipulated which local institutions (e.g., the municipal senate) were to try different types of cases;[86] it was the praetor's job to ensure that the correct procedures were followed and to appoint the panels of judges if necessary. Verres violated the law by failing to follow the proper procedures and especially by appointing his own friends to hear cases.[87] It is largely by his influence over the courts that he secures his aims; for example, he rigs a panel to find against a defendant in a property dispute in return for a kickback from the plaintiffs.[88]

Jurisdiction, however, is something constantly open to negotiation under Verres and probably under other governors as well;[89] it would be a mistake to assume that laws like the Rupilian Law had the effect of dictating or simplifying the distribution of legal authority. Well-connected provincials might get a property dispute before the governor if they thought they might benefit from that, or in Verres' case, if the corrupt governor could benefit.[90] It was apparently customary for the governor to hear some criminal cases himself; Verres hears one case that his predecessor also heard.[91] Like property disputes, these cases arose out of local conflicts and rivalries, where enemies went after enemies (public prosecutors did not exist in antiquity; one was prosecuted by one's enemies and defended by one's friends).[92] Here Cicero criticizes Verres' choice of advisers to sit on his council; the corrupt governor appoints only close friends and retainers, some of low status,[93] rather than local Roman citizens or upstanding Sicilians as appropriate.

Legal proceedings, then, were an important nexus of interaction between the Romans and their subjects; certainly this was true in the better-documented imperial period, during which governors and the emperor heard cases of all kinds.[94] Local law and legal institutions continued to operate, but the Roman governor was another source of authority. His function was to resolve the cases before him rather than to impose some overarching legal system. Naturally, the social connections between the disputants and the governor would be a major factor in determining the outcome. Cicero's case against Verres is precisely that traffic in cash and commodities has replaced the normal traffic in social influence and favours – a typically Roman understanding of corruption. But even in its most abusive form – the form that Cicero attributes to Verres' regime – the administration of justice in the provinces is a very complex system that arises out of local rivalries and enmities and that involves collaboration and negotiation among provincials, their friends, their Roman or Romanized patrons, and the Roman state as represented by Verres and his staff – but Verres could also be patron or friend, and these categories were not distinct. No large bureaucracy or public labour force was dedicated either to collecting taxes or to the administration of justice; both were done largely through social mechanisms.

So far I have not taken account of the fact that some parts of Sicily may have been entirely independent of Roman control even in Verres' day. In a famous article Brent Shaw[95] demonstrated how at any given time large regions of the empire were dominated by the 'personal power' of bandits and pirates, who constantly negotiated the boundaries of their influence with local landowners, municipal officials, kinship groups, and the Roman state. Banditry was a problem not only in frontier regions but in the heart of the empire as well, including Italy and Sicily in the late second century BCE. Many scholars trace the origins of two slave revolts in Sicily to the high number of shepherd-bandits in some regions.[96] Cicero of course mentions banditry and piracy many times in his indictment of Verres,[97] but it is difficult to know how to interpret this, because failing to control bandits was a standard accusation against bad governors. Still, it would not be surprising if banditry were still a problem. While I would disagree with Shaw's programmatic distinction between state and personal power – I see no such meaningful distinction in the Roman sociopolitical system – it is important to remember that the network of Roman power was weak in some areas at the very heart of the empire.

Caesar and Cicero were highly educated thinkers and philosophers but not in the works I have discussed here. In these works they do not philosophize. In fact, apart from Cicero (whose ideas are discussed eloquently by Geoffrey Kellow in this collection), the Romans produced very little that deserves the title of political philosophy or, especially, the philosophy of empire; even Cicero's *De re publica* is mostly about the idea of the state, not how (or why) to acquire and rule an empire. This does not mean that the Romans had no understanding of what they were doing or that they applied no rational set of ideas. Indeed, both Caesar and Cicero show an acute understanding of how imperialism works as a social system. A question that arises is whether Roman subjects understood the system in the same way that the Romans themselves did. It is easy to see how, in the normal course of imperial conquest or rule, each party might interpret the same situation, the same speech or set of circumstances, in a different way; they might even disagree on whether the 'subject' was really a subject at all, or about what its obligations were. In fact that would seem inevitable.

I have been asked to comment on what lessons or insights from the Roman world might be applied today. I approach this task with hesitation as I am not an expert on the foreign policy of any modern nation. But to the extent that we see foreign policy as policy at all – as a realm of grand ideas and theories – we neglect the example of the texts I have discussed here. Caesar would tell us that big ideas such as liberty or democracy don't really matter – they won't help you win the hearts and minds of the people among whom you pursue your interests and ambitions (though they may make good slogans in a revolt, but that is a separate issue). At best, such ideas will appeal to certain sectors of the population who believe they can benefit materially from manipulating your desire to impose those ideas. The world of Caesar and of Verres is a dark and Machiavellian one where innumerable parties exploit the international situation to the maximum extent of their ability to do so. And throughout Roman history it is always the same. The conquest of any province, where it is known in any detail, resembles Caesar's story in Gaul – the Greek East, Judaea, even Spain to the extent that that story is known, all can be read the same way.

It is not hard to see the universal truths of the Roman imperial example. Conquerors always represent a small minority among their so-called subjects. Occupation of overseas territory is extremely difficult in any era. Military might and imperial bureaucracy alone never explain how a dominant nation rules. There is a sense in which one does not conquer a people or territory; nor, strictly speaking, is one drawn into it; rather, a previously existing web of connections is activated and reconfigured. And in areas already long and deeply entangled in the web, an even more complicated network of power governs the interactions between ruler and subject. This is not to say that imperialism is not traumatic or damaging. Gaul under Caesar and Sicily under Verres both suffered enormously (though archaeologists have long argued that in the long term, both economies flourished under the Roman empire). But invoking a simple narrative to explain that misses something essential about how imperial power works: it can only be understood as a negotiation, one in which the deeply complicated social structures, motives, and agendas of the subjects are as important as those of the conquerors. In this model, what might determine the success of an empire is how well subjects and conquerors communicate or understand one another and not, for example, logistical or strategic issues nor even commitment and willingness to sacrifice. Imperialists who truly understand why they have become involved in a conflict – this means not only their own motives but those of the parties who have asked for their support – and who understand the subtle mechanisms by which power is negotiated in the would-be subject nation may be more likely to achieve their aims than those who do not.

NOTES

1 Susan Mattern, *Rome and the Enemy: Imperial Strategy in the Principate* (Berkeley: University of California Press, 1999).
2 Here the most important contribution is that of Kallet-Marx; see Robert Morstein Kallet-Marx, *Hegemony to Empire: The Development of Roman Imperium in the East from 148 to 62 BC* (Berkeley: University of California Press, 1995), 11–30.
3 Thus Benjamin Isaac, *The Limits of Empire: The Roman Army in the East*, 2nd ed. (Oxford: Clarendon, 1992), 394–401, argues that the Romans thought of

themselves as conquering people, not territory, even in the imperial
period. However, geographical boundaries do play an important and
complex role in Caesar's *Gallic War*.

4 Peter A. Brunt, *Italian Manpower, 225 BC–AD 14* (Oxford: Clarendon, 1971),
432–3.

5 E.g., 1.1.5, but this is a theme throughout.

6 See Mattern, *Rome and the Enemy*, 118–19, 191–2.

7 Brunt, *Italian Manpower*, 432–3, n. 4.

8 Most studies of Caesar's Gallic war are heavily military in emphasis, but
Joachim Szidat, *Caesars Diplomatische Tätigkeit im gallischen Krieg* (*Historia*
Einzelschrift 14, Wiesbaden: Steiner, 1970), is an illuminating study of its
diplomatic aspects.

9 Caesar, *BG*, 1.3.

10 *Fratres consanguineique*, 1.33, 36, 45.

11 *Hospitium atque amicitia*, 1.31.

12 Ibid., 1.33, 35, 43.

13 Ibid., 1.45.

14 Ibid., 1.3, 30.

15 Ibid., 1.11, 18–19.

16 Ibid., 1.6, 11, 14.

17 Ibid., 1.10.

18 Ibid., 1.11, 14.

19 Ibid., 1.1. See also Gerold Walzer, *Caesar und die Germanen: Studien zur
politischen Tendenz römischer Feldzugsberichte* (*Historia* Einzelschrift 1,
Wiesbaden: Steiner, 1956), 1–7, on Caesar's portrayal of the Helvetians
and their motives.

20 *BG*, 1.31.

21 Ibid., 1.31, 36.

22 Ibid., 1.33, 36.

23 Ibid., 1.31.

24 Ibid., 1.35, 39, 43, 44.

25 See Walzer, 21–36, on Caesar's complex portrayal of Ariovistus.

26 See, for example, 1.14: 'if hostages were given to him [Caesar] by them [the
Helvetians], so that he might believe that they would do what they promised' (*si obsides ab iis sibi dentur, uti ea quae polliceantur facturos intellegat*).

27 Ibid., 1.35, 43.

28 For a thorough discussion of the diplomatic concept of *amicitia*, see Erich
S. Gruen, *The Hellenistic World and the Coming of Rome*, 2 vols. (Berkeley:
University of California Press, 1984) ch. 2.

29 Ibid., ch. 2, n. 14 and passim; for example, 31–2, 63, 68, etc.; cf. Kallet-Marx, *Hegemony to Empire*, 23.

30 *BG*, 1.43, 44.

31 On the autonomy of Roman generals to conduct diplomatic negotiations in the field, see Arthur M. Eckstein, *Senate and General: Individual Decision Making and Roman Foreign Relations, 264–194 BC* (Berkeley: University of California Press, 1987). Caesar describes receiving delegations after successful campaigns in *BG*, 1.30.

32 *BG*, 1.19.

33 Ibid., 1.46, 52.

34 Ibid., 1.35, 43; cf. 1.40, encouraging Ariovistus not to reject 'the favor of himself or the Roman people.'

35 Ibid., 1.44.

36 The best exposition of this war, stressing its personal elements, is Kurt Raaflaub's classic work, *Dignitatis contentio: Studien zur Motivation und politischen Taktik im Burgerkrieg zwischen Caesar und Pompeius* (Munich: Beck, 1974). For the armies of Caesar and Pompey, see Brunt, *Italian Manpower*, 473–80 and App., 29.

37 *BG*, 1.24–6.

38 Ibid., 1.48–53.

39 For a brief discussion of Caesar's army in Gaul and its composition, see Brunt, *Italian Manpower*, 446–66. A legion was in theory about five thousand men, but they could be underenrolled.

40 *BG*, 1.42.

41 Ibid., 1.15.

42 The very prominent role of supply in both of Caesar's *Commentaries* is difficult for even a cursory reader to overlook. Ever since the seminal work of Donald Engels, *Alexander the Great and the Logistics of the Macedonian Army* (Berkeley: University of California Press, 1978), scholars have emphasized the degree to which armies on campaign were dependent on local resources, though the Romans also developed a logistical infrastructure that maintained its standing army and that could to some extent supply it in hostile territory. Two good recent studies of the Roman army's methods of supply are Paul Erdkamp, *Hunger and the Sword: Warfare and Food Supply in Roman Republican Wars (264–30 BC)* (Amsterdam: Gieben, 1998); and Jonathan P. Roth, *The Logistics of the Roman Army at War (264 BC–AD 235)* (Leiden: Brill, 1999).

43 *BG*, 1.16.

44 Ibid., 1.23, 40, 48.

45 Conversely, allies must refrain from supplying the armies of his enemies: *BG*, 1.26.

46 Michel Rambaud's classic work *L'art de la déformation historique dans les Commentaires de César* (2nd ed., Paris: Les Belles Lettres, 1966), illuminates the depth and complexity of Caesar's ideological agenda.

47 Good discussions of Caesar's construction of Germans and Gauls include Walzer, *Caesar und die Germanen;* Colin Wells, *The German Policy of Augustus: An Examination of the Archaeological Evidence* (Oxford: Clarendon, 1972), 14–32; Allan Lund, *Zum Germanenbild der Römer: Eine Einführung in die antike Ethnographie* (Heidelberg: Winter, 1990), 82–100; and Charles R. Whittaker, *Frontiers of the Roman Empire: A Social and Economic Study* (Baltimore: Johns Hopkins University Press, 1994), 74–8. The distinction between Gauls and Germans is probably traceable to Posidonius – the word *Germanoi* is attested in a surviving fragment of his work – but it is likely that most of the schema are Caesar's own.

48 Cf. Maureen Carroll, *Romans, Celts, and Germans: The German Provinces of Rome* (Stroud: Tempus, 2001), 10–11.

49 *BG*, 1.30–2.

50 The most famous incidence is Tacitus' portrayal of Arminius and Flavus of the Cherusci, *Annales,* 2.9–10.

51 *BG*, 1.3, 9, 17, 18.

52 Ibid., 1.31, 36, 53.

53 Ibid., 1.20, 31, 32.

54 Ibid., 1.11, 17–18, 30–2, 37.

55 Cicero, *Ver.,* 2.2.7.

56 Ibid., 2.2.8, 2.3.67.

57 Ibid., 2.27.68, 2.29.74, 2.31.79.

58 A good introductory history of Sicily under the Republic is Roger Wilson, *Sicily under the Roman Empire: The Archaeology of a Roman Province, 36 BC–AD 535* (Warminster: Aris and Phillips, 1990), 17–32.

59 Cic., *Ver.,* 2.3.13–15. On taxation and tax collectors in Sicily, see Christopher Schäfer, 'Steuerpacht und Steuerpächter in Sizilien zur Zeit des Verres,' *Münstersche Beiträge zur antiken Handelsgeschichte* 11 (1992): 23–38, with full bibliography.

60 For example, Segesta and the Scipiones, Cic., *Ver.,* 2.4.78–80; Syracuse and the Marcelli, 2.2.36, 50–1; Messana and Verres, 2.4.17–26.

61 Cic., *Ver.,* 2.1.50; 2.2.9, 11; 2.2.122.

62 Ibid., 2.3.204.

63 Ibid., 2.2.8; 2.1.16–17; 2.2.122.

64 *socii atque amici populi Romani, mei autem necessarii* (2.1.15); cf. 2.4.80, *clientes tui, socii populi Romani atque amici*.

65 Cic., *Ver.*, 2.2.12, 2.2.27.

66 Ibid., 2.1.67, 2.2.69.

67 Ibid., 2.1.64, 66; 2.2.27.

68 Ibid., 2.2.11, 22.

69 Ibid., 2.1.67, 2.2.11.

70 Ibid., 2.2.49.

71 Ibid., 1.13, 2.3.186.

72 Cicero calls them *Venerii*; see, for example, 2.3.61, 62, 65, and many more references. On the cult, see Wilson, *Sicily under the Roman Empire,* 282–4.

73 Cic., *Ver.*, 2.2.6

74 2.2.169ff, 2.3.167; see Ernst Badian, *Publicans and Sinners: Private Enterprise in the Service of the Roman Republic* (2nd ed., Ithaca: Cornell University Press, 1983), 76, 78; Schäfer, 'Steuerpacht und Steuerpächter in Sizilien,' 24–5.

75 Cic., *Ver.*, 2.3.21, 66, 75.

76 Ibid., 2.3.77.

77 Ibid., 2.3.98; cf. 2.2.6.

78 See, for example, 2.1.7. It was an important theme throughout, as outrages against Roman citizens made for the most moving rhetorical arguments; for prominent individual cases, see, for example, 2.3.36–7, 60–1. On Italian immigration to Sicily and Roman landowners in Sicily, see Wilson, *Sicily under the Roman Empire,* 28–9.

79 Enfranchised provincials included Dio of Halaesa (2.2.19–20), Sextus Pompeius Chlorus (2.2.23), and Gnaeus Pompeius Philo (2.4.48); Wilson, *Sicily under the Roman Empire,* 29, counts fourteen enfranchised Sicilian provincials in Cicero's works.

80 Brunt, *Italian Manpower,* 220–4 on *conventus*.

81 For example, Wilson, *Sicily under the Roman Empire,* 29; Brunt, *Italian Manpower,* 204–33.

82 For example, 2.2.24, 83, 96; 2.3.18; 2.4.25, 49, etc.

83 Cf. Koenraad Verboven, *The Economy of Friends: Economic Aspects of Amicitia and Patronage in the Late Republic* (Collection Latomus 269, Brussels: Éditions Latomus, 2002), 51, 58.

84 Cic., *Ver.*, 2.4.18–19.

85 2.2.110; cf. 2.2.113, where he is acquitted by Pompey, another former guest; Sthenius is Cicero's own *hospes* also, 2.2.227.

86 Ibid., 2.2.32–3.

87 Ibid., 2.2.35–42. He does the same with the panels of *recuperatores* who hear tax cases: 2.3.28, 54, 68–9, 137.

88 Ibid., 2.2.25, 35–42, 53–61.

89 Ibid., 2.2.90–1.

90 Ibid., 2.2.89–91.

91 Ibid., 2.2.68.

92 See 2.2.134 and the cases of Sopater (2.2.68–75) and Sthenius (2.2.83–118).

93 Ibid., 2.2.71, 75.

94 The classic discussion of Roman law as a bottom-up, rather than top-down, system is Fergus Millar, *The Emperor in the Roman World (31 BC–AD 235)* (2nd ed., Ithaca: Cornell University Press, 1992).

95 Brent Shaw, 'Bandits in the Roman Empire,' *Past and Present* 105 (1984): 3–52.

96 See ibid., 40n10.

97 Cic., *Ver.*, 2.1.12, 2.3.186, 2.4.21.

10 The Rise of Global Power and the Music of the Spheres: Philosophy and History in Cicero's *De re publica*

GEOFFREY KELLOW

> Forgetfulness, and I shall even say historical error, form an essential factor
> in the creation of a nation; and thus it is that the progress of historical stud-
> ies may often be dangerous to the nationality. Historical research, in fact,
> brings back to light the deeds of violence that have taken place at the com-
> mencement of all political formations, even of those the consequences of
> which have been most beneficial.
>
> Ernest Renan, *What Is a Nation?*

Cicero is popularly known as the last great republican statesman. From
the standpoint of politics and political history, this characterization is
indubitably just. Nonetheless, Cicero was much more than a politician.
His contributions to Roman life were as expansive as the borders of the
republic and nascent empire that was the almost singular object of his
extraordinary attentions. Cicero was an orator, lawyer, poet, translator,
political theorist, and philosophic historian of Rome. It is these last two
in particular – philosophic historian and political theorist – that press
most profoundly on our present politics. Of especial interest is the manner in which Cicero perceived these twin tasks as bound up, inextric-
ably, one with the other. This connection – in particular, the necessity of
a political theory embedded in a philosophic approach to history – is an
underappreciated yet essential element of his thinking on political
questions – questions that continue to concern us today. Indeed, the
mutual entailment that Cicero recognized between these two modes of
inquiry grounds one of his principal insights into the nature of imperial
politics.[1] I will argue that Cicero's magnificent, if tragically fragmentary, *De re publica* constitutes his best effort at a threefold reconciliation:

between republic and empire, politics and history, and ultimately, political philosophy and historical necessity. In this attempt at reconciliation, Cicero reveals himself as a patriot, a statesman-historian and ultimately, a philosopher.

Both in Cicero's time and in our own, the republican and imperial citizenry is characterized by a historical consciousness. Cicero recreates and renders luminescent this consciousness with clarity and elegance, most conspicuously in his paired dialogues *De re publica* and *De legibus*.[2] With their explicit subjects – the ideal regime and its laws, respectively – the two dialogues consciously echo yet carefully contrast with their eponymous Platonic precursors. However, when we compare the Ciceronian and Platonic dialogues, the most striking difference we find relates to the extended historical exegesis present in the former.[3] In *De re publica* in particular, Cicero distinguishes his own enterprise from that of Plato in explicitly historical terms. In the second book of the dialogue, he has Scipio assert: 'I will have an easier time in completing my task if I show you our commonwealth as it is born, grows up, and comes of age, and as a strong and well-established state, than if I make up some state as Socrates does in Plato.'[4]

Why will Cicero have an 'easier time' if he writes a philosophic history? There are a number of viable answers. The dialogue's sheer topical breadth and stylistic variety necessarily mean that no single assessment need serve to the exclusion of all others.[5] Nonetheless, the multiple meditations on the importance of history to politics and on Roman history per se, when combined with Cicero's circumspect presentation of that history, strongly suggest that history is Cicero's central political and philosophic concern. This essay will argue that this 'easier time' is far more than a philosophic recognition of or resignation to the special place of history in Roman life.[6] Cicero ultimately aims to enchant Roman history – to discern, in the apparent action of historical necessity, the revelation of a Roman ideal.

History and Reconciliation

Leo Strauss famously wonders, in the very heart of his *Natural Right and History,* whether 'a self-respecting society cannot become reconciled to the notion that its foundation was laid in crime?'[7] This is the central challenge that history poses to the politics of a republican empire. Cicero recognized that empires, almost by definition, are historical entities. Empires are creatures of change over time; their institutions and their boundaries develop, expanding or contracting over time. Unlike the ancient Hellenic republics, empires are neither founded in an ideal (and invisible) past nor established by an original lawgiver. The constant change in imperial boundaries and institutions constitutes a continual refounding. Moreover, the historical processes of political, institutional, and geographic growth definitively preclude the possibility of a mythical and hence morally unambiguous founding. Indeed, Cicero rejects the authenticity of such claims, even when the political form is sufficiently ancient and static to entertain the possibility of an untroubled founding. Exploring this theme early in *De re publica*, Cicero depicts the world-weary Philus, compelled by his colleagues, arguing on behalf of injustice as the *sine qua non* of successful rule. In so contending, Philus specifically derides the Athenian and Arcadian claims to a morally unambiguous autochthony by suggesting that 'they pretended that they arose from the earth like these mice from the field.'[8] Empires can entertain no such illusions of original possession. Their ascent inevitably entails popular cognizance of a secondary – or even tertiary – seizure from prior inhabitants. The possibility of a morally unambiguous founding, and therefore of a founding to which a self-respecting society is easily reconciled in Strauss's terms, is simply unavailable to imperial polities.[9] Indeed, Cicero broadcasts the rough nature of imperial politics from the very outset of *De re publica*. His Scipio, a man who in some important senses serves as the Ciceronian Socrates, enters the dialogue surrounded by the violence and victory of his illustrious family. At the outset of the dialogue his family's martial history is invoked as the proud legacy of having 'put out with their own blood the rising flames of the Second Punic war.'[10] In so commencing, Cicero makes it clear that history, even bloody history, is an intractable element in Roman political life, discourse, and philosophy.

History's profound role in Roman political life forces upon Cicero an alternative conception of founding, one that is not territorially, temporally, or philosophically unitary. The alternative foundation he discerns amounts to recasting Rome's political and historical development as the wisdom of generations engaged in the incremental founding of the state. Particularly significant is the implication of underlying action that, he suggests, gradually reveals Roman and eternal principles through the work of generations in history. In a remark he attributes to the greatest of the noble Catonii, Cicero asserts: 'Our commonwealth, in contrast, was not shaped by one man's talent but by that of many: and not in one person's lifetime, but over many generations. He said that there never was a genius so great that he could miss nothing, nor could all the geniuses in the world brought together in one place at one time foresee all contingencies without the practical experience afforded by the passage of time.'[11]

These words, with their attribution to Cato and their connection between wisdom and contingency, hint at Cicero's philosophic/historic strategy. They further justify Cicero's insistence that he will have an 'easier time' if he begins not with an ideal city in speech but rather with an account of the historical ascent to political wisdom that the republic experienced over its history. Rome, Cicero acknowledges, is the work of generations. However, with uncharacteristic imprecision, he leaves open the manner in which time affords opportunities for insight to arise.

The ambiguity in Cicero's account of the rise of wisdom within the passage of time serves a set of very particular and complementary purposes whose specificity is belied by the imprecision that permits them. First among these is the conversion of the study of history into a second-best *paideia*. As Cicero writes in his *Orator*: 'To be ignorant of what occurred before you were born is to remain always a child. For what is the worth of human life, unless it is woven into the life of our ancestors by the records of history?'[12]

Cicero deliberately employs the language of growth and maturation on the part of the individual to explain the value of historical knowledge. A lack of historical knowledge is not simply a type of ignorance; it is a radical form of immaturity, an incompleteness in the soul. To be ignorant is to fail to realize, to ascend, to attain the natural end of citizenship and civic virtue through contact with the Roman ideal in history. The growth of the individual in wisdom through life both mirrors and is prompted by an understanding of the historical development of Rome. As Cicero states later in *De legibus*, the lack of such contact leads citizens to miss the justice for which they were born.[13] In this way, contact with the history of Rome serves the same periagogic and pedagogic purpose that the dramatic turn towards the light and escape from the cave serves in Plato's *Republic*.[14]

Indeed, Cicero hints subtly at this connection in the very first dramatic encounter in his own *De re publica*. Therein the youthful and precocious student Tubero presents himself to the august General P. Scipio Africanus on the occasion of the Latin Holidays[15] and asks of the great soldier: 'Then since you seem to invite it and give me hope of your attention, shall we first consider (before the others arrive) what the meaning is of the second sun, which has been reported in the senate.

The witnesses are neither few nor frivolous, so that isn't so much a question of believing them as of explaining it.'[16]

The dramatic action of *De re publica* begins with an account of a second sun, a parhelion. With great subtlety, Cicero echoes the central moment in his great precursor's masterwork.[17] With this second sun, a pale reflection of the original, Cicero indicates the philosophic possibility of the conversation. In the Ciceronian rendering of the ascent from darkness to illumination, from ignorance to knowledge of the ideal, the ascent culminates only in the refracted light of a second sun. The Roman atmosphere is too thick with history for the full light of philosophy to break through.[18]

Imperial Settings in Ciceronian Dialogue

Cicero is the author of a novel form of philosophic dialogue, a form that captures the essential elements of republican politics through its structure and equally captures specifically Roman and imperial political qualities in its historical content. By subtly depicting the influence of historical and imperial contexts on superficially republican dramatic action, he judiciously discloses the limits and possibilities of philosophy in an imperial age. The substance of Cicero's dialogues, especially *De re publica*, perfectly captures the refracted and diminished possibility imposed on politics and philosophy by an atmosphere saturated with history.

Any study of late republican Rome cannot avoid the radical disconnect between origins and current conditions, between the city of Romulus and the nascent world state that awaits the Caesars. Indeed, the Roman failure to confront this disconnect in institutional terms can be compellingly asserted as a proximate cause of the demise of Senate rule.[19] In the construction of his dialogues, Cicero indicates his awareness of the political distance that Rome has travelled by repeatedly contrasting its rustic origins with its cosmopolitan present. Moreover, he reiterates the implicit correlations among philosophic, historic, and political growth by linking Athens and Rome via the media of dialogue and attendant setting. He accomplishes this end with fullest effect by explicitly invoking Platonic and bucolic settings and then placing them in a subtly cosmopolitan setting. Cicero's *De legibus* invokes the Cretan wildness of Plato's dialogue of the same name[20] but then draws attention to the new Roman reality. In Plato's *Laws* the conversation between Kleinias, Megillus, and the Athenian stranger begins with Kleinias' description of the pastoral landscape through which they will travel.[21] In such a setting the Athenian stranger feels comfortable speaking with candor and inquiring into the potentially divine origins of law.[22] Cicero, both in his choice of title and in the dramatic action, suggests a similarity of setting but then presents Atticus' telling declaration in response to a controversial definition of the gods: 'Of course I will grant it, if you wish: the singing of the birds and the noise of the river give me reason not to fear that any of my fellow students will hear.'[23]

Atticus' remarks reveal a crucial facet of empire. While outward appearance suggests rusticity, Atticus' fear of being overheard suggests the true nature of an imperial countryside. The potential for being witnessed, the absence of a sufficiently remote locale to permit full philosophic exposition, is a hallmark of the imperial social and political environment. Citizens are everywhere. Civilization is everywhere.[24] Politics and its consequences, both benign and malignant, are everywhere.[25] All action, all speech in imperial settings, must be considered as potentially a matter of record.[26] What is lacking in an imperial society is the seclusion that permits full philosophic candor;[27] in its place is an awareness that speech and action are likely to become part of history, possessing the fullness of consequence that entails. History, understood both as the events of the past and as the ever expanding record of the present, is the unavoidable circumstance in which philosophy find itself in. Philosophy's illuminations must inevitably refract through this atmosphere.

History, Necessity, and Ideal

It is into this irreducibly historical milieu that Scipio begins his account of the rise of Rome and of the emergence of its governing principles in history. It becomes clear at the outset of Scipio's account of the rise of Rome that this task will entail imperatives distinct from those of the historian. Scipio seeks in historical narrative to achieve the same end that Plato realizes with the internal dialogue of the laws in his *Crito*; in Plato's famous meditation on law, obedience, and obligation, the interior dialogue concludes with Socrates enchanted by his own creation. Speaking to his friend of his ultimate resignation to his fate, Socrates declares: 'Crito, my dear friend, be assured that these words I seem to hear, as the Corybants seem to hear the music of their flutes, and the echo of these words resounds in me, and make it impossible for me to hear anything else. As far as my present beliefs go, if you speak in opposition to them, you will speak in vain. However, if you think you can accomplish anything, speak.'[28]

The intellectual and elenchic motion of Socratic philosophizing possesses a supervening musicality that enchants Socrates at the same time as the argument itself convinces. The combination of rational conviction and musical enchantment further immunizes Socrates to the arguments of others. Beyond conviction, his words have rendered him 'unable to hear anything else.'[29] Turning to Scipio's account of Rome's origins, the same dual appeal is at work, only the medium has changed: instead of interior dialogue, Scipio presents an enchanting historical enterprise that culminates – as does the *Crito*'s discussion of laws – with music.

Scipio's history commences with an admission that his narrative must mix fable and fact in treating Romulus' divine origin and bizarre childhood.[30] Considering Romulus' famous Lupine rearing, Cicero conceals from view the specific animal that nurses Rome's august founder. Instead of a wolf (*lupus*) Scipio describes Romulus as being suckled simply by a 'woodland beast' (*silvestris beluae*).[31] This careful concealment of explicit detail serves an essential civic purpose and reveals the imperatives behind his account of Rome's founding. Cicero does not intend to fabricate a fantastic and propagandistic account of Rome's past; he is confined by what occurred – or perhaps more precisely, by common beliefs about what occurred. He makes this clear when he declares that 'lies are particularly intolerable when we can see that they are not only inventions but completely impossible.'[32] At the same time, his reckoning is not concerned with – indeed, is even hostile to – the surface details. If Cicero's object is the construction of an enchanting history, he is equally cognizant of history's ability, even its subversive propensity, to demystify. By withholding the graphic image of Romulus suckling at the teat of a wolf, Cicero draws the reader's attention upwards away from the mere detail and towards its grand significance: the instilling in Rome's founder of a fierce spirit sufficient for the founding of a great city. This initial example, with its attention to larger significance and the concomitant escape from what we may call the tyranny of mundane detail, transforms history into a vehicle for the conveyance of something higher. That something higher, which Cicero prefers to subtly insinuate rather than completely commit to, is the possibility that Roman history possesses an underlying *ratio*.[33] Cicero hints that the historical action of the Roman past moves through a self-revealing ideal, veiled in apparent necessity and revealed only to the careful and philosophic student of history.

Cicero's account of the rape of the Sabine women further illuminates this vision of history's role. Moreover, it brings to the fore one of the starkest examples of criminal founding to which any community must reconcile itself. In considering the great crime of Romulus and the original Romans, as with the woodland beast, the specifics of Cicero's circumspect account are all-important. The actual crime is deliberately underdescribed. Romulus' order that the Sabine girls (*virgines*) be seized (*rapi*) and forced into marriage 'with the most important families' passes deliberately over the details of what is euphemistically described as a 'crude plan.'[34] Cicero proceeds with blinding speed from the initial and massive crime to a description of the reconciliation with the Sabine monarch and especially the period of co-rule between Romulus and Titus Tatius, the Sabine king. The dramatic arc of the story draws upwards with almost impossible rapidity from the initial events to the broader political significance. Cicero transforms the rape of the Sabine women from Rome's original crime into the historical circumstance that freed Rome from the narrow politics of autochthony. The crime against the Sabine women, in bringing into existence a first generation of Romans who are really Romano-Sabines, freed Rome from the self-limiting politics of blood and belonging. Indeed, from Cicero's perspective, the perspective of a *homo novum*, this is perhaps *the* critical moment in Roman history: the emergence of a central Roman principle justifies a founding that is otherwise *literally* criminal and hence unreconcilable to a self-respecting society. What emerges in Cicero's telling of this infamous history is the central element in Rome's future success: its ability not merely to conquer but to accommodate.

Later, in Scipio's account of the regicide that transforms Rome from monarchy into republic, Cicero explicitly adopts the language of self-revelation that previously operated as implied principle, *tertium quid*, in his philosophic narrative of Rome. The refounding of Rome and its transformation from monarchy to republic are drawn on a background of sexual criminality that is the reflected moral and political opposite of the original crime against the Sabines. In the latter case, Tarquinius Superbus' eldest son Sextus rapes Lucretia. In so doing, he brings about the end of the rule of kings in Rome and the emergence of the signal civic virtue of Republican society. In avenging Lucretia, 'Lucius Brutus, a man of outstanding talent and virtue, threw off from his fellow citizens the unjust yoke of harsh slavery. Although he was a private citizen, he upheld the whole commonwealth: he was the first in this state to *show that in preserving the liberty of citizens no one is a private person.*'[35]

As with the rape of the Sabine women, Cicero's recounting of the rape of Lucretia emphasizes not criminality, or even vengeance, but the historic opportunity for the signal virtue of republican life to reveal itself.[36] In Cicero's accounting, historical necessity seems to conspire with Roman ideal to create the necessary conditions for the revelation of the latter. Note that Cicero never actually says this, but his construction of history as a series of moments of revelation connected by a narrative constructed along the lines of Rome's rise cannot help but imply as much. Cicero intimates the superphenomenal: he insinuates a connection, and he subtly posits the possibility – even the hope – for a hidden connective melody of Roman history.

Scipio's friend and formidable interlocutor Laelius responds to the Scipionic representation of history, to the subtle insinuation of a concealed reason, by asserting that it equates the ideal with the necessary. Laelius charges Scipio with combining the perceived idealism of Plato with the irreducibly historical perspective of Rome and the Roman citizen. Demurring from the Scipionic mode of history, Laelius contends:

> That great man [Plato], the greatest of all writers, chose his own territory on which to build a state to suit his own ideas. It may be a noble state, but it is totally alien to human life and customs. All the others wrote about the types and principles of states without any specific model or form of commonwealth. *You seem to me to be doing both:* from the outset, you have preferred to attribute your discoveries to others rather than inventing it all yourself in the manner of Plato's Socrates; and you ascribe to Romulus' deliberate planning all the features of the site of the city which were either the result of chance or necessity.[37]

Cicero, through Scipio, is doing both. Scipio's history of Rome almost imperceptibly collapses each of the dichotomies that Laelius constructs. This is possible only if one accepts that the relationship between the two enterprises, history and philosophy, is more complex than Laelius' strict dichotomies allow. Instead of producing antinomy, Scipio insinuates that the reconciliation of historical necessity with philosophic ideal discloses a heretofore concealed creative sympathy. Scipio employs history to demonstrate the substance of the ideal, but he also almost inaudibly implies that history is not merely the source of demonstrative example but the visible action of an underlying principle serving to bring the ideal into existence. Finally, he is insinuating, again without ever *explicitly* asserting, the presence and action in history of a supervening reason. Laelius accuses Scipio of attributing to Romulus' planning what is actually the motion of historical contingency.[38] What Laelius misses is the underlying attribution of a plan and reason (*ratio*) to Roman history itself.

The Dream of Scipio and the Music of History

The Dream of Scipio was the only substantial portion of Cicero's *De re publica* to pass intact without interruption into the present. This remarkable set piece, a dialogue within a dialogue,[39] remains one of the most elegantly constructed and poignant of Cicero's prose works. Scipio's Dream gracefully traverses vast topical territory; Cicero moves with ease between historical and cosmic vistas and tightly drawn intimate portraiture. Despite being textually located in the same position as the Myth of Er in Plato's *Republic,* the Dream of Scipio serves a very different purpose. The descriptive austerity of the account of the afterlife reveals his alternative purpose in striking terms. In marked contrast to the traversed landscapes of Plato's Myth of Er, consider the stark economy of Cicero's account of the celestial reunion of Cornelius Scipio with his late father Lucius Aemilius Paullus: '"Yes indeed," he said, "these people are alive; they have escaped from the chains of the body as if from a prison, and what is called life among you is in fact death. Don't you see your father approaching you?" And when I saw him I wept heavily, but he embraced me and told me not to weep.'[40]

Cicero's account is all foreground.[41] Where did Paullus come from? What was it that had initially concealed him from view? Scipio's dream lacks the background and broader vision necessary to any satisfactory account of the afterlife. Instead of the Myth of Er, the image of enchainment both resembles literarily and serves philosophically a purpose closer to the oft invoked Myth of the Cave of the *Republic.*

The Dream of Scipio reveals itself, especially in its account of celestial motion, not as poetic cosmology but rather as philosophic and pedagogic metaphor. The Dream serves as a compelling rejoinder to Laelius' critique of the Scipionic vision of Roman history. Cicero indicates this purpose, and its compelling aspect, first in the opening dramatic action of the Dream. Among all of Scipio's guests, it is Laelius who shouts out, attempting to 'wake' Scipio from his reverie and thereby thwart his rejoinder.[42] With his shout, Laelius literally attempts to bring the ascending Scipio back down to reality, to the world of necessity.[43] As Scipio escapes into philosophic slumber, he moves between sleep and waking, reliving his night journey to the eternal home of his great ancestors. In this metaxic state he perceives both the necessary and the ideal within history. In philosophic slumber, Scipio metaphorically straddles Laelius' dichotomies.[44] He occupies a number of halfway points, in cosmos, in consciousness, and in philosophy.

The cosmological elements of the Dream of Scipio, in its description of the motion of the universe, reveal the cosmic reconciliation of the necessary with the ideal that Laelius' challenge demanded. From his sublunar position, the youngest Scipio asks his august ancestor what the beautiful sound is that overwhelms his senses, filling his ears 'so great and so sweet?'[45] To this query the elder Africanus responds: 'This is the sound that is caused by the action and motion of the spheres themselves. Its harmony is based on uneven intervals, but the inequality of the intervals is proportional and based on reason, and by blending high notes with low causes balanced music.'[46]

The relationship between motion and melody, the music of the spheres, reveals in its imagery the relationship between Roman history and Roman ideal. The elder Africanus observes matter-of-factly that 'such vast motions cannot proceed without sound.' The Laelian dichotomy is not so much reconciled as bypassed altogether. Instead of a dichotomous relationship, the dream posits one wherein, counter-intuitively, the ideal is the consequence of the necessary. In its historic motion the expansion and development of Rome sounds the music of the ideal. The eternal and the temporal are not at odds; rather, the motion of the latter ushers into audibility the music of the former.

The Dream of Scipio turns as it must to the world of the waking. The younger Scipio cannot help but gaze downwards.[47] In light of what the dream has revealed, what is most distressing about the mundane now appears to be not its smallness but its deafness to the music of the spheres. Closing the dialogue with a final invocation of the Myth of the Cave with which the dramatic action commenced, the elder Scipio contends: 'The sound made by the rapid revolution of the universe is so great that human ears cannot grasp it, just as you are unable to look directly into the Sun, because your sight and sense are overcome by its rays.'[48]

Like the prisoner first freed and brought up into the sunlight in Plato's myth, the terrestrial and historical citizen's senses are overwhelmed by the sheer enormity of stimuli. The passage through history, combined with the experience of engulfment in history so central to Roman life, deafens the citizens to the music of the ideal. Cicero's history clarifies and distils the sound into the comprehendible and essential. He deliberately leaves out some of the 'noise,' the tyranny of mundane detail that overwhelms the senses. In considering the particulars of Romulus' rearing, the seizure of the Sabine Women, and the fall of Tarquinius Superbus, he carefully filters his account and seeks to tune the ear of the reader to the music behind. Ultimately, this clarified historic account of the dynamic and expansive motion of early Rome serves to prick up the ears of his audience; it permits citizens to hear the ideal reveal itself in the motion of the spheres.

The central element of the Dream that must be recalled when employing it to interpret the rest of Scipio's speech is its status as *a dream*. Even the dream itself has some curious characteristics. As Laelius tries to prevent the slide into reverie with his shouts, Scipio responds: 'Hush, please or you will wake me up.' Scipio is not really falling asleep. He is bringing on a condition, a reverie, that allows him to see the reconciliation of historical necessity with philosophic ideal. Like Socrates in the interior dialogue with the laws in *Crito*, Scipio conjures from within himself an enchantment that renders him immune to the arguments of others. But what is the status of a claim about history made only in dream, recounted only in reverie, explained only in the words of long dead ancestors? Ultimately, the merit of the exercise is twofold. On the political level, it provides a means by which a historical community can reconcile itself to the inevitable injustices and tragedies that invariably attended its expansion in history. On a more profound level, Cicero's history provides the philosophic student residing in a historical culture with a ladder of ascent to knowledge of the ideal. As such, the student of Scipio's history stands both reconciled to the past and educated to the eternal.

History's Music in the Sphere of American Politics

There is a constant temptation to apply ancient structures to modern politics and employ ancient examples to explain modern phenomena. The appeal of Rome's example to explain America's current position in world politics is undeniable. The two most obvious reasons for this are mutually reinforcing. First, Americans themselves, especially the Founders, appealed to Roman example to understand, explain, and justify their own actions. Second, and more germane to the purposes of this chapter, the United States, like the Roman Republic of Cicero's time, has undergone almost unimaginable expansion over the first two-and-one-third centuries of its existence.

For the term 'empire' to mean anything, in either the ancient or the modern world, we must eschew the facile equation Rome with America. In its own era, each enjoys a position of unrivalled global dominance. However, mere dominance is an insufficient definition of empire. The political, institutional, economic, and cultural structures of these two states are at such profound variance that to assign them the same political signifier is to will unknowing. At the same time, while their institutions bear little resemblance to each other, their positions and certain elements of their historical experience permit fruitful comparison. On the most obvious level, the rapid expansion of a small republic to *the* world power cannot help but generate commonalities. The single greatest commonality, connected to the development from republic to world power, is almost certainly the record and historical consciousness of that transformation. Like Romulus, the American founders have had their lives and acts presented in admixture of fable and fact. Equally, and more significantly for politics, the American republic is surrounded by history. It cannot make morally convenient claims to autochthony and original possession. Like Rome's, America's politics are so run through with history that ignoring that history is impossible. Finally, as Cicero's circumspect treatment of the historical record implicitly acknowledges, mundane history may serve civic purposes either salutary or subversive.

The enchantment of history that Cicero seeks is distinct from propaganda. Recall that Scipio's dream is a dream. It is a self-enchanting way of viewing history that seeks within necessity the emergence of ideal, of truth. It seeks to induce in the citizen a philosophic reverie that reveals a purpose in history. Politically this purpose serves to reconcile, to make in important ways bearable, that very history. Unfortunately, it seems impossible, in an age exponentially more historically conscious than that of Cicero, to imagine history serving his second purpose, as mode of ascent to the ideal. Fortunately, the civic purpose endures; more than enduring, it has served America's highest purposes.

Consider in this light Martin Luther King's famous invocation of history at the conclusion of his extraordinary 'Letter from Birmingham Jail': 'One day the South will know that when these disinherited Children of God sat down at lunch counters, they were in reality standing up for what is best in the American dream and for the most sacred values in our Judeo-Christian heritage, thereby bringing our nation back to those great wells of democracy which were dug deep by the founding fathers in their formulation of the Constitution and the Declaration of Independence.'[49]

In this famous passage King appeals to the verdict of history. He believes clearly that history is more than a mundane record. It possesses a revelatory and sanctifying quality. Just as Lucius Brutus brought into view the signal virtues of Roman republicanism, Meredith and others across the South sound the American ideal in their own history. With the declaration and prayer that 'one day the South will know,' King is assigning to history the task of revealing the ideals of the American Republic. This is true. It is also an enchantment. Martin Luther King, positioned in prison like the Socrates of the *Crito*, to whom he explicitly refers in his letter, writes to convince but also to induce a hopeful reverie. By the conclusion of his letter, Dr King appears equally convinced that 'as far as my present beliefs go, if you speak in opposition to them, you will speak in vain.'[50] However, like Cicero rather than Plato, King makes his case in philosophic *and* historic terms. In so arguing, King presents a clarified history akin to that of Cicero. In explaining and justifying civil disobedience, he refers to biblical figures, Shadrach, Mechach, and Abednego, and (admittedly somewhat ironically for my purposes) to Christians tortured and murdered in the Roman forum, uniting these events with the ideals of the Civil Rights Movement. In Dr King's reading, these events are variations on a theme. In his presentation, as in Cicero's, there are intimations of an arc, a plan, a motion that is gradually rendered audible, the music of the ideal. For King, unlike Cicero, this contention is surely rooted in a Christian conception of history and the action of God in that history. Nonetheless, it possesses the same political characteristics that allowed Cicero to reconcile himself to his own history. It transforms, even if only in moments of reverie, the action of necessity into the expression of something larger. For a community deeply permeated with history this may be the only means by which the injustices that all political communities participate in, but that are unique to the extent that they are woven into the accounts of the founding of both Rome and America, can be reconciled to the ideals that sustain them.

NOTES

1 I will use the terms 'empire' and 'imperial' here while granting their potential anachronism at the time of Cicero's authoring. Indeed, a forceful argument could be made that Rome becomes irretrievably imperial as opposed to republican only with Cicero's murder.

2 These dialogues have come down to the present only in a fragmentary form. Cicero's *De legibus* in particular is severely fragmented. Moreover, Cicero may never have completed it. While this challenges the modern interpreter of Cicero's intentions, this essay will focus primarily on the atmospheric elements of empire – a focus that is perhaps least liable to the hermeneutic perils of an incomplete document.

3 Structurally, Cicero's decision to place himself in his own dialogues – and in particular, *De legibus* – as a dramatic character is another profound distinction. However, while acknowledging the blurred lines between argument and action in the dialogue form, I would contend that the role of history is at least equally important.

4 Marcus Tullius Cicero, *On the Commonwealth* and *On the Laws*, trans. James E.G. Zetzel (Cambridge: Cambridge University Press, 1999), 2.3.

5 For a list of such alternatives and a powerful argument in favour of another motivation for Cicero's historical form from that contended herein, see Walter Nicgorski, 'Cicero's Focus: From the Best Regime to the Model Statesman,' *Political Theory* 19 (1991): 230–51.

6 Bertrand L. Hallward, 'Cicero Historicus,' *Cambridge Historical Journal* 3, no. 3 (1931): 233.

7 Leo Strauss, *Natural Right and History* (Chicago: University of Chicago Press, 1953), 130. Tellingly Strauss specifically references the earliest passages of Scipio's argument in *De re publica* I:39–41.

8 *De re*, 3.25. The use of that most diminutive of mammals is no accident. Consider the imagery of Lion and Fox in both Cicero's *De officiis* and in its precise inversion in Machiavelli's *The Prince*. Consider J. Jackson Barlow, 'The Fox and the Lion: Machiavelli replies to Cicero,' *History of Political Thought* 20 (1999): 627–45.

9 Strauss, *Natural Right and History*, 130.

10 *De re*, 1.1. It is perhaps of particular relevance to Strauss's challenge that the figure Cicero selects to recount the Roman founding, in all its moral shades, is most famous for declaring that at his own hands 'Carthago delenda est.' Scipio is famous not for founding cities but for ending them.

11 *De re*, 2.3.

12 Cicero, *Orator*, trans. Harry M. Hubbell (Cambridge, MA: Harvard University Press, 1962), 120.

13 *De leg.*, 1.28.

14 Plato, *Republic*, trans. Allan Bloom (New York: Basic, 1991), 515c–e.

15 Consider the opening of Plato's *Republic*, 327a.

16 *De re*, 1.15.

17 Seth Benardete, *Plato's Laws* (Berkeley: University of California Press, 2000), 356.

18 Further emphasizing that his account of Rome's past is more than simply history, Cicero commences *De legibus*, *De re publica's* companion dialogue, with a lament addressed to the lack of such a history or of a historian capable of generating one. To the demands for a Roman history made by his Atticus and Quintus, Cicero rejoins: 'I realize there have been demands

for some time that I undertake this task, Atticus, and I wouldn't refuse if I had any free and unencumbered time' (*De leg.*, 1.8). Cicero clearly indicates that a historical recording of Rome's emergence as the power in the known world was neither the intent nor the consequence of his historical exercises in the preceding dialogue.

19 Christian Meier, *Caesar, A Biography* (New York: MJF, 1982), 492.

20 *De leg.*, 1.15.

21 *Laws*, 625c.

22 Ibid., 625a.

23 *De leg.*, 1.21.

24 Consider Cicero, *De oratore* I.vii.28–9.

25 Consider here also ibid.

26 Of course, Cicero is one of the best examples of this contention: his voluminous speeches represent one of the largest literary legacies to survive into the present and remain an invaluable source on late Republican Roman life.

27 Woldemar Gorler, 'Silencing the Troublemaker: *De legibus* 1.39 and the Continuity of Cicero's Skepticism,' in *Cicero the Philosopher,* ed. Jonathan G.F. Powell (Oxford: Clarendon, 1999), 94.

28 Plato, 'Crito,' in *Five Dialogues,* trans. George M.A. Grube (Indianopolis: Hackett, 1981), 54d–e.

29 Ibid.

30 Consider in this light *De legibus* 1.1 and its discussion of the 'Tree of the People' at Arpinum: 'its roots are in the imagination.'

31 *De re*, 2.4. See James G. Zetzel's note on the translation of this passage in *On the Commonwealth*, n34.

32 *De re*, 2.28.

33 R.F. Hathaway, 'Cicero's Socratic View of History,' *Journal of the History of Ideas* 29 (1968): 12.

34 *De re*, 2.13.

35 *De re*, 2.45 (italics added).

36 Consider also the contrast between the two sexual crimes that bracket the monarchic age of Rome. In the first instance the fact that the Sabine women are married off to the 'best families' possesses a clear exculpatory quality. In the second case the Tarquinii are arguably the very best family, yet in considering the crime against Lucretia this detail is irrelevant.

37 *De re*, 2.21 (emphasis added).

38 Ibid.

39 Recall the dialogue, also an enchantment, that concludes Plato's *Crito*.

40 *De re*, 6.14.

41 Consider the extraordinary opening chapter, 'Odysseus' Scar,' in Eric Auerbach's *Mimesis* (Princeton: Princeton University Press, 2003).
42 *De re*, 6.12.
43 Compare with the opening action and recumbent Socrates of the *Crito*, 43a–c.
44 Consider Plato, *Laws*, 644e–645b.
45 *De re*, 6.18.
46 *De re*, 6.19.
47 Ibid.
48 Ibid.
49 Martin Luther King, 'Letter from Birmingham Jail,' in *Ideals and Ideologies*, ed. Terence Ball and Richard Dagger (New York: Pearson Longman, 2003), 347.
50 *Crito*, 54d.

11 Machiavelli's Model of a Liberal Empire: The Evolution of Rome

WALLER R. NEWELL

Empires were not unknown to the classical political philosophers either in theory or in practice. Plato and Aristotle were well aware of the alternative to the Greek *polis* presented by the Persian empire and, in Aristotle's case, the Alexandrian empire. Cicero defended the idea of the *res publica* against the emerging imperial ambitions of Pompey, Caesar, and Octavian. Nor is it the case that classical political philosophy was simply hostile to the concept of empire. Both the Platonic and the Xenophontic Socrates used Cyrus the Great and the Persian Empire as a foil for the *polis*, sometimes to the detriment of the latter. Indeed, for Xenophon, an idealized Persian Empire under Cyrus the Great provided an alternative version of the best regime to that of Plato's idealized *polis*, the *Republic*. Aristotle is ambivalent as to whether a republican aristocracy or a monarchy patterned on *oikonomia* – the art of household management – is the best form of rule, and in the latter case explicitly extends the concept of monarchy to a multinational authority over 'many cities and peoples.'[1]

For all that, however, it cannot be denied that classical political philosophy as a whole has a preference for the small, self-governing republic. Even Xenophon arrives at the conclusion that the Persian republic from which the young Cyrus emerged – a blend of real-life Sparta and something akin to Plato's best regime – is in some ways superior to the vast multinational household he creates through his conquests. Plato's best regime is of course a *polis*, and Aristotle ends the *Politics* by endorsing his own version of the neighbourly homogeneous republic. What explains this republican preference? Plato, Xenophon, and Aristotle all identify empire with the elevation of the art of household management – the production of material goods and the division of labour – over the cultivation of the moral and intellectual virtues solicited by civic deliberation about the common good. Whereas republics foster the common good, empires allow individuals to maximize their private gain.[2] Whatever their merits, therefore, they fall short of the highest human excellence. Even in their relative approbation for empire, the ancient thinkers do not so much stress the conquest and power-seeking necessary to establish it as the unity of the finished product – for Xenophon, Cyrus' perfected empire embodies the art of household management that his Socrates establishes as a path to the Good, the conception of an ordered *cosmos*. Much the same is true of Cicero with respect to the imperial dynasts and of Tacitus with respect to the Augustan principate: if it is necessary to accept that the republic has been superseded by the empire, one must endorse the empire only insofar as it guarantees the settled peace and the rule of law. All the classical thinkers are at one in downplaying and severely criticizing the kind of dynamic and expansionist foreign policy that is needed to establish the path to imperial rule.[3]

Bearing this in mind will enable us better to appreciate what is novel about the specifically modern conception of empire that I will argue is first theoretically elaborated by Machiavelli in his *Discourses*. That novelty has two main components, which I hope to bring out through a reading of the opening chapters of book 1 dealing with the crucial theme of how cities are founded and ordered. First, Machiavelli denies the classical contention that the pursuit of wealth and power rank below the pursuit of moral and intellectual virtue on the scale of human excellence. On the contrary, he maintains that the honour of success in this pursuit is constitutive of human excellence, as well as beneficial to all. Second, Machiavelli's endorsement of empire is not limited to its end state of established peace and law. On the contrary, he focuses on and praises the dynamic rise of republic to imperial power through an expansionist foreign policy that enriches all classes. For the classics, such approbation as could be extended to empire was based on the degree to which it might mirror the settled orderliness of the *cosmos*. For Machiavelli, it is the dynamism of the rise to empire – embodied in the career of Rome – in response to 'chance' and 'the occurrence of accidents' that achieves whatever perfection politics can sustain by imitating the flux of *fortuna* in its clash of interests and pursuit of power.[4]

According to the classics, one must choose between the communal honour of a republic and the individual security and well-being fostered under an orderly empire. According to Machiavelli, the ambitious energies bred by the laws of an honour-loving republic can be harnessed to a project of imperial expansion, resulting in individual security and well-being. This combination of what the classics regarded as very difficult or even impossible to combine is what I mean by terming Machiavelli's vision a *liberal* empire, an empire in which republican virtue is the basis for the liberty of the individual. The challenge to statesmanship is not, as it would have been for the classics, to encourage the rise of empire to arrive as soon as possible at the peace and orderliness of its end state, but rather to embody in the very institutions of the regime the vitality and ambition of its rise; to unleash recurrently the power seeking of individuals in all classes as the mainstay of the regime's stability. For Machiavelli, a way must be found of consciously enacting the rise of republic to empire that Rome achieved spontaneously and unpredictably, so that the new empire to come – a discovery even greater than that of the New World across the seas that would become its future home – might be methodically established.[5]

The Origin of the City and the Virtue of Necessity

In discussing the founding of cities, Machiavelli stresses that the origin of the city is in necessity and adversity.[6] Plato and Aristotle, by contrast, stress the ends for which the city comes into being and downplay its origins. But more than this, for Machiavelli, necessity is actually *constitutive* of virtue. He provides not merely a more realistic fleshing out of the classical ideal, but a new basis for the political order. Founders, he writes, are 'free' when they are 'constrained' to flee some disaster, as were Aeneas or Moses. As in the discussion of founders of the greatest virtue in chapter 6 of *The Prince*, a pagan prince is equated with a biblical prophet, and Fortuna provides nothing but adversity against which such men must test themselves. In both cases, Machiavelli omits their obedience to a religious command.

'Men work either by necessity or choice,' Machiavelli concludes, and 'there is greater virtue to be seen where choice has less authority.' This is a major contrast with classical thought. For Aristotle, choice (*prohairesis*) is what makes us capable of virtue and distinguishes us from animals.[7] For Machiavelli, the hostility of the world compels us to fight back through our labour to survive. So it may therefore be best to choose a sterile region for founding a city, where necessity 'constrains' people to be industrious, therefore less idle, therefore more united and less exposed to discord.

On the face of it, the praise of industriousness and dispraise of idleness sounds in accord with both elements of the Great Tradition, Christianity and the pagan classics. But to make industriousness the *ground* of virtue in the absence of other virtues takes what for the tradition was regarded as a comparatively low virtue and elevates it into one of the highest. The Christian and classical traditions did not approve of laziness. But they did not praise industriousness to any great degree either, and certainly not as the basis of political order and unity. One need only consider Plato's and Aristotle's strictures on excessive commerce, the unlimited pursuit of *oikonomia*, echoed by Thomas. Laziness is bad because it is a sign of a character falling beneath itself at the most rudimentary level of mastering one's passions, antecedent to higher virtues involving deliberative choice rather than mere self-repression.[8]

For Machiavelli, on the other hand, civic disunity or discord comes from 'idleness,' from a condition that, for the tradition, properly directed, made contemplation or devotion possible. What Machiavelli calls 'idleness' includes the leisure (*scholé*) that according to Aristotle enables us to dwell on what most unifies us, which is philosophy and deliberative citizenship.[9] Indeed, Machiavelli collapses Aristotle's distinction between mere relaxation and leisure into idleness. For Aristotle, idleness might, if properly cultivated, become the leisure that is indispensable for the actualization of civic virtue through a full-time devotion to public affairs and, at the highest level, cultivating the contemplative virtues. Far from preferring labour to idleness (properly improved as leisure), Aristotle argues that the correct employment of idleness as leisure requires that we not have to labour for survival. Those who labour for a living are not capable of the fullest citizen virtues.[10] Idleness is acceptable to the extent that it provides us with the opportunity to pursue those civic and philosophic ends that are the surest source of friendship and unity among humans in the *polis*. For Machiavelli, by contrast, this drifting away into the contemplation of 'imagined republics'[11] afforded by idleness is precisely what is most likely to undermine a republic's unity, discipline, and vigour.

While both the classics and Christian revelation focus on the ends, for Machiavelli, leisure to contemplate the higher world is what distracts us from *virtu*. Labour compelled by necessity overcomes poverty as a source of discord. By contrast with making the conquest of poverty a chief theme of politics, all Aristotle could do to ameliorate the harmful effects of poverty on the common good was to suggest the mixed regime, polity, as a way of mitigating the worst effects of excessive wealth and poverty while encouraging public virtue.[12] For Machiavelli, collective labour itself forges the unity of the city. Aristotle assumes that the material wherewithal for the practice of virtue, and the founding of the city to ensure minimal order, are already largely taken care of when he turns to the prescription for the best regime.[13] Machiavelli uncovers these preconditions and makes their achievement – and continuing reachievement – the sole and sufficient basis for the common good. For the classics, the necessity for physical survival and commodious living, the realm of *oikonomia*, is, because it necessarily individuates, the least likely basis for the common good. Once the material wherewithal is achieved, we can turn towards virtue and wisdom, which transcend individuation and therefore unite us in the actualization of virtues of soul. For Machiavelli, by contrast, the necessity for material survival that individuates, for the very reason that its dangers cannot be avoided, drives us to labour in common with others and so create a bulwark of order.

Choosing a sterile location that engenders virtue through labour would be sufficient for founding a city if 'men were content to live off their own and did not wish to seek command over others.' But because others do wish not merely to survive and prosper but to exercise command, any city wishing security must choose a fertile spot that 'affords the means of becoming powerful.' A people cannot look inward, as the classics advise, and content itself with self-government.[14] Even if it wants to, the world will stimulate and necessitate that people in the form of outside aggressors to expand, both to 'defend itself from whoever might assault it and crush anyone who might oppose its greatness.' A fertile spot confers wealth and power. But it also leads to effeminacy in the soldiers, which is the natural outcome of the softness of their climate. Severe laws can offset the pleasures and softness with the rigours of severe discipline to produce 'better soldiers there than in countries that have naturally been harsh and sterile.' In other words, laws can take the place of the compulsion that nature would supply directly in a sterile spot. In a fertile spot, the luxurious fecundity of Fortuna or chance flourishes, leading to enervation, self-indulgence, and disorder. Laws can enable us to consciously replicate the severity unconsciously produced by necessity – nature's reversals and hostility, the sterile side of Fortuna. Devising an institutional imitation of nature's hostility stimulates the acquisition of the mastery to fight back, channelling the hostility of Fortuna in order to fight Fortuna.

In this way, Machiavelli writes, 'one prudent orderer' can provide a corrective to too much bounty from nature. The severity of such founders cuts nature's fecundity back, tapping its power while keeping it from dissipating in ease and pleasure.[15] Even though power is the goal, to give in to the rewards of power undermines the vigour and self-control needed to acquire and maintain power. We must avoid the delusion of the world's beneficence. Here we might detect a connection between what came to be known as the 'worldly asceticism' of the bourgeois virtues – the deferral of gratification – and the inwardness and self-denial sought by the Reformation's repudiation of 'the theology of glory' (Luther's derogatory term for Thomism), a synthesis arguably indispensable for the emergence of modern liberal democracy.[16] In discussing the comparative merits of a sterile and fertile spot for the founding, Machiavelli is arguing that, while nature can be either sterile or bounteous, the sterility is fundamental. Chance and disorder are the substance, peace and bounty are the accidents, reversing classical metaphysics. To imitate the bounteous side alone must lead to the teleology of the 'imagined republics' and the delusion that the passions possess an immanent potentiality for virtue leading us to peace, the eternal, the divine, and their instantiation in a just republic. Therefore, it is more prudent to imitate the necessitous side. As in his advice in *The Prince*, founders and rulers must let the hostility of Fortuna fuel their actions so as to be able to turn the tables on 'her' treacherous reversals and fight back. Recognizing that the passions are not a mixture of beast and soul, but all beast, lion and fox, will enable a leader to alternate methodically between their release and control for the sake of maximizing power.[17]

According to Aristotle, when founding a city you should choose a spot neither sterile nor bounteous.[18] That search for the middle way reflects the mean, the orderliness and moderation at the core of the world. For Machiavelli, by contrast, nature as Fortuna oscillates between sterility and fertility, necessity and dissolution. The sterility is closer to the truth, which is that the fertility cannot be relied upon. We achieve freedom through our consciousness of nature's hostility, which engenders in us the mastery to fight back. This requires a new understanding of law. For Aristotle, law is subordinate to the *politeia*, which embodies a division of offices based on a partial account of justice and virtue.[19] Law depends on the distinct regime. For Machiavelli, since nature is uniformly indifferent to human purpose and supplies no such teleological ordering, law is the abstract regulator of nature as a field of forces or happenstance. We imitate nature's hostility by distancing ourselves from a reliance on nature. This denaturing or abstraction of self from nature is necessary for mastery. Law, far from being subordinate to the regime, supersedes it as the core of statecraft. Constitutions are the most useful and efficacious arrangements of political 'bodies' subject to the uniformity of law as the controller of hostile chance or, on the other hand, its deliberate reinjection into the body politic to jolt it out of the enervation and complacency of too long a period of success. In this way, the regime becomes a local historical modality of the law, and the distinction between good and bad regimes is replaced by the criterion of legitimacy.

Rome is the proof of how to combine fertility and prosperity (with the attendant danger of relying on the spurious and merely apparent beneficence of nature) with law-bred severity, with the result that 'they maintained it full of as much virtue as has ever adorned any other city or republic.' The Senate uses the people to fight its wars and buys it off with land and booty. The people and nobles of the conquered areas join the Roman people and nobles and press outward to a new perimeter. Like a cell dividing and redividing, the republic becomes a cosmopolitan empire containing (to borrow a phrase from chapter 17 of *The Prince*) 'men of all nations.'

The Founding of Cities and the New Relationship of Reason to Nature

The issue of the origin of cities in *Discourses,* I.i, leads to the issue of the founder, the constitution, and the best regime in I.ii, a traditional rubric that Machiavelli endows with a subversive new content: how the alternation between prosperity and law-bred sterility can be institutionalized. Some republics are founded by one man and never undergo danger because of his prudence. The most illustrious case, Sparta founded by Lycurgus, lasted eight hundred years. Others, most notably Rome, 'become perfect' through 'the occurrence of accidents.' Their growth is always accompanied by danger, because only danger convinces people of the necessity to change. Does this suggest that a statesman might want to imitate 'the occurrence of accidents' by introducing seemingly chance stimuli such as the threat of a foreign aggressor (or the depiction of such) in order to keep the danger fresh?[20]

The contrast between Rome and Sparta leads Machiavelli to what appears to be a discussion of the traditional view of the regimes by those 'who have written on republics.' Some distinguish among three regimes: monarchy, aristocracy, and democracy. Others, 'wiser according to the opinion of the many,' distinguish six: three good, three bad. Aristotle is chief among the latter. Does this suggest that 'the many' lean towards the moral distinction between good and bad regimes – that classical political philosophy is in truth the prejudice of the mob? Machiavelli collapses the distinctions, for example, between aristocracy and oligarchy and between monarchy and tyranny in chapter 9 of *The Prince*: *nobiles* is simply a fair-sounding word for oligarchs, and 'prince' obscures the difference between monarch and tyrant. Or, as he puts it here, over time the good regimes degenerate into the bad, 'for no remedy can be applied there to prevent it from slipping into its contrary because of the likeness that the virtue and the vice have.'[21] The distinctions made by Aristotle and the other writers on republics between good and bad regimes *sub specie aeternitas* are historicized, launched into the ebb and flow of chance events and the clash of natural bodies, so that their categorical distinctions break down and meld under the impact of Fortuna. There is no stable order of being that transcends temporality.

To collapse the distinction between good and bad regimes might seem to restore ancient conventionalism. While there are similarities between Machiavelli's argument and ancient conventionalism, however, there are more important differences. According to the Sophists, you can react to the meaning of nature as chance by (a) private vice and the manipulation of convention through rhetoric to create a public appearance of virtue; (b) the defence of convention as a bulwark against the chaos of the state of nature; or (c) the embrace of tyranny as the natural way of life. But because the Sophists tend to see nature as the upsurge of spontaneous motions, they doubt that it can be methodically controlled on the political level. Those who claim that it can, run into difficulties. Thus, for example, Thrasymachus' search for a *techné* of injustice is frustrated by Socrates' demonstration that *techné* is self-forgetting, not self-aggrandizing, and leads to order, harmony, and beneficence. Protagoras, more insightful, doubts that statecraft is rigorous knowledge, seeing it as more akin to a local 'way.'[22]

Machiavelli is after much bigger stakes: the disorder of nature is the source of political power, stability, and rationality. It can be tapped and channelled by correctly designed institutions. By imitating the impetuosity of Fortuna, we can gain methodical control over 'her' reverses by anticipating them, pre-empting them, and fighting back. It is the belief in convention – in political order – that leads to decay, chaos, and weakness;

that belief does not, as Protagoras maintained, act as a bulwark against them. So chance (*tuché*) does not have to be fenced off or concealed under a rhetorical guise that preserves *nomos*. Rather, Machiavelli says: Let chance in, let selective spurts of chaos invigorate and set in motion the levers of power. Statecraft will be more methodical and more consistent if we allow politics to be empowered by disorder. We need not be helpless in the face of the rise and decline of regimes because we will undertake no mistaken search for permanence in the first place whose inevitable failure could disillusion us. This calls for a new notion of *techné* – not, as it is for Socrates, an intimation of, and path towards, the *taxis* and *sunounia* of the *cosmos*, a harmony of proportions that grounds subject and object, lover and beloved, citizen and citizen, *polis* and *cosmos*.[23] Instead, *techné* is to be seen as the imposition by man of form on matter, the conquest of nature for the sake of power, the act of resolve whereby a prince, like God, can 'introduce into matter whatever form he pleases.'[24]

I would like speculatively to suggest that this revaluation of the relation between virtue and nature has three stages:[25]

1 Nature is viewed as hostile and alien to man. Reason is seen as anthropocentric, with no immanent link to nature.
2 Having alienated yourself from the world, you must also let the disorder of the world empower your desires while remaining conscious of how the intoxication of those passions can undermine your self-mastery – in the terms of *The Prince*, you must know how to alternate methodically between the lion (allowing the world to empower you) and the fox (reasserting your alienation from the world and your own passions).
3 A certain strain of Christianity – more Augustinian than Thomistic, perhaps more Protestant than Catholic – has paved the way in several senses:
   (i) It supplies the concept of a radically pure will that is able to create out of nothing and oppose itself to all natural limitations. This power to alienate the will entirely from nature so as to aim at its complete mastery is transferred from the Abrahamic God to the secular prince.
   (ii) The Abrahamic God's ability to uproot Himself from nature, once transferred to human agency, fortifies man's ability to assert freedom and mastery over nature by treating it as an alien other, as a foe. Classical philosophy could not provide this fortification even if the claims of philosophy were dismantled from its

defence of civic virtue because classical philosophy, strictly speaking, has no conception of a pure antinatural will that parallels that of the Abrahamic faiths. For the ancients, virtuous acts derive from the proper ordering and balancing of passions such as *eros* and *thumos*, while vicious and tyrannical acts stem from their disharmony. Both virtuous and vicious acts take place within the boundaries of nature. You can be educated to pursue *eros* toward its highest objects, civic virtue and philosophy. But you cannot extirpate *eros* or step outside of nature. *Thumos* can be kept at bay through laws and education, but not overcome. The thumotic man is angry, moralistic, and self-righteous, and therefore, for Machiavelli, not cold-blooded and methodical enough – too much lion, not enough fox.

(iii) By draining the natural world of transcendental purpose and placing it in the otherworldly Beyond, a certain strain of Christianity reduces nature to Fortuna. Once we part ways with our loyalty to that otherworldly kingdom, we can allow the natural world of purposeless happenstance already drained of teleological purpose by Christianity to itself empower us with its sheer force and impulse. These passions contain no immanent potential for transcendence. Not only can we aim to control the external world, but we can also treat our own inner passions as pure other, pure foe or fodder to be imprisoned until needed.

In these ways, then, Machiavelli prepares a new synthesis: reason can and should still govern the city, just as Plato and Aristotle maintain. Viewing nature as chance does not require us to view politics as tragic in the sense that chance and necessity must doom reason. The assimilation of reason to willpower promises to free man altogether from nature, or at least to an extraordinarily greater degree than anything envisioned by the classics. The clarity of the Platonic Ideas becomes the goal to be imposed on nature through the will power of the Abrahamic God's efficient cause, the power to create ex nihilo, transferred to the secular prince.

The Cycle of Regimes and the Superiority of Rome

What follows in the *Discourses* is a genealogy of how regimes rise and decline in a world drained of classical and Christian transcendence in which time does not participate in the eternal, a profane cycle of shaky stability and more fundamental decay. No longer are we to see regimes as solicited into being by the final cause towards which they partially and imperfectly arise. The end is replaced by unfathomable happenstance: 'these variations of governments arise by chance among men.' This genealogy has two phases.

Phase One resembles arguments made by Sophists like Protagoras to the effect that human beings lived at first 'like beasts' in a primitive and dispersed condition, coming together in rudimentary associations for the sake of survival. They placed whoever was 'more robust and of greater heart' at their head, and obeyed him in exchange for protection. At this point, when a crude despotism has provided enough organization to stave off extinction by natural disaster or external attack, sentiments of justice and injustice, virtue and vice, first arise. With the emergence of these first moral sentiments, people look for a ruler who is wise and just rather than merely courageous. When this monarchy becomes hereditary, however, the rulers are no longer necessarily the best men but come to 'surpass others in sumptuousness and lasciviousness and every other kind of license.' The hatred these arrogant libertines provoke in the people leads their rulers in turn to become more tyrannical. Finally, certain citizens who surpass the others 'in generosity, greatness of spirit, riches and nobility who were unable to endure the dishonest life of that prince' establish an aristocratic republic in which 'they governed themselves according to the laws ordered by them, placing the common utility before their own advantage.'

Now we are at the transition to Phase Two, the transition from the primitive origin of authority in the pre-political state of nature to the cycle of regimes as we know them now, and similar to the typologies of Plato and Aristotle. The difference is that, while for Plato and Aristotle the regimes are present at any time in principle, for Machiavelli they are first historically created by those possessing 'greatness of spirit.' In effect, the Platonic and Aristotelian typologies are engendered historically out of the pre-political state of nature and the primitive compact. Somewhat as in book 8 of the *Republic*, decline sets in after the original high point of an aristocratic regime devoted to the common good. However, for Machiavelli, the high point is the regime that Socrates describes as 'timocracy' – for Machiavelli, those possessing 'greatness of spirit.' Socrates' 'aristocracy,' the regime ruled by philosopher-kings, is absent. Just as Socrates depicts the decline of regimes as a series of rebellions by less virtuous sons against their fathers, Machiavelli observes that the children of the aristocracy (his version of aristocracy, the men possessing generosity, greatness of spirit, riches, and nobility) succeeded the fathers and turned to 'avarice, to ambition [and] to usurpation of women,' causing the aristocratic government to degenerate into oligarchical tyranny. The people rebel against the oligarchy and institute a popular government. But, echoing Plato's strictures against popular government, Machiavelli observes, 'it came at once to license, where neither private men nor public were in fear, and each living in his own mode, a thousand injuries were done every day.' In order to escape from anarchy, they returned to the government of a prince, starting the cycle over again.

The upshot, as Machiavelli concludes with an allusion to book 3 of Aristotle's *Politics*, is that all the regimes are defective.[26] A new approach is needed. Two solutions are explored: a 'mixed' regime, and Rome. Just as Aristotle's observation that all six regimes in his typology are defective inasmuch as they provoke outrage among those excluded from offices and honour precedes his discussion of polity, the mixed regime, so now Machiavelli proceeds from the typology of regimes to describe the mixed regime. In this case, prudent founders choose a constitution that 'share[s] in all' the regime types, 'for one guards the other, since in one and the same city there are the principality, the aristocrats and popular government.' But this is not the mixed regime of Aristotle; it is the Spartan regime founded by Lycurgus. Aristotle criticized Sparta for being too disunited and too focused on military courage. By contrast, polity blended the claims of oligarchs and democrats to foster a moderate middle class. For Machiavelli, the internal clash of powers, checks, and balances criticized by Aristotle is precisely what is admirable about Sparta; it earned Lycurgus 'the highest praise.' It was in every way superior to Athens, which ran through the entire cycle because it tried to set up a distinct regime each time, as if it were imitating the writers on republics who maintain that regimes must serially embody the claims of monarchy, aristocracy, and democracy rather than, as did Sparta, containing them within one regime and allowing them to clash and check. We recognize, of course, an anticipation of the modern constitutional theory of checks and balances in the mode of students of Machiavelli such as Montesquieu, probably the chief philosophical influence on the U.S. Constitution.

'But let us come to Rome.' Rome is even better than Sparta because Rome let in the full sweep of chance. Rome became a 'perfect republic' through 'disunion,' a reversal of classical metaphysics, according to which perfection comes from the degree to which the regime participates in rest (the inward-looking deliberation on domestic public affairs) and avoids motion (the outward-looking tyranny over other peoples requiring tyrannical leadership at home).[27] As Machiavelli observes of Rome, 'so many accidents arose in it through the disunion between the plebs and the Senate that what an orderer had not done, chance did.' A founder can be great, but the power of chance, the pulse of Fortuna, is even greater when harnessed to energize the republic's institutions. Lycurgus institutionalized conflict, but only to maintain inner unity. Unlike Sparta, on the one hand, Rome developed historically. 'Fortune was so favourable to Rome' because she opened herself up to the shifts of history. Unlike Athens, on the other hand, Rome did not change regimes serially from one principle to another, but let the claims of people, nobles, and monarchy clash and check.

In sum, Rome's historical success defied those 'who have written on republics' by combining what they decreed could not be combined: a mixed regime capable of imperial expansion. Dynamic, dialectical, and flexible, Rome retained whatever was useful from the regime's previous evolution and incorporated it in response to necessity. The cycle of regimes in Phase Two above is now shown to be contained within *one* evolving mega-regime, a progression in which one regime's principle is never entirely superseded by the next. The monarchs became the consuls answerable to the Senate, while the Senate's arrogance was restrained by the tribunes of the people. Remaining class conflicts were submerged in the joint project of imperial expansion, which gave scope for honour and brought land and riches to all strata.

The career of Rome is the unique case of how a regime can deliberately open itself to Fortuna so as to let Fortuna provoke the necessary new modes of statecraft. The law-bred internal severity praised in the initial discussion of foundings can be supplemented by the regime's recurrent self-exposure to the prospect of conquering or being conquered. The ensuing chapters illustrate this premise through a discussion of the conflict between the Senate and the people. Men are only 'good' – orderly and disciplined, and therefore able to acquire power – through being subjected to some external compulsion (necessity, fear, the hostility of Fortuna).[28] Freedom without the stimulus of compulsion degenerates into the disorder and confusion produced by too much ease and comfort and by the relaxation of vigour. This is the central and most difficult paradox of the new political science: the republic's achieved goal of power, wealth, and security is precisely what unravels into effeminacy and laziness. Its *virtu* is its own grave digger. Rome provides the best model to date because, during her rise to empire, the ceaseless struggle between the people and the Senate imposed necessity on each, keeping each strong and orderly through mutual opposition and thereby preventing degeneration. This enabled each to get what it wanted as the regime expanded outward.

Machiavelli is aware that the traditional writers on politics tended to look askance at the 'extraordinary and almost wild' means by which Rome gained her empire in comparison with the standards set by the best regimes of Plato and Aristotle, and their followers. He entertains this viewpoint, but quickly abandons it: 'One should blame the Roman government more sparingly,' for its internal tumults 'frighten whoever does no other than read of them.' Thought and action may not have a common end. Could Rome have achieved its greatness without the ongoing dissension between Senate and people? To consider this fully, Machiavelli argues, we have to return to the two alternatives posed by Rome and Sparta. By implication, the typology of regimes has been disposed of, superseded by these two archetypes, which combine all regime principles within them – people, nobles, monarch – as powers that reciprocally check one another.

Sparta and Rome may be said to parallel the alternation between caution and impetuosity recommended in chapter 25 of *The Prince*. Both modes are useful, but when the situation is uncertain, go with impetuosity – it more closely mirrors the inner dynamism of Fortuna herself.

Let us look at Machiavelli's assessment of the merits of each regime. Sparta with its equality of poverty and martial vigour is the perfection of that law-bred severity and institutionalized necessity set forth in the modes of founding in *Discourses* I.i. This is not the equality of citizens who, as Aristotle prescribes, rule and are ruled in turn, engaging in a common deliberation about justice and injustice that solicits the cultivation of our moral and intellectual virtues through open discourse and the leisure to reflect. Machiavelli prefers the taciturn Spartans to the chatty Athenians, who lived out the Aristotelian typology in their fruitless lurching from one exclusive regime type to another. Sparta instead embodies the repression of our natural longing for happiness, and therefore degeneration, by an abstract general necessity. Antagonism and repression replicate the lawfulness that holds the forces and clashing bodies of nature in a dynamic equilibrium. The monarchy restrains the nobles on behalf of the people (rather like the advice given in chapter 9 of *The Prince*). The citizens are few in number in order to maintain cohesion. Sparta is the only possible real-world version of what Plato and Aristotle idealize and render fanciful by adding the superfluous and dangerous concerns with choice and open discussion. There is no 'middle way.' You cannot combine a small, austere, self-governing republic with grandeur of soul. As suggested in chapter 16 of *The Prince*, you can have an austere and orderly small republic, or an empire that provides the scope and wherewithal for grander virtues of pride and liberality. The 'middle way' of Aristotle, where the grander virtues can be exercised within a small, orderly *polis*, does not exist.

You must choose between Rome and Sparta. Rome could not have been great without the disorder, class conflict, and selfish ambitions that the classics would have regarded as political vices: 'if Rome wished to remove the causes of tumults, it removed too the causes of expansion.'[29] Moreover, there is no infallible choice as between Sparta and Rome, only the least bad choice under the circumstances. One or the other may best suit the times. Regimes like Sparta (or the Venice of Machiavelli's day) are undermined by war and by the need to conquer or be conquered, because these things invite masterful personalities to assert themselves, who then unravel collective discipline and austerity by dangling the prospect of greater riches and power. But as we know from chapter 1, the rise to empire cannot be avoided: even if you choose a sterile environment to breed toughness through labour, the world will crash in on your orderly small republic in the form of external aggressors. Sparta is the best example of a regime that resisted the compulsion to empire, and is, to repeat, the real-life version of the best regime of the classics: Machiavelli cannot even endorse its partial virtues without reformulating it and dispensing with the classical original. A regime like Sparta is neither too weak nor too strong. It does not threaten others and therefore avoids to the degree possible being menaced. It remains quiet within its borders while the laws forbid expansion.

Such 'balance,' Machiavelli grants, 'would be the true political way of life and the true quiet of a city.' But in the long run it cannot be, because 'one cannot balance ... this thing nor maintain this middle way exactly.' The only fundamental alternatives are rise or decline. Necessity compels a republic – even a Sparta or Venice – either to expand or to go down. Reason has no influence on this cycle – it cannot be transcended by choice, leisure, or deliberation. A republic must recurrently undermine its own constitutional foundations by imperial expansion in order to survive and prosper, as did Rome. If a small republic remains at peace for a long time, this can only be because 'heaven' is 'so kind that it did not have to make war.' To rely on this peace to last forever is to rely on Fortuna in the bad sense of disarming oneself literally and psychologically.[30] Even when the peace is long-lasting, it leads to internal dissension and 'effemination' – we recall from I.i that the flourishing side of nature in a fertile spot makes men soft, vain, and unruly (the beginning of Aristotelian leisure is the end of public virtue). In another parallel to the advice in chapter 25 of *The Prince* that, in a pinch, impetuosity is to be preferred to caution, Machiavelli here concludes that, since there is no exact 'middle way' between the archetypes embodied by Sparta and by Rome, one must choose 'the more honourable part,' the course of imperial expansion, wealth, and glory enacted by Rome. Sometimes rest or moderation is better than motion or impetuosity, but rest is only the temporary pause in an underlying and ongoing motion, so when unsure, leap towards honour. We are reminded of those men possessing 'greatness of spirit,' the pre-political great men of the state of nature, who began the cycle of regimes. In this way, Machiavelli as it were encourages the revolt of the Auxiliaries in book 8 of the *Republic* and the decoupling of prudence from contemplation.

Is America Today's Rome?

The foregoing scarcely constitutes even an adequate preliminary presentation of Machiavelli's teaching, but it does, I hope, uncover enough of its basic premises that we can make some broader observations about the theme of empire. Machiavelli claims that his *Discourses* open 'a path as yet untrodden by anyone,' paralleling the exploration of 'unknown waters and lands' – very likely an allusion to the discovery of the New World. It is an eerie and prophetic parallel, since it can certainly be argued that the greatest imperial republic since Rome emerged in the New World and enacted many of Machiavelli's prescriptions. America was indeed a regime founded on the checks and balances among branches of government; it deliberately harnessed and played off against one another the power of the people (the House of Representatives), the notables (the Senate), and the chief executive (the Presidency). Its pedigree through Montesquieu, Locke, and Harrington back to the original 'Machiavellian moment' is well documented.[31] It is, moreover, a republic that from its origins harnessed the ambition of the common people for a better life and projected this outward to forestall internal class strife and a popular assault on the remnants of the Old World gentry (the original Whig–Federalist ruling class) while furthering the interests of that class as well. The first object for expansion was the American continent itself, through the displacement of the indigenous peoples and the development of agriculture and commerce through successive waves of immigrants ('men of all nations'). With the nineteenth and twentieth centuries came the projection of economic and military power throughout the world, accompanied by the crusade to extend the individual's liberty to achieve a better life to all peoples on earth. In all of these ways, America embodied Machiavelli's claim that one need not choose, as the classics had maintained, between a virtuous self-governing republic and an imperial *oikonomia* – that, on the contrary, the democratic energies of the people could be the vehicle for a republic's expansion into an empire in which all classes would benefit.

Whether and to what degree one would assess the American crusade to extend its version of republican liberty to the rest of the world as idealistic, or as a mere ideology for exploitation, or as some blend of the two, is beyond the scope of this chapter. Clearly, it has been all three from one event to another. My task is to offer a judgement about whether and to what degree it is a *Machiavellian* crusade. The central paradox of the *Discourses*, illustrated by the career of Rome and already implicit in the limited segment of book 1 we have considered, is that eventually the expansionist republic has nowhere left to expand, at which point those cravings to enjoy the settled peace sap the vigour of the empire, leading to a disenchantment with honour and war and a longing for the otherworldly peace. Christianity thus emerged as the spiritualization of the universal safety promised by the Augustan principate at its zenith in the Antonine age. It is not clear to me that Machiavelli believed he had found a way whereby even his prescription for a consciously re-enacted duplication of Rome's 'chance' career could in the long run avoid this inner degeneration and the longing for a counter-factual utopia of permanent peace and safety.[32] Might it not be the case presently that, as America extends her power, influence, and economic might to the farthest reaches of the globe, two challenges are emerging to the empire's sway that Machiavelli would immediately recognize? On the margins of the empire, hardier and angrier peoples who either have not tasted the promised material benefits or despise them are stoking the fires of communal honour and a fear of being overwhelmed. These are motives that, as we have seen, Machiavelli certainly appreciates as preconditions for the continued rise of healthy and vigorous republics into a greater historical sphere. More significantly, within the population of the imperial heartland itself, there is growing an ever more powerful counter-factual longing for a global peace, a universal society 'beyond' politics with its unedifying compromises and clash of interests – the parallel of that 'effemination' that Machiavelli was obliged to concede was inevitable even for Rome. Within today's imperial republic, during the apparently endless sunny noon of its Antonine age, with the legions securing the borders and unprecedented wealth and relaxation enjoyed within them, the citizens grow ever more bored with the republican vigour of their origins, ever more enervated through their hedonistic satiation, and ever more attracted to the dream of that coming global paradise when all conflict will end forever.

So there is a sense in which Machiavelli not only showed the route to the new Rome but foresaw its downward spiral. Machiavelli thought that Rome had contained 'as much virtue as has ever adorned any other city or republic,' and he hoped that the rise to such greatness could begin again. But he knew that even Rome would have to atrophy due to her very success, and that even the methodical and conscious imitation of her spontaneous career would carry this same long-term inner decay. While Machiavelli argues that the mastery of Fortuna is possible to an extraordinarily greater degree than anything entertained by the classics, he also appreciates that it is ultimately limited and that all things, including the peaks of human greatness, must pass.[33] In this respect, he remains at one with the classics and offers a sobering reminder that, whatever may be the comparative merits of empire and republic, human or even political perfection is not available on this earth or within the limits of nature.

NOTES

1 *Politics*, 1285b30–5. Consider also Plato, *Alcibiades*, 1:121–4; Xenophon, *Oeconomicus*, 4.1–25, 21.12; idem, *Memorabilia* 3.9.10–13. See also Waller R. Newell, 'Tyranny and the Science of Ruling in Xenophon's *Education of Cyrus,' Journal of Politics* 45 (1983); idem, 'Superlative Virtue: The Problem of Monarchy in Aristotle's *Politics,' Western Political Quarterly* 40 (1987).

2 This is implicit, for example, in Aristotle's remark that, if economics were the chief end of politics, all cities could be united in a single state, as happens with multinational trade agreements (*Politics* 1280a35–40).

3 Though Cicero never forsook his dream of the republic, he recognized that Caesar's dictatorship, a monarchy in disguise, provided stability and security, especially for the plebs, welcome after many years of civil war, and he conceded that the continuing strife between the dynasts Antony and

Octavian highlighted the comparative merits of monarchy as well as the likelihood that the republic would never be restored. Virgil endows Rome's founder, Aeneas, with Stoic qualities of duty and perseverance that are transferred to Augustus, divinely appointed to carry out Rome's divine destiny of bringing peace to the world. Syme notes that many of Augustus' apologists airbrushed, so to speak, Julius Caesar and especially his dictatorship out of the prehistory of the 'restored' republic as an unseemly precursor owing to his deliberate subversion of the old regime (Ronald Syme, *The Roman Revolution* [Oxford: Oxford University Press, 1982], 144–6, 318–22). Tacitus grudgingly concedes that the principate was necessary to bring peace after the civil war years and that it was popular, especially in the provinces (*Annals* 1.2; *Histories* 1).

4 Niccolo Machiavelli, *Discourses on Livy*, trans. Harvey Mansfield and Nathan Tarcov (Chicago: University of Chicago Press, 1998), I.ii. The following essay extends and develops some themes I explore in 'Is There an Ontology of Tyranny?' in *Confronting Tyranny: Ancient Lessons for Global Politics*, ed. David Edward Tabachnick and Toivo Koivukoski (Lanham: Rowman and Littlefield, 2006).

5 See the likely allusion to the discovery of the New World in the preface to book 1, and the conclusion to this essay below.

6 *Discourses*, I.i.

7 *Nicomachean Ethics*, 1111b–1112a.

8 Consider, for example, Plato, *Republic*, 419a–422a; Aristotle, *Politics*, 1252b.25–1253b, 1255b–1256a; Thomas Aquinas, *Commentary on the Politics*, 13, 31, 38.

9 *Nicomachean Ethics*, 1176b–1178b.

10 *Politics*, 1278a20–7.

11 *The Prince*, ch. 15.

12 *Politics*, 1293b22–1297b35.

13 Ibid., 1258a20–30.

14 Ibid., 1325b23–33, 1324b22–41.

15 *Discourses*, I.ii. Cf. II.iii: 'For the Romans wished to act according to the usage of the good cultivator who, for a plant to thicken and be able to produce and mature its fruits, cuts off the first branches it puts forth, so that they can with time arise there greener and more fruitful, since the virtue remains in the stem of the plant.' One can hardly avoid thinking of the allegorical figure of the Gardener in Shakespeare's *Richard II* (3:iv), whose maxim provides a backdrop for the rise of the Machiavellian new prince Henry Bolingbroke and the fall of the flawed Christian monarch Richard: 'All must be even in our government ... We at time of year do wound the bark, the skin of our fruit-trees, lest, being over-proud in sap

and blood, with too much richness it confound itself … Superfluous branches we lop away, that bearing boughs may live.'

16 Consider, for example, George P. Grant, 'In Defense of North America,' in *Technology and Empire* (Toronto: House of Anansi, 1991); and Richard H. Tawney, *Religion and the Rise of Capitalism* (London: Peter Smith, 1950).

17 *The Prince,* chs. 17 and 25. On why the Machiavellian prince must reify the external world by personifying it as a woman, see Hanna Fenichel Pitkin, *Fortune Is a Woman* (Chicago: University of Chicago Press, 1999).

18 Aristotle, *Politics,* 1326a.25–1326b.10; 1326b.26–1327a.40.

19 Ibid., 1278b.15–30; 1280a.7–21; 1276a.34–1276b.16

20 Consider the following enigmatic observation by Tocqueville about the need to stimulate honour in democracies: 'I think then that the leaders of modern society would be wrong to seek to lull the community by a state of too uniform and too peaceful happiness; and that it is well to expose it from time to time to matters of difficulty and danger, in order to raise ambition and to give it a field of action.' Alexis de Tocqueville, *Democracy in America,* vol. 2, trans. Henry Reeve (New York: Colonial, 1900), 259.

21 *Discourses,* I.ii.

22 Consider Plato, *Theaetetus,* 166d, 172a–b, 177d–e, 180a–c. For an extended discussion of the political ontology of the Sophists, see Waller R. Newell, *Ruling Passion: The Erotics of Statecraft in Platonic Political Philosophy* (Lanham: Rowman and Littlefield, 2000), ch. 2.

23 Plato, *Gorgias,* 506d–e.

24 *The Prince,* ch. 6.

25 As further background for what follows, allow me to refer the reader to my exploration of the relationships among will, nature, and statecraft in *Ruling Passion,* esp. 69–71 and 139–40; to 'Is There an Ontology of Tyranny?'; and to 'Machiavelli and Xenophon on Princely Rule: A Double-Edged Encounter,' *Journal of Politics* 50 (1988): esp. 128–9.

26 *Politics,* 1283a25–30.

27 Ibid., 1325a5–1325b30.

28 *Discourses,* I.iii.

29 Ibid., I.vi.

30 In II.i, Machiavelli wants everyone to 'know better how much more virtue could do than [the Romans'] fortune in acquiring that empire.'

31 John G.A. Pocock, *The Machiavellian Moment* (Princeton: Princeton University Press, 1975).

32 I offer the following inferences in support of this assertion. In *Discourses* II, 'Introduction,' Machiavelli depicts the world's virtues as first arising in Assyria, then migrating to Media and Persia, then to Italy and Rome.

Greece, the home of philosophy, is omitted. However, after the Roman Empire and its fall, this complete set of virtues finds no new home. We find only fragments of them scattered among France, the Turkish empire, Germany, and the Saracens. Something about the Roman Empire's rise and fall prevents all the virtues from migrating intact to a new empire. What is that something? It can only be Christianity, a religion that developed under the empire and that inhabited its dead husk when it fell, replicating its universal political order as a universal religious order (*The Prince*, ch. 12). In *Discourses* II.ii, he begins by making a sharp distinction between the pagan religion of Rome and 'our' religion: the Roman religion promotes glory while our religion promotes humility. He goes on to suggest that it is a false interpretation of Christianity to conclude that it must make us effeminate and unable to defend our country. But he then suggests another reason for this effeminization, one that shows that there is a link between Rome and the version of Christianity he decries. Through her conquests, Rome extinguished republican liberty everywhere ('eliminated all republics and all civil ways of life'). By extinguishing the spirit of liberty everywhere, the Roman Empire effeminated itself and prevented the world's virtue from finding a new imperial homeland. Finally, in *Discourses* III.i., he remarks that all religious republics will decay over time unless returned periodically to the vigour of the original rise by recurrent refoundings. Though the notion of a religious republic might seem to refer exclusively to modern Christian states, Rome, too, was a religious republic – religion was essential to its success, according to Machiavelli – and the examples he uses to illustrate the need for refounding are drawn from Rome as well as from modern times. In *Discourses* III. xvii, in remarking that officials could commit outrages even during the early republic when Rome 'was still uncorrupt,' he concludes that 'it is impossible to order a perpetual republic because its ruin is caused through a thousand unexpected ways.' While everything possible should be done to return a republic to the vigor of its origins, there is nothing more true than that all the things of this world have a limit to their existence (III.i).

33   See, for example, *Discourses* II, 'Introduction': 'human appetites are insatiable … since from nature they have the ability and the wish to desire all things and from fortune the ability to achieve few of them.' See also III.i. cited in note 32 above.

12 Post-9/11 Evocations of Empire in Light of Eric Voegelin's Political Science

JOHN VON HEYKING

Empire as a Scientific Problem

In a 1961 speech that was later published as 'World-Empire and the Unity of Mankind,' Eric Voegelin (1901–1985) stated that the 'age of empire is coming to its end in our time' because imperial evocations could no longer be considered coherent.[1] Voegelin did not live to see the end of the Cold War and the subsequent ascension of the United States to 'hegemon' and 'hyperpower' status. Nor did he live to see the resurgence of political Islam, with its aspirations for a global caliphate. While these phenomena might disprove Voegelin's claim, their characteristics, and the ideologies that purport to legitimate them, actually confirm his claim.

Empires evoke comprehensive world rulership: 'To establish an empire is an essay in world creation, reaching through all the levels of the hierarchy of being.'[2] But to create a world demands giving an account of that world, which is why empires frequently attract the attention of philosophers of history, who describe empires as constituent elements of human development. Few contemporary scholars, not even Francis Fukuyama, attempt such grand theorizing any more. Instead, one finds historians, including Charles Maier, pragmatically focusing on structures and institutions but avoiding seeing anything meaningful in them. On the other hand, Michael Hardt and Antonio Negri have embraced the 'post-metaphysical' project of evoking a revolution of the seemingly marginalized to oppose global capitalism.[3]

Despite this uncertainty, man's noetic participation in reality suggests that meaning in history is an ineluctable problem, which means that history is more than a meaningless imperial gigantomachia. If one grants that contingent events, including the death of Socrates, the Crucifixion of Jesus, or the French Revolution, play a constituent role in the way humans understand themselves and their world, then the actions of empires take precedence because of their scope and aspiration for universality. Voegelin frequently dismissed such philosophies as 'stop-history' ideological programs. Hegel was the most sophisticated act of 'sorcery' because he provided a deformed account of noetic reason to wedge the empirical materials of history into his system. Even so, Voegelin shared Hegel's philosophical interest in the 'absolute epoch,' in which empires play a role in shaping the discovery of human consciousness of their humanity:

> For the enlargements of the social horizon from tribal society to city-state, and further on to an empire which comprises the whole area of a civilization, are not mere quantitative increases in the number of population, but qualitative jumps in social organization which affect the understanding of human nature. They were experienced as creative efforts by which man achieved a differentiated consciousness both of himself and of the divine origins of an order that is the same for all men. Through the hard reality of empire there begins to shine forth, as the subject of history, a universal mankind under God.[4]

Unlike Hegel, Voegelin did not think that empire exhausts the meaning of man's existence. Between the grinding wheels of imperial drives of the past, the 'constitution of reason through revelation,' which moves beyond pragmatic history, mysteriously gets discovered as the core of man's humanity.[5] This discovery of the mystery at the heart of human temporal existence, made by a variety of philosophers and mystics, including Plato, reminds human beings that they participate in a historical process not of their making. Instead of the 'stop-history' theories of Hegel and the Enlightenment, Voegelin points to the necessary 'suspense' faced by the thinker who is genuinely luminous of his humanity. Gaining insight into the contemporary significance of this 'suspense' is the purpose of this essay.

This essay considers Voegelin's understanding of empire in order to discern whether indeed our current situation in the early twenty-first century proves his 1961 declaration that the age of empire is over. Voegelin's understanding of empire contains some ambiguities, in part because he does not provide a systematic treatment of them with an eye towards constructing a set of typologies. His discussions of empire are set within analyses of broader topics concerning lines of meaning in history and structures of consciousness. Even so, the theme of empire resides near the centre of his concerns because he thought that empires are a constituent element of human existence and self-understanding.

Voegelin seems to distinguish five categories of empire: (1) cosmological, (2) ecumenic, (3) orthodox, (4) national, and (5) totalitarian.[6] These five types have a chronological dimension, but for Voegelin they are more conceptually clear, and less deterministic, than the commonly used ancient–medieval–modern categories. Drawing on the work about comparative civilizations of Max Weber, Eduard Meyer, and Arnold Toynbee, as well as the philosophies of Giambattista Vico and F.W.J. Schelling, Voegelin found that the ancient–medieval–modern categories arose from the emphasis placed on the Roman Empire in Western self-interpretations. The utility of such categories for understanding non-Western empires is limited because they derive from Western political myths instead of from science. Moreover, they fail to explain how the participants of empire understand themselves. For instance, neither Charlemagne nor St Thomas Aquinas considered himself 'medieval,' but both were concerned with evoking the idea of the *corpus mysticum* as the unifying substance of their civilization.

After considering these five types of empire, we will consider our contemporary situation and its three rival evocations of empire: the Islamist ideal of the caliphate, the Bush Doctrine of pre-emption and its rhetoric of democracy, and the 'humanitarian' democracy espoused by various proponents of 'global civil society' and those who look forward to an international society composed of universal humanity.

Cosmological Empire

Cosmological empires, such as the ancient Egyptian and the Babylonian, are the earliest types of empire in recorded history. They represent themselves as analogues of cosmic order and its cyclical rhythms, with the empire corresponding to the heavenly order and the earth's four points.[7] Gods and men share a common, visible world, dominated by the cosmic rhythms of coming and passing that reflect the motion of the stars and the seasons. The interpenetration and mutual reinforcement of cosmic and political analogies means that there are not two realms, but a single compact order.

City-states are the earliest known political form. In the Mesopotamian case, each city-state had its own gods, and all of these gods had enough in common to be united in a common religious culture, under the highest god, Enlil of Nippur (whose authority compared with that of Delphi in ancient Greece). Conquests of one by another led to empire, which in turn led to a corresponding change in political symbolism. Imperial symbolism in its cosmological mode saw the emperor's rule correspond in the earthly world to Enlil's rule in the cosmos, as one sees in the preamble to the Code of Hammurabi.[8] The sun god Marduk (son of Enlil) is appointed ruler over all peoples, while his earthly analogue, Hammurabi, 'rises like the sun over the people and lightens up the land, dispensing the essentials of just order.'[9] Unlike ecumenic, orthodox, or totalitarian empires, cosmological empires were self-contained, which meant they felt no obligation to subjugate foreign populations; they could tolerate other analogues of the cosmos.[10] Imperial conquests were for pragmatic purposes, including population growth, scarcity of resources, and rulers' desire for self-aggrandizement, not for reasons of ideology. Even so, imperial expansion put pressure on the cosmological symbolic form, which could not always withstand the symbolic systems of conquered peoples (or of the ones who conquered them).

The Babylonian and Egyptian empires endured for a long time. However, the very instability of the cosmos undermined the compact mode of symbolization of cosmological empires. For instance, Babylonian court astronomers noticed that the sun god (i.e., not just the planets) was irregular in its course, which undermined trust in the cosmos as well as in the empire. Cosmological symbolization is compact, which means that political, cosmological, and theological speculations are combined. The anxiety engendered by the discovery that the cosmos is unstable – which compounded the anxieties inherent in imperial conquests and setbacks – was profound because the unity of cosmic and divine order was no longer tenable: 'Society and the cosmos of which society is a part tend to be experienced as a sphere of disorder, so that the sphere of order in reality contracts to personal existence in tension toward the divine Beyond. The area of reality that can be experienced as divinely ordered thus suffers a severe diminution.'[11]

This anxiety also led to a new form of imperial symbolization – one that is important for our analysis – which Voegelin called historiogenesis, whereby court historiographers/cosmologists described their own imperial order as the culmination of a linear historical process going back to the creation of the world. In Voegelin's more technical terms, 'historiogenesis is a mytho-speculative extrapolation of pragmatic history toward its cosmic-divine point of origin.'[12] Examples of historiogenetic speculation include Sumerian (c. 2,050 BCE) and Egyptian king lists (c. 1,345–1,200 BCE), according to which kings closer to the divine origin live for hundreds or even thousands of years.[13]

While different examples vary in intensity of imperial aggressiveness, the imperial purpose of historiogenetic speculations is clear: 'One cosmos, it appears, can have only one imperial order, and the sin of existence must be atoned by posthumous integration into the one history whose goal has been demonstrated through the success of the conqueror ... The relevant course of events descends ineluctably from the cosmic origin down to the present authors whose society is the only one that matters.'[14] Voegelin compared the anxious and deliberate misreadings of historical sources found in ancient historiogenetic speculations with 'modern' ones, including Hegel's *Lectures on the Philosophy of History*, and with the general Enlightenment myth of 'progress,' which was shared by many thinkers, such as Turgot, Condorcet, Voltaire, and Marx. Hegel thought that Christianity and political events such as the French Revolution required philosophical explanation, and his system, in which history unfolds in a linear fashion that ends with the French Revolution, constituted a mythopoetic and 'magical' speculation whose predecessors in human history could be traced back to the Sumerian court historians.[15]

Ecumenic Empires and the Ecumenic Age

The instability of cosmological empires led eventually to spiritually more differentiated symbolizations of order. For instance, the inadequacy of the cosmos led Abraham to seek the God beyond the cosmos, and Socrates to 'bring philosophy down from the heavens' by locating man's experience of order in his individual soul.[16] The fragmentation of reality that occurs under empires also leads to the discovery of the soul as the focal point of man's participation in divine presence. The cosmos gets differentiated into its various strata, which produces symbolisms including 'the world' and 'the Beyond' – or *civitas terrenas* and *civitas Dei*, as St Augustine expressed it.

In the ecumenic age, which dates approximately from the rise of the Persian Empire to the collapse of the Roman Empire, that differentiation took place in a plurality of civilizations. Ecumenic empires (e.g., Rome) did not start off seeking imperial power so much as they fell into it as the result of successful defensive wars; that is, they fell into power vacuums and then had to expand their power in order to maintain it (one thinks of chapter 11 of *Leviathan*, in which Hobbes lists diffidence or fear as one of the causes of war). Ecumenic empires began 'by accident' as projections of power over subject peoples who could not organize themselves.[17]

Even so, the 'accidental' beginnings of ecumenic empires led to efforts to develop historiogenetic accounts to legitimate imperial rule, as well as to philosophical efforts to understand the meaning of the new universal humanity that had opened up. Voegelin labelled the former the 'concupiscential exodus,' and the latter the 'spiritual exodus.'[18]

The transformation of the term *oikoumene* provides a summary expression of how, in the ecumenic age, the entire world became a project of imperial expansion: 'The term *ecumene*, which originally means no more than the inhabited world in the sense of cultural geography [as in Herodotus], has received through Polybius the technical meaning of the peoples who are drawn into the process of imperial expansion. On this Polybian stratum could later be superimposed the meaning of the mankind under Roman jurisdiction (Luke 2:1; Acts 17:6; 24:5), and ultimately of the messianic world to come (Heb. 2:5).'[19]

Voegelin's reading of sources, including Herodotus, Polybius, and scripture, indicates that *ecumene* (what today we might call 'the world') evolved from a symbol of geography into an object of empire, and finally into the *eschaton*. Today one might draw a comparison with the evolution of the term 'space,' which originally meant extension but has since become reified for conquest by space tourists.[20] The *ecumene*, as the inhabited world and the object of imperial expansion, can never be coterminous with any empire simply because human beings can never control the whole in which they participate. Ecumenic empire is ultimately a fantasy.

The primary difference between a cosmological empire like that of Babylon or Egypt, and an ecumenic one like Rome or that of Alexander the Great, is that the former is a subject of order – it is an analogue of the cosmos – whereas the latter is an object of conquest, an organizational shell with no inner spiritual substance that expands indefinitely to engulf former concrete societies.[21] Cosmological empires consisted of two realms in one world, connected by a divine representative such as the Egyptian Pharaoh or by an access point to the divine, such as *omphalos* (e.g., Delphi); whereas in ecumenic empires the spiritual and pragmatic orders of human existence were split apart: 'The universality of spiritual order, at this historical epoch, meets with the indefinite expansion of a power shell devoid of substance.'[22] For people living in cosmological empires, human existence is surrounded by *okeanos*, the horizon of mystery. For ecumenic imperialists, *okeanos* becomes the ever receding limit of concupiscential exodus. The history of the ecumenic age, from Persia to Rome, is the history of human efforts to reconnect those two realms, to reconcile the concupiscential with the spiritual exodus. Examples of efforts at such reconnection include Alexander the Great's attempts to cast himself as a divinity over his worldwide empire; attempts by various thinkers, including the Stoics and Philo, to concoct syncretistic myths by incorporating the gods of other empires into their own; and Gnostic deformations that took imperial destruction as the prelude to ecumenic transfiguration. But these attempts were doomed to failure because *okeanos* can never be an object of imperial conquest. The syncretistic constructions were achieved at the expense of losing sight of the animating experience that first motivated those individual symbolizations (i.e., the objects of philosophy and theology had become reified).[23] Augustine's *City of God*, with its division between *civitas terrenas* and *civitas Dei*, amounts to a eulogy for ecumenic empires: 'And when universal humanity was understood as deriving from man's existence in presence under God, the symbolism of an ecumenic mankind under an imperial government suffered a serious diminution of status. Philosophically, the ecumene was a miserable symbol.'[24]

For Voegelin, authentic human existence consists of giving each stratum of humanity its due weight, which requires avoiding ideological and monistic deformations of humanity. He regarded the 'balance of consciousness' achieved by Plato and Aristotle as 'one of the principal events, not in the Ecumenic Age only but in the history of mankind.'[25] Faced with the 'concupiscential exodus' whereby emperors turned the historical field into a field of senseless violence, philosophers and mystics like Plato, Aristotle, and St Augustine committed themselves to a 'spiritual exodus' whereby they found human order a matter of attunement to the divine. Voegelin pointed to Plato's *Symposium*, the 'Apocalypse of Abraham,' Paul, the Tao Te Ching, the Upanishads, and St Augustine's *Confessions* as prime examples of the discovery made by the ecumenic age: that the human soul is the site of the divine irruption into the world and history. This is more than the discovery of 'the self' or of individuality, because to become conscious of oneself is in fact to become conscious of one's soul as the in-between (*metaxy*, a term Voegelin takes from Socrates' speech in the *Symposium*) that is the site of the search. Put another way, one does not fully experience oneself as seeking the ground of one's existence in a philosophical sense until one recognizes that the one doing the seeking is also the one sought: 'It is the site where immanence and transcendence meet, but that is itself neither immanent nor transcendent ... The tension of God seeking man, and man seeking God – the mutuality of seeking and finding one another – the meeting between man and the Beyond of his heart.'[26] While this formulation seems to conflate reason with revelation, for Voegelin, philosophically speaking, there is no such thing as 'unassisted reason' because reason does not ground itself nor does it motivate its own questioning. Man experiences his philosophical questioning retrospectively as a discovery of something that has been moving him.[27] The constitution of reason through revelation was the great discovery of the ecumenic age, during which the grinding wheels of imperial ambition to conquer the *ecumene* inadvertently bore the insight, by philosophers and mystics, that universal humanity is found under God and that this covenant cannot be fully expressed politically.

Orthodox Empires

Amidst the struggles for order in the Roman Empire, Cicero in *On the Nature of the Gods* defended philosophy against the false myths of Roman mythopoetic speculation. He retrieved an older Latin term, *religio*, to become a symbol that 'comprehends protectively both the truth of existence and its expression through cultic observance and doctrine.'[28] St Augustine followed in treating *religio* as an apologetic term, in *De Vera Religione* (On True Religion) and more generally in *The City of God*.[29] The great philosophical and mystical spiritual outbursts had taken place in ecumenic empires; now, while imperial structures remained, the successor empires understood that those outbursts had to be defended against deformations, including heresies. Moreover, according to Voegelin, the Augustinian two cities – which were to frame thinking during the European Middle Ages – gave too little weight to historical events; this led to later Gnostic and ideological efforts to seek immanent political meaning.[30] The protection of orthodoxy distinguishes orthodox empires from other types.

In 'World-Empire and the Unity of Mankind,' Voegelin cited the following as examples of orthodox empires: 'the Western Latin and the Eastern Greek Christian empires, the Islamic empire, and the Neo-Confucian empire in the Far East. The case of India displays certain peculiarities – a Hinduist orthodoxy without formal power organization.'[31] Unfortunately for the purposes of this chapter, Voegelin did not explicate the problems of orthodox empires in his late work after the publication of volume 4 of *Order and History*, *The Ecumenic Age* (1974). Nor did he examine the orthodox empires on this list. Voegelin's most extensive examination of an orthodox empire is his study of the political ideas of the European Middle Ages.[32] It appears in his *History of Political Ideas* (hereafter HPI), which he wrote before he published the first three volumes of *Order and History* in 1956. HPI was only published in full, in seven volumes, in 1997 as part of his *Collected Works*. Its methodological limitations relate to its exclusive focus on European history and to its partial reliance on ancient–medieval–modern categories, whose limitations motivated him to abandon the project in favour of the methodology of *Order and History*.

These qualifications aside, the European orthodox empire is central to his overall understanding of empire. In the 1940s he devoted considerable attention in his writings to the Germanic part of the empire. His understanding of European politics, and of later totalitarian empires, is rooted here, as he writes in an essay on Nazi geostrategy published around this time: 'The German center of Europe is the old empire core, a residue, one might say, burdened with the imperial tradition ... Around this empire core lies, then, the zone of the old national states that separated gradually from the empire ... Carrying on the original imperial drive they created empires of their own. The third zone is formed by the overseas extension of the European national states, by the former colonies, some of which have grown into the British dominion states ... and one, the United States, into a great power in her own right.'[33] The events of the 'empire core' form the basis of Western ideological history, as well as of the history of empires that extends to the present day.

The lever that moved ecumenic empires like the Roman one was the belief in universal jurisdiction over the known world. The lever that moved the European Middle Ages was *sacrum imperium* (Holy Empire), referring to the cooperation between papacy and empire to form a unitary political order that was eschatologically oriented.[34] As with the Roman *ecumene*, the *sacrum imperium* was an ideal only. Even so, because of the wealth of empirical materials documenting its rise and fall, *sacrum imperium* provides an excellent case study for those formative processes whereby a 'universal empire as a power organization and the universal spiritual community tended toward each other and finally met, but they did not amalgamate.'[35] With papacy and emperor, two central institutions cooperated and competed in a single unity. However, this arrangement's eschatological orientation made it unstable as a political entity, as the symbols it developed to justify and legitimate political order frequently meant that the authenticity of faith was mortgaged to political forces. *Sacrum imperium* evoked a transcendent ideal for which the realities of power politics could not easily get legitimated; this cast the seeds for later national and totalitarian empires.

The *sacrum imperium* arose in Europe in the fifth century and reached its apex in the twelfth century: 'But the long preparatory period of the imperial evocation from the fifth to the twelfth century extended right into the period of culmination, overlapping the beginning of the disintegration of the empire into national units. The history of the Middle Ages consists of two long, drawn-out processes of integration and disintegration of the imperial idea, joined in an ephemeral climax around 1,200.'[36]

The *sacrum imperium* ideal began after the collapse of the Roman Empire, as the evocation of a new imperial ideal that would be legitimated in terms of the Augustinian two-cities scheme. Later it would disintegrate under the pressure of its inner contradictions – most notably, by the failed attempt to incorporate political authority into the charismatic order of the *corpus mysticum* (the mystical body of Christ) and by the rise of regional and national identities that resisted both papal and imperial authority.[37]

Voegelin identifies two phases of this history: 'The evocation of the Carolingian empire constitutes the first phase of the process, and the great reform movement of the eleventh and twelfth centuries, with the dramatic high point of the Investiture Controversy, constitutes the second phase.'[38] The first phase runs from Pope Gelasius' declaration on the division between temporal and spiritual power to the establishment of the Carolingian Empire. Imperial debates in the ninth century revolved around the evocation of the empire in terms of the Pauline notion of the body of Christ, along with the Pauline doctrine of the *charismata* according to which the gifts of grace differentiate the functions of different members of that body. The coronation of Charlemagne was the high point of this evocation because he was consecrated emperor by the will of God: 'With the coronation of Charlemagne the idea of empire had been created that was to dominate the centuries of medieval political history. The church had found again an orthodox Christian power that could raise the claim of being the universal temporal organization of the Christian people; the kingdom of the Franks had become through the conquest of Italy more than a national Christian realm and had gained the stature of a multinational empire.'[39]

The attempt to incorporate the requirements of imperial power politics into the *charismata* of the *corpus mysticum* was bound to unravel. This unravelling constituted the second phase of the *sacrum imperium*, which lasted until the twelfth century's Investiture Controversy and the rise of national identities. Thereafter there would be no emperors as powerful as Charlemagne. The empire and the papacy came to be entrenched in a struggle over the political control of the *corpus mysticum*; this culminated in the Investiture Controversy. As a result of the struggle over political control, the Church lost its ability to absorb spiritual movements, especially those proclaiming universality. Hence, this period is characterized by efforts to articulate a spiritual mystical community that could serve as the overarching canopy of the *ecumene*. Voegelin's analysis of Joachim of Fiore, as the precursor for modern ideologies and historiogenetic constructions, in the *New Science of Politics* is best known.[40]

Another illuminating example is Voegelin's analysis of a lesser-known work, *De recuperatione terre sancta* (1306) by the French lawyer Pierre Dubois.[41] Joachim's evocation of a spiritual community is 'idealistic'; Dubois, for his part, evokes a 'realist' international order dominated by the French monarchy. Papal possessions are to be ceded to France; this would help the papacy purify itself by concentrating on its spiritual functions. Dubois proposed a league of European sovereign states, organized along the lines of collective security, which some have called a precursor to the League of Nations (and the United Nations, in Voegelin's time). Voegelin found Dubois's imperial evocation significant because it did not appeal to a Christian *sacrum imperium*, and 'a reconstruction of Europe out of the forces of the particularized nations under a hegemon seemed advisable.'[42] The purpose of Dubois's league of nations was not to evoke the *charismata* of the *corpus mysticum*, but rather to ensure the flow of commerce and to advance European interests in the Mediterranean. Voegelin notes that 'the idea of the hegemonic league of nations and the intellectual creed that the unity of Western mankind can be produced synthetically by lawyers have remained ever since an important strain in the political ideas of the West.'[43]

Behind the ideal of *sacrum imperium* lies the philosophical and theological speculation that articulates the understanding of the *corpus mysticum*. For Voegelin, the two figures that stand out in the European orthodox empire are St Thomas Aquinas and Nicholas of Cusa. In order to incorporate an understanding of political authority into theological doctrines such as the *corpus mysticum*, one needs a developed account that integrates reason and faith. By the time St Thomas Aquinas produced his great intellectual works, the *sacrum imperium* ideal was in decline. Even so, while Aquinas was no simple advocate of empire, his integration of faith and reason provided a grounding for these ideals: 'Faith and reason cannot be in conflict because the human intellect carries the impression of the divine intellect; it is impossible that God should be guilty of deceiving man by leading him through his intellect to results conflicting with the revealed faith. It follows that the human intellect, though capable of errors, will arrive at the truth wherever it goes.'[44] Unlike Joachim or Dubois, Aquinas' intellect can 'embrace the natural contents of the world as well as the human intellect and mankind organized in a plurality of commonwealths.'[45] His 'naturalism' allows for a diversity of political societies that need not be subsumed under empire. Conversely, his universalism is found in his understanding of the mystical body of Christ: 'It is Thomas Aquinas who considers the Christ to be the head of the *corpus mysticum* that embraces, not only Christians, but all mankind from the creation of the world to its end. In practice this means that one has to recognize, and make intelligible, the presence of Christ in a Babylonian hymn, or a Taoist speculation, or a Platonic dialogue, just as much as in a Gospel.'[46]

The evocation of the *concordantia* of mankind by Nicholas of Cusa possesses similar 'balance' between an affirmation of particular nations (and religions) and an affirmation of a mystical human community grounded in the interpenetration of reason and faith.[47] For instance, in *On the Peace of Faith*, Nicholas bases his argument for the toleration of religions in the context of a mystical vision of the divine. National customs are authentic expressions of their participation in the *corpus mysticum*, which is glimpsed most completely in mystical vision. Voegelin admires Cusanus' 'balance' even though it is expressed less systematically than that of Aquinas:

> Precisely at the moment when the medieval *sacrum imperium* was disassociated into the *societates perfectae* of the church and the nations, precisely at the time when the category of the mystical body was transferred from universal Christianity to the particular national bodies, the new *concordantia* of mankind was evoked by the Cusanus out of the forces of the new intellectual mysticism. The nations emerging from the *sacrum imperium* did not become a plurality of brute power facts without grace: the mystical faith in the *concordantia* of mankind was still extended over them as the eternal arc, far outreaching the discord of the times.[48]

Even so, the European orthodox empire dissolved into a complex of nation-states that inaugurated their own empires.

National Empire

Nation-states arose when the 'mystical body' idea of the orthodox empire was transferred to smaller territorial units, which were evoked as closed, autonomous societies, each led by its own *imperator in regno suo*. National aspirations to universality sometimes expressed themselves as the carriers of Western Christianity. However, universality could also result from the penetration of modern, scientistic political thought, according to which man's condition of living without the shelter of a cosmion (expressed most clearly by Hobbes's state of nature) required him to extend his will into the 'open, infinitely extending universe evoked as a projection of the human mind and of its infinity into space.'[49] Being emperor in one's own realm constituted a rejection of the *sacrum imperium* idea. Spiritual and commercial pressures then led nation-states into imperial activity.

Voegelin considers the conflictual situation of the nation-state in his chapter on Richard Hooker's *Of the Laws of the Ecclesiastical Polity*, in which Hooker treats the Church of England and the 'Church of Rome' as equivalent and separate expressions of parochial Christianity.[50] Voegelin criticizes Hooker for his handling of the problem of universal Christianity. For Hooker, the visible church is simply too large to have institutional expression, yet Christianity's current historical form has been achieved in the form of English society. Against the Puritans, who would logically follow through with his rejection of Rome's universality with their own rejection of the Church of England in favour of local assemblies of churches, Hooker simply states that the early Church's model of assemblies is outdated. Hooker's mystical historicism reveals a threefold historical structure: the Church in pagan antiquity, universal Christianity, and the Church of England. Voegelin dismisses Hooker's failure to delve more deeply into the problems of universal Christianity as an example of English parochialism. In the era of national empires, the idea of universality was largely buried as a substantive problem.

The work of the Spaniard Francisco de Vittoria (1480–1549), who theorized about interpolity relations, comes closest to uncovering universality, because he had to respond to concrete cases brought about by Spanish imperial activity; for example, he had to consider the nature of the duties that Christians owed non-Christian Indians. His efforts to formulate *ius gentium* for mankind, composed of nation-states, were an attempt to reverse the trend towards localism found in Hooker. However, *ius gentium* extended only so far as the peoples of *Christianitas*. As with Hooker, Vittoria saw the nation-state – namely, Spain – as the carrier of Christianity's universal civilization: 'Imperial expansion is impermissible if the agents are emperor and pope, while it is permissible if the agent is the king of Spain.'[51] Voegelin observes that whatever prohibitions against the conquest of foreign civilizations (outside *Christianitas*) Vittoria makes in Parts One and Two of *Relectio Prior, De Indis Recenter Inventis*, his theory in Part Three 'demolishes with judicious thoroughness every conceivable legal claim of non-Western mankind to preserve the integrity of its civilizations.'[52] There Vittoria argues that non-Westerners are obliged to grant Spaniards the right to promote commerce and trade, as well as to propagate Christianity. Persistent failure to do so means they must be treated as *perfidi* who are incapable of peaceful relations and who thus deserve to be deprived of property and reduced to captivity. Voegelin concludes, however, that Vittoria was no 'fervent imperialist': his judicious list of just causes for war was meant to moderate Spanish imperialism, whose contributions to the Spanish treasury made expansion inevitable.

The ambivalent position of Vittoria, whose evocation of universal mankind retains the parochialism of the Spanish nation as well as Western Christianity, brings to the foreground the ambivalence of national empires. They seek universality but their spiritual object seems non-existent, which gives greater prominence to international commerce as its evocative symbol. Yet nation-states themselves are beset with populations with divided loyalties, as evidenced by the wars of religion during the Reformation and by subsequent forms of internationalism that are at odds with their host nations. Voegelin identifies three features of ambivalent national empires that remain to this day: (1) the rise of spiritual, revolutionary movements that transcend national limits; (2) countermovements of largely national reaction; and (3) temporary stabilization. Historical examples of these features include (1) the Reformation, with its Counter-Reformation, followed by the period of stabilization, including the Treaties of Westphalia (1648) and Utrecht (1713); (2) the French Revolution and the reaction to it, with stabilization through the Congress of Vienna and the subsequent Concert of Europe; and (3) Marxist movements and revolutions, which culminated in 1917, and subsequent twentieth-century efforts to counter them.[53]

We will consider Voegelin's second and third historical examples in the next section. However, it is noteworthy that for Voegelin, the European political situation becomes increasingly complicated with each new outburst and subsequent stabilization because none of the competing universalist evocations is victorious. Moreover, each outburst brings into play increasing numbers of non-European forces, and this requires thinkers to consider how non-Westerners fit into their notions of universality. Applying Voegelin's categories to the present situation, one could suggest that we have passed the period of stabilization following Marxism (and totalitarian empire in general) and have entered a new period of outburst in the West's confrontation with political Islam. The nature of this confrontation will be addressed below.

Totalitarian Empire

With the rise of revolutionary expansion in roughly the middle of the fifteenth century, the task of 'modern' political thought has been to evoke a political unity in universality. For the most part, this has taken the form of the 'stop-history' movements first seen in the ecumenic age. The great discovery of the ecumenic age was the differentiation of the philosopher's experience of the Question, whereby man discovers his 'consciousness as the site where the movement of the Whole becomes luminous for its eschatological direction.'[54] But 'man' is better understood as concrete individuals in concrete societies and situations responding to the disorder of their times by inquiring into the mystery of existence. Thus, Voegelin concludes his study of the ecumenic age by confessing that his own mode of questioning took its form 'by a philosopher's resistance to the distortion and destruction of humanity committed by the "stop-history" Systems' of totalitarian ideologies and by the philosophies of history developed by thinkers such as Hegel and Marx.[55]

'Stop-history' systems inspired the totalitarian empires of the twentieth century. Like the historiogenetic speculations of ancient Babylon, these systems viewed history as a linear movement towards an absolute point; like the orthodox empires, they attempted to incorporate the transfigurative processes of history into their realm; and they radicalized the 'modern' notion of technological reason as an instrumentalist faculty capable of manipulating the world according to its designs.

Modern revolutionaries reject the transcendent orientation of the Christian symbol of *corpus mysticum*, but they retain the dream of transfiguration, transferring it, like Joachim of Fiore, from the *eschaton* to the historical process; and, like national imperialists, they regard the globe as the *ecumene* across which they direct the revolution. Accordingly, ideologues regard the historical process as one in which the aggregate talents and achievements of humanity, from its origins, have culminated in the present generation, which is led by a cadre of propagandist intellectuals who view themselves as representative of 'enlightened' humanity. The totalitarian ideologue concocts a historiogenesis according to which history ends with him. Voegelin's analysis of such efforts, including those by Turgot, Comte, Hegel, and Marx, shows how they distorted historical materials to force them into their systems. He regards this as an act of violence that comes to be replicated in the violence of totalitarian imperialists such as Hitler and Stalin.

Voegelin's analysis of the *Discourses* by French encyclopedist Anne-Robert-Jacques Turgot reveals the seeds that become amplified in more radical revolutionaries, but also the manner in which liberal ideals become bound up in empire. The central imperial symbol for Turgot's Enlightenment is the *masse totale*. It is universal humanity moving in a progressive fashion towards its culmination in Turgot's own representative humanity.[56] This liberal progressivist ideal contains three principles:

> The first principle is the historical individuality of every man, as the substance from which the whole of the *humanitas* is built; the second is the continuity of cause and effect linking the generations; the third is the accumulation of substance through collective memory in language and script. A *trésor commun* accumulates, is transmitted from one generation to the next, and passed further on to future generations. Moreover, the accumulation has progressive character … and the criteria of progress can be identified as (1) the softening of mores, (2) the enlightenment of mind, and (3) the intensified commerce between formerly isolated nations to the point of global intercourse.[57]

The *masse totale*, which is meant to replace the *corpus mysticum*, compares with the thirteenth-century Latin Averroeist doctrine of monopsychism found in Siger de Brabant and Dante.[58] One of the problems with this construction is that the collective consciousness of humanity is merely asserted by the Enlightenment intellectual. 'Humanity' thus conceived is an illusion: 'the meaning of the whole is inaccessible to the intramundane thinker because he is living in his finite presence and the whole, extending into an infinite future, is unknown to him. The meaning of the whole is an unsolvable problem from the intramundane position.'[59] From this, a deformation results whereby past generations are reduced to mere fodder for the present one.[60] The notion of 'universal humanity' as an entity waiting for universal political form, empire, was a key ideal of· the Enlightenment, one that animated Western colonialism. For example, Tocqueville saw it as the basis for the universality of democracy. John Stuart Mill was attracted to the divinized humanity of Comte's *Grand-Être*, though his own position came closer to that of Turgot in his late essay 'Theism.'[61] One can hear its echoes in contemporary evocations of 'humanitarian' democracy and global trade. Unfortunately, as Voegelin diagnoses, it is incoherent, which leads to ruin.

With Auguste Comte's *Grand-Être* and Marx's socialist man, one proceeds to more radical visions of universal humanity. Comte views his *Grand-Être* as a divinized humanity to replace the *corpus mysticum* of Christ. His proclamation of world leadership was reprinted on the first page of the *Catéchisme positiviste*: 'In the name of the past and the future, the theoretical servants and the practical servants of humanity assume befittingly the general leadership of the affairs of the earth in order to construct, at last, the true providence, moral, intellectual, and material; they irrevocably exclude from political supremacy all the various slaves of God, Catholics, Protestants, or Deists, since they are retrogrades as well as perturbators.'[62] Osama bin Laden's *fatwas* and attempts to lead the global Islamic caliphate find their Enlightenment counterpart in the representative humanity of Comte's positivist intellectual.

With Marx's socialist man, one reaches an end point in the development of Western revolutionary consciousness. The proletariat is, of course, universal, and the tactics of bringing about socialist revolution ignore national, 'bourgeois' boundaries, not the least because socialist revolution is permanent. Voegelin was most damning of Marx's intellectual 'swindle,' the lie at the root of his ideological construction. Socialist man is a metaphysical category as much as an economic one. Voegelin was relatively sympathetic towards socialism's economic dimension insofar as Marx resisted the destruction of personal freedom caused by industrialization's specialization and by its creation of degrading conditions (something that Marx shared with Adam Smith).[63] The metaphysical construction of,socialist man, whereby men regain their 'self-activity' (*Selbstbetätigung*) in the face of alienation, is the source of Marxian totalitarianism. 'Self-activity' entails the abolition of property along with any kind of dependence on another human being or part of creation:

A man who lives by grace of somebody else is dependent; and I live most completely by the grace of somebody else when he 'has created my life,' when the source of my life is outside myself. Creation, Marx reflects sadly, is an idea that is rather deeply rooted in the consciousness of man ... Man knows himself as a link in the chain of being, and of necessity he will ask: where is this chain suspended? And what can we answer to this inopportune questioner? Marx gives the same answer as Comte: don't ask such questions; they are 'abstractions'; they have 'no sense'; stick to the reality of being and becoming! As in the case of Comte, at the critical moment we are faced by the demand not to ask idle questions. The man who does not ask such questions is, by definition, 'socialistic man.'[64]

Such prohibition of questioning, Marx's 'swindle,' is the source of totalitarian terror, as he observes in another context: 'One thinks of Rudolf Höss, the commandment of the extermination camp in Auschwitz. When asked why he did not refuse to obey the order to organize mass executions, he replied: "At that time I did not indulge in deliberation ... I do not believe that even one of the thousands of SS leaders could have permitted such a thought to occur to him. Something like that was just completely impossible."'[65]

Voegelin states that the overall effect of ecumenic empires is the 'contraction and fragmentation of man's experience of order and reality.'[66] The overall effect of totalitarian empires is the intensification of that contraction and fragmentation of human existence to such a degree that humans are so morally, intellectually, and spiritually deformed as to share more with demons than with gods. Voegelin rejected Hannah Arendt's conclusion that totalitarian empires seek to 'change human nature' as nonsensical: either humans have a nature or they do not.[67] The 'empire' of totalitarian empires is geographic as well as anthropological: they purposely distort man's participation in the transfigurative process of the Beyond; they dominate bodies and souls under the banner of 'humanity' – an intellectual 'swindle.'

By 1961, Voegelin believed that the age of empires had ended because their intellectual foundations had become exhausted: the swindles had been exposed – clearly, no organization could organize mankind. Human history had reached a point 'when the meaning of universal order as the order of history under God has come into view.'[68] We had reached 'an epoch in the original sense of suspense.' *Suspendere*, of course, means to hang from a point, and it is this consideration that guides our analysis of post-9/11 evocations of empire.

Three Rival Versions of Imperial Evocation

Our current historical moment seems to disprove Voegelin's contention that the age of empire is over. Less true seems his assertion that 'the order of history under God has come into view,' unless one takes his statement as anticipating the 'resurgence' of religion in world affairs.[69] But evidence suggests that our epoch of 'suspense' means more than this. Our current moment of uncertainty is characterized by a struggle among three rival imperial evocations: (1) the Islamist *jihad* for a global caliphate; (2) the 'global sheriff' of the Bush Doctrine, which promotes democracies in areas strategic to the United States; and (3) the notion of 'humanitarian' democracy organized by the United Nations and global civil society (largely in opposition to the United States).

Islamists seek a global caliphate, a political empire to unify the Islamic community (*umma*), though they express it in different and sometimes contradictory ways. Osama bin Laden characterizes the *umma* as spreading 'from the Far East, from the Philippines, to Indonesia, to Malaysia, to India, to Pakistan, reaching Mauritania.'[70] 'The *umma* is asked to unite itself in the face of this Crusaders' campaign, the strongest, most powerful, and most ferocious Crusaders' campaign to fall on the Islamic *umma* since the dawn of Islamic history. There have been past Crusader wars, but there have never been campaigns like this one before.'[71] Behind the political goal of unifying the *umma* is a vision of history which begins with the ideal state of the early caliphate and which declares that Muslims are currently facing their greatest existential threat ever. While bin Laden is the figurehead and longtime organizer of al-Qaeda, the intellectual foundations for this empire can better be seen in the ideas of Sayyid Qutb, whose brother taught bin Laden and whose writings are studied in al-Qaeda training camps.[72]

Qutb's political writings consist mostly of a critique of the West and an evocation of Islamic empire; they contain little of what can be characterized as discursive analysis of political principles and structures.[73] The West, along with the despotisms in the Islamic world, is in a state of *jahiliyya* – that is, a state of ignorance resulting from having usurped divine sovereignty (*hakimiyya*). The moral degeneracy of the West is the cause of its injustices and inequalities and will lead to its downfall. The world has reached an end of history insofar as all of its ideologies have failed to provide for human happiness. Only Islam remains. Among the subtexts of *jahiliyya* are that the West is inherently violent and imperial; and that the part of the world not ruled by Islam (*dar*

al-Harb) is warlike (the literal meaning of *dar al-Harb* is 'realm of war').
Jihad is necessarily defensive and necessarily permanent so long as *dar
al-Harb* can threaten the *dar al-Islam*. Qutb envisages permanent war.
Nasiri reports that *jihadi* fighters learn that though the laws of *jihad*
make for strict rules on how to treat enemies, the concept of 'enemy' is
infinitely plastic and expandable: 'The definition of "enemy" can be
expanded to include the entire supply chain: anyone who supports
the enemy with money or weapons, or even food or water; even to
those who provide moral support – journalists, for instance, who write
in defense of the enemy's cause ... If [a young boy] carries food or
even a message to an enemy fighter, then he becomes an enemy. I came
to understand how, in the mind of an extremist, almost anyone could
become the enemy.'[74]

The logic of 'defensive' jihad propels Islamists towards a universal
empire by default in the same way that the 'defensive' wars of Rome
and other ecumenic empires led those powers to fill the power vacuum
that those very wars had created.

However, one finds in Qutb a more substantive evocation of empire
than the default position of *jihad*. *Jahiliyya* has divided human beings
according to inferior principles, including tribe, race, and nationality.
Islam, rooted in man's highest faculty, faith, is the only universal expression of political rule: 'It is in the very nature of Islam to take initia-
tive for freeing the human beings throughout the earth from servitude
to anyone other than God; and so it cannot be restricted within any
geographic or racial limits, leaving all mankind on the whole earth in
evil, in chaos and in servitude to lords other than God.'[75] Qutb's imperial evocation is a world empire in the making, comparable to that of
Genghis Kahn.[76] Territories, rulers, and peoples may be de facto beyond
the sphere of influence of *dar al-Islam*, but they are de jure and potentially members of the empire. The *ecumene* consists of *dar al-Islam* and
dar al-Harb, and for Qutb, our epoch is one in which the latter will submit to the former. However, the truly radical and totalitarian nature of
Qutb's imperial evocation is found in his elliptical statements of what
dar al-Islam should look like. While it is an 'open and inclusive
community,'[77] Islam and *shari'ah* cannot be summarized in terms of
doctrine or propositions. It is an activist faith revealed only in its instantiation.[78] The important point is the magical belief that the sovereignty
of God alone brings about just political rule. In another context, Voegelin
called this belief that one's individual mystical faith brings about world
transformation, 'metastatic faith.'[79] However, like another example of

metastatic faith, Marxist History, the god of the Islamists needs the help of an imperial vanguard, the 'few noble souls' who genuinely understand the Oneness of God.[80]

Qutb's vision, like that of Marx, is an intellectual 'swindle.' It reflects a consciousness deformed by what Voegelin called 'pneumopathology,' whereby the ideologue purposely and knowingly offers a deformed account of reality to fit with his system.[81] Qutb's pneumopathology expresses itself in a promise of defensive *jihad* that will cease only when the world submits to Islam. Yet his argument is circular: *dar al-Islam* is the realm of peace, but this realm of peace cannot truly be at peace until it has conquered the *ecumene*. The source of this double-think is his equation of imagination (*tasawwur*) with faith, which supports his belief in the unity of thought and action as the root of Islam's historical unfolding. This equation accounts for Qutb's heterodoxy, or rather, his vision for totalitarian empire in the wake of the dissolution of Islam's orthodox empire.[82] It also allows him to state that he is not offering an interpretation of Islam, but Islam itself – his visionary imagination. The pneumopathology of Qutb better explains the radicalism of Islamism than do accounts of intellectual influences, whether they argue that Qutb, Khomeini, and others were influenced by French neo-Marxists; whether their apocalyptic vision derives from more home-grown beliefs in the return of the Mahdi; or whether their radicalism is part of the continuity of some ill-defined 'millenarian' impulse in Islamic history.[83] Their pneumopathology sustains these other 'influences' and allows Islamists to develop syncretic and ecumenic symbols that give their ideas their religious and ideological flavour.

It is against this conception of Islamic totalitarian empire that the Bush Doctrine of American foreign policy is directed.[84] Put briefly, the Bush Doctrine calls for offensive operations, including pre-emptive war, to defend the United States and its allies. In its realism, it echoes Dubois's hegemonic model for the French monarchy over the European imperial core. As Daniel Mahoney points out, the promotion of democratic 'regime change' serves as the Bush Doctrine's moral compass.[85] The public defence of this moral compass shares somewhat in the Enlightenment hope for a progressive future.[86] But to whatever degree Bush leavens his personal faith by recognizing man's limitations and fallen condition,[87] his political rhetoric of democracy betrays a simplistic belief in humanity's yearning for freedom. In his Second Inaugural he spoke of the administration's policy 'to seek and support the growth of democratic movements and institutions in every nation and culture, with the ultimate goal of ending tyranny in our world.' According to this view, man naturally yearns for freedom, 'as if "democracy" arises automatically once impediments are removed.'[88] As Mahoney pointedly observes, one's yearning for one's own freedom does not necessarily translate into respect for another's freedom. Bush's rhetoric of democracy raises expectations for those living under tyranny; it also risks accusations of hypocrisy in cases where the United States works with despots like Pakistani President Musharraf in fighting Islamism (while preventing Islamists from entering electoral politics).

Bush's rhetoric of democracy shares too much with the universalist ideals of 'postmodern' or 'humanitarian' democracy and civil society. Bush speaks of man's universal desire for freedom, and then leaves it up to specific policy judgements to determine the extent to which the integrity of nation-states should be maintained. Conversely, partisans of 'humanitarian' democracy are suspicious of any kind of assertion of national interests (especially those by the United States), and look instead to the United Nations and 'global civil society' to evoke a universal *imperium*.[89] 'Humanitarian' democracy evokes a more direct vision of universal humanity, but rarely is this vision as flamboyant as that of Comte and Marx. The logic of 'humanitarian' democracy is meant to supersede the self-rule of nation-states, yet its proponents retain the Kantian reservation that historical progress conflicts with human dignity. Neither the proponents of the Bush Doctrine nor the proponents of 'humanitarian' democracy are willing to liquidate populations in the name of a 'stop-history' ideology that would legitimate imperial rule over humanity. They reside within the parameters of liberal-democratic thinking and the heritage of classical-Christian dignity that gave birth to it.

Conclusion

The three rival versions of empire that mark today's international political scene are only half-hearted empires. The Bush Doctrine and 'humanitarian' democracy evoke a universal humanity, but the proponents of these are less than serious about giving it unified political shape. The Islamist caliphate is the only genuinely imperial evocation. However, it is also a totalitarian vision that expresses the anxiety associated with the destruction of an orthodox Islamic empire and any kind of meaningful political life. It is as much a product of Islam's contact with the West as it is home-grown.[90] The evocation of the caliphate has taken a great deal of its shape from its opposition to the imperial *dar al-Harb* and from its own barely articulated political principles. Even so, though Qutb's *tasawwur*, which grounds his 'praxis'-oriented understanding of Islam, can be compared with Marx's view that the dictatorship of the proletariat executes the immanently apocalyptic end of history, at least Marx had to appeal to a tradition of discursive philosophical thinking about politics – something that Qutb avoids. *Dar al-Islam* is supposed automatically to follow submission to God, without the intermediary steps, guided by *phronesis*, of constructing the political structures and institutions of a political society. Even so, even unreflective evocations can cause a great deal of destruction for a very long time, especially when motivated by a desire to destroy an enemy identified as the rest of the world.

· If Voegelin's own questioning was motivated by resistance to 'stop-history' ideological movements, he also considered our epoch to be one of 'suspense' because the range of history was again open for philosophical investigation. The twentieth century (now continuing into the twenty-first century) saw an explosion of comparative knowledge about many civilizations. As he observes in the case of Max Weber, the broad range of empirical materials makes it nearly impossible to develop an ideological system into which they can be reduced for a political program.[91] Such range requires the scholar not only to keep up to date in many different fields, but also to keep an open mind to the manifold of human possibilities. It requires the scholar to recognize the limits of his intellect's ability to organize those materials, and also to confront the possibility – contrary to what the secular Enlightenment holds – that his own intellect has been brought into being and moved by the mysterious whole in which he participates. This broad range helps account for the sense of 'postmodern' fragmentation we experience today, and for why contemporary evocations of empire, especially in the West, remain incomplete in their ecumenism. For Voegelin, the symbol, 'the Question' was the central achievement of philosopher-mystics, including Plato and St Augustine. The end of empire today still leaves open the possibility that imbeciles will evoke empire, but 'the Question' is retained as the central form of human experience – and this question, moreover, cannot be wholly crushed by imperial and historiogenetic deformations. In addition to thinkers like Voegelin, the world today has thinkers and artists, including, in the Muslim world, Nobel Prize winner Orhan Pamuk and Iranian philosopher Abdolkarim Soroush, who have taken 'the Question' as the centre of their personal existence and of their resistance to untruth.[92] Their efforts, and those of others, in maintaining 'suspense' mean that the age of empire will remain closed.

NOTES

1 Eric Voegelin, 'World Empire and the Unity of Mankind,' in *Published Essays, Collected Works of Eric Voegelin*, vol. 11, ed., Ellis Sandoz (Columbia: University of Missouri Press, 2000), 155. Originally published in *International Affairs* 38, no. 2 (1962). References are to *Collected Works* edition (WE).

2 WE 145. For Voegelin's understanding of 'evocation,' see the comments of Peter von Sivers, 'Editor's Introduction,' in Eric Voegelin, *History of Political Ideas*, vol. 2, *The Middle Ages to Aquinas: The Collected Works of Eric Voegelin*, vol. 20 (Columbia: University of Missouri Press, 1997), 5. Hereinafter HPI2.

3 Typical of the emphasis on structures at the expense of philosophical meaning is Charles Maier's definition of empire: 'a territorially extensive structure of rule that usually subordinates diverse ethnolinguistic groups or would-be nations and reserves preponderant power for an executive authority and the elites with whom this power is shared. Thus an empire is characterized by size, by ethnic hierarchization, and by a regime that centralizes power but enlists diverse social and/or ethnic elites in its management.' Charles Maier, *Among Empires: American Ascendency and its Predecessors* (Cambridge: Harvard University Press, 2006), 31; Michael Hardt and Antonio Negri, *Empire* (Cambridge, MA: Harvard University Press, 2000). On post-metaphysics and empire, see James Ceaser, *Reconstructing America: The Symbol of America in Modern Thought* (New Haven: Yale University Press, 1997), 187–244; Stefan Rossbach, "Corpus Mysticum': Niklas Luhmann's Evocation of World Society,' *Observing International Relations*, ed. Mathias Albert and Lena Hilkermeier (New York: Routledge, 2004), 44–56.

4 Voegelin, *The Ecumenic Age* (Baton Rouge: Louisiana State University Press, 1974), 95, 309. Hereinafter OH4. Useful treatments of this work and of Voegelin's understanding of empire include Geoffrey Barraclough, 'Eric Voegelin and the Theory of Imperium,' *The Philosophy of Order*, ed. Peter Opitz and Gregor Sebba (Stuttgart: Klett-Cotta, 1981), 173–89; Stephen McKnight, 'The Ecumenic Age and the Issues Facing Historians in the Twentieth Century,' *Political Science Reviewer* 27 (1998): 68–96; Michael Franz, 'Editor's Introduction,' *The Ecumenic Age, Order and History IV, Collected Works of Eric Voegelin*, vol. 17, (Columbia: University of Missouri Press, 2000), 1–28; Barry Cooper, *Eric Voegelin and the Foundations of Modern Political Science* (Columbia: University of Missouri Press, 1999).

5 OH4, 228.

6 WE, 136–7. Voegelin referred to these five types as late as 1982 in his Commencement Address to the Dominican School of Philosophy and

Theology (Berkeley), though there he replaces totalitarian with ideological (Voegelin Archives, Hoover Institution, Stanford University, o HHoover-Box 3, Folder 1). See also Voegelin, *Autobiographical Reflections* (Baton Rouge: Louisiana State University Press, 1989), 102–7. Hereinafter AR.

7 Voegelin, *Israel and Revelation, Order and History*, vol. 1, (Baton Rouge: Louisiana State University Press, 1956), 25. Hereinafter OH1.

8 See OH1, 24.

9 OH1, 26.

10 OH4, 146–7.

11 OH4, 21-2. While Voegelin's comments are directed towards the impact of ecumenic empires on ancient traditional societies, the same could be said about the impact of modern society on contemporary aboriginals and on non-Western cultures. Indeed, scholars of militant Islam, or Salafism, have observed its greater appeal for Muslims who are alienated from their traditional rural backgrounds and who have gone into the cities. For example, see Olivier Roy, *Globalized Islam* (New York: Columbia University Press, 2004); Barry Cooper, *New Political Religions, or An Analysis of Modern Terrorism*, (Columbia: University of Missouri Press, 2004), 16–24.

12 OH4, 101.

13 OH4, 82–96. The same construction animates the Hebrew Bible's presentation of the patriarchs.

14 OH4, 65–6.

15 OH4, 67.

16 For details, see the first three volumes of *Order and History* (Baton Rouge: Louisiana State University Press, 1956). He provides a concise account in 'Reason: The Classic Experience,' *Published Essays, 1966–1985, Collected Works*, vol. 12, ed. Ellis Sandoz, 265–91.

17 OH4, 117. The reluctantly imperial role the United States plays in trying to prop up 'failed states' is comparable to this dynamic. See Robert D. Kaplan, *Imperial Grunts* (New York: Random House, 2005).

18 OH4, 197, 308.

19 OH4, 124.

20 OH4, 211.

21 OH4, 117–25.

22 OH4, 117.

23 OH4, 20–58, 153–65.

24 OH4, 172.

25 OH4, 183–92; 218–28.

26 OH4, 324. Voegelin's discovery of the constitution of reason through revelation sets him apart from Enlightenment thinkers, and also

distinguishes his approach from that of Leo Strauss, who separated revelation from what he sometimes called 'unassisted reason.' See *Faith and Political Philosophy: The Correspondence between Leo Strauss and Eric Voegelin, 1934–1964*, ed. Peter Emberley and Barry Cooper (University Park: Penn State University Press, 1993). The volume contains key essays, 'Gospel and Culture' and 'Immortality: Experience and Symbol.' See also 'In Search of the Ground,' *Collected Works*, vol. 11, 224–52.

27 Voegelin, *In Search of Order, Order and History*, vol. 5 (Baton Rouge: Louisiana State University Press, 1987); 'In Search of the Ground.'

28 OH4, 44.

29 The form of the *City of God* is a combination of apologetics and meditation, written for different types of readers, including philosophical ones. In a letter, Augustine wrote that *City of God* – all twenty-two books and more than one thousand pages in some English editions – required multiple rereadings to discern its deepest meaning (Ep. 231A). For details, see Heyking, *Augustine and Longing in the World* (Columbia: University of Missouri Press, 2001), ch. 1.

30 On twentieth-century efforts to retrieve in modernity a meaningful sense of historical existence within an Augustinian framework, see Heyking, 'From a Wooded Summit: Learning to Love through Meditation at Ascona,' *Pionere, Poeten, Professoren: Eranos und der Monte Verità in der Zivilisationsgeschichte des 20. Jahrhunderts*, ed. Elisabetta Barone et al. (Würzburg: Königshausen und Neumann, 2004), 83–96.

31 WE, 137; see also AR, 106.

32 HPI2; *The Later Middle Ages, History of Political Ideas*, vol. 3, *Collected Works*, vol. 21, ed. David Walsh. Hereinafter HPI3.

33 Voegelin, 'Some Problems of German Hegemony,' in *Published Essays, 1940–1952, Collected Works*, vol. 10, ed. Ellis Sandoz, 63. Originally published in the *Journal of Politics* 3 (May 1941). See HPI3, ch. 21.

34 While the sentiments of a holy empire characterize the age, the term *sacrum imperium* as such appeared only during the reign of Frederick I Barbarossa (1152–1190) (Peter von Sivers, 'Editor's Introduction,' HPI2, 7n17).

35 HP2, 66.

36 HPI2, 30.

37 HPI2, 62–6, referring to Rom. 12:3–8, 1 Cor. 12:12–31, Eph. 4:15–16.

38 HPI2, 66.

39 HPI2, 59.

40 *New Science of Politics*, in *Modernity without Restraint, Collected Works*, vol. 5, ed. Manfred Henningsen; HPI2, 126–34.

41 HPI3, 61–5.

42 HP3, 64.

43 HPI3, 64. Other imperial evocations include Dante's vision of a universal monarchy and William of Occam's vision for a world government through an aristocracy of national kings and popes (HPI3, 75–7, 122–3).

44 HPI2, 209.

45 HPI2, 214.

46 Voegelin, citing *Summa Theologiae* III.8.2 in 'Response to Professor Altizer,' *Collected Works*, vol. 12, 294. Voegelin's affirmation of this universality needs to be read in light of the above quotation on the centrality of the Question discovered in the ecumenic age. See also his 'Equivalences of Experience and Symbolization in History,' *Collected Works*, vol. 12, 115–33.

47 HPI3, 256–6; see Heyking, 'Prophecy and Politics in Nicholas of Cusa,' in *Propheten und Prophezeiungen – Prophets and Prophecies*, Eranos – Neue Folge nr. 12, ed. Matthias Riedl and Tilo Schabert (Würzburg: Königshausen and Neumann, 2005), 143–60.

48 HPI3, 266.

49 Voegelin, *Religion and the Rise of Modernity*, *History of Political Ideas* 5, *Collected Works* 23, ed. James L. Wiser, 136. Hereinafter HPI5.

50 HPI5, 84–6.

51 HPI5, 122.

52 HPI, 123.

53 HPI5, 110–11. Writing in the 1940s, Voegelin mentions the League of Nations, and today we could add the Cold War and the following (brief) period of stabilization in the 1990s, which President George H.W. Bush referred to as the 'new world order.'

54 OH4, 335.

55 Ibid.

56 *Crisis and the Apocalypse of Man, History of Political Ideas*, vol. 8, *Collected Works*, vol. 26, ed. David Walsh, 111–15. Hereinafter HPI8; WE, 147.

57 WE, 147.

58 HPI2, 192; HPI3, 75.

59 HPI8, 111.

60 Voegelin recalls how Kant observed how historical progress conflicts with the categorical imperative (OH4, 224, 325).

61 John Stuart Mill, 'Theism,' in *Three Essays on Religion*, (Amherst: Prometheus, 1998), 255–7; on Mill and Comte, see Linda Raeder, *John Stuart Mill and the Religion of Humanity* (Columbia: University of Missouri Press, 2002), 38–86; Alexis de Tocqueville, *Democracy in America*, trans. Harvey

Mansfield and Delba Winthrop (Chicago: University of Chicago Press, 2000), 2.1.7, 2.1.17, 2.4.8.

62 Quoted in Voegelin, HPI8, 168–9, citing *Catéchisme positiviste* (Paris: Garnier, 1852).

63 HPI8, 370.

64 HPI8, 358–9.

65 In *Science, Politics, and Gnosticism*, in *Collected Works*, vol. 5, 264.

66 OH4, 85.

67 'The Origins of Totalitarianism,' *Collected Works*, vol. 11, 21. Voegelin's review of Arendt's book prompted a response, and subsequent exchange of views, between the two as well as with Carl Friedrich. The point of contention was Voegelin's criticism of what he regarded as Arendt's failure to organize the historical materials according to a meaningful philosophical anthropology. For her part, Arendt dismissed Voegelin's appeal to human nature as 'essentialist.' See the commentary by Barry Cooper, as well as the suggestion that Arendt's response was motivated more by moral than by scientific concerns (*Eric Voegelin and the Foundations of Modern Political Science*, 145–53).

68 WE, 155.

69 See Peter L. Berger, *The Desecularization of the World: Resurgent Religion and World Politics* (Grand Rapids: Eerdmans, 1999); Pippa Norris and Ronald Inglehart, *Sacred and Secular: Religion and Politics Worldwide* (Cambridge: Cambridge University Press, 2004); Heyking, 'Secularization: Not Dead Yet, But Never What It Seemed,' *International Studies Review* 7 (2005): 279–84.

70 Osama bin Laden, *Messages to the World: The Statements of Osama bin Laden*, ed. Bruce Lawrence (London: Verso, 2005), 120 and 134. See also Efraim Karsh, *Islamic Imperialism: A History* (New Haven: Yale University Press, 2006), 220–8.

71 Bin Laden, *Messages to the World*, 121.

72 For details on how the jihadis-in-training spend Friday evenings studying Qutb, see Omar Nasiri, *Inside the Jihad: My Life with Al Qaeda* (New York: Basic, 2006), 150. A recent study of authors read by Islamists suggests that the entire jihadist movement be renamed 'Qutbism' in recognition of Qutb as the most cited author by jihadi propagandists (William McCants et al., eds., *Militant Ideology Atlas: Executive Report* [West Point: United States Military Academy, 2006], 10).

73 Sayyid Qutb, *Milestones* (Cedar Rapids: Mother Mosque Foundation, n.d.). American Trust Publications of Indianapolis has also published an edition (1990).

74 Nasiri, *Inside the Jihad*, 148.

75 Qutb, *Milestones*, 73. See also 8, 21, 37, and 56.

76 See Voegelin, 'The Order of God,' in *Anamnesis, Collected Works*, vol. 6, ed. David Walsh, 253.

77 Qutb, *Milestones*, 49.

78 Ibid., 9, 39.

79 OH1, 452–5, 475–81.

80 Qutb, *Milestones*, 27.

81 Cooper, *New Political Religions*, 119–28.

82 In *Islamic Imperialism*, Efraim Karsh argues for the continuity of contemporary Islamic imperialism with the early caliphates, as well as with that of the Prophet Muhammad. On the other hand, Patricia Crone and L. Carl Brown argue for a separation on the basis that emperors did not always base their authority on explicitly Qur'anic grounds (Crone, *God's Rule: Government and Islam* [New York: Columbia University Press, 2004]; Brown, *Religion and State: The Muslim Approach to Politics* [New York: Columbia University Press, 2000]).

83 For the French connection, see Waller Newell, 'Why Is Ahmadinejad Smiling? The Intellectual Sources of his Apocalyptic Vision,' *Weekly Standard*, 16 October 2006. http://www.weeklystandard.com/Content/Public/Articles/000/000/012/795hlmvk.asp; for the Mahdist interpretation, see Timothy R. Furnish, *Holiest Wars: Islamic Mahdis, Their Jihads, and Osama bin Laden* (Westport: Praeger, 2005), 150–67; for Islamic 'millenarianism,' see Karsh, *Islamic Imperialism*, 2.

84 See Elisabeth Bumiller, 'White House Letter: Watchword of the Day – Beware the Caliphate,' *New York Times*, 11 December 2005 (http://www.iht.com/articles/2005/12/11/news/letter.php).

85 Daniel J. Mahoney, 'Conservatism, Democracy, and Foreign Policy,' *Intercollegiate Review*, Fall 2006: 6.

86 Though not to the same degree as some critics believe. Francis Fukuyama's evocation of the end of history seemed to have aggravated the ecumenic ambitions of a few Republican policy wonks in the 1990s, but the Bush administration seems not to have been overly influenced by it.

87 Joseph Knippenberg, 'A President, Not a Preacher,' *Claremont Review of Books* (Fall 2004).

88 Mahoney, 'Conservatism, Democracy, and Foreign Policy,' 9.

89 Examples of this kind of thinking include Paul Kennedy, *Parliament of Man: The Past, Present, and Future of the United Nations* (Toronto: HarperCollins, 2006); David Held, *Democracy and the Global Order: From the Modern State to Cosmopolitan Governance* (Stanford: Stanford University

Press, 1995). The most sophisticated expression of this evocation remains Alexandre Kojève, *Introduction to the Reading of Hegel*, ed. Allan Bloom, (New York: Basic, 1969).

90 Bernard Lewis, *What Went Wrong? The Clash between Islam and Modernity in the Middle East* (Toronto: HarperCollins, 2003); Olivier Roy, *Globalized Islam*.

91 AR, 13.

92 See my 'Mysticism in Contemporary Islamic Political Thought: Orhan Pamuk and Abdolkarim Soroush,' *Humanitas* 19, nos. 1 and 2 (2006).

13 Athens as Hamlet: The Irresolute Empire

BARRY STRAUSS

Readers of Thucydides come away with an impression of Athens as the original example of imperial hubris. Athens preached freedom at home while ruling fellow Greeks abroad; it committed notorious war atrocities such as those on the island of Melos, where it massacred all the men and enslaved the women and children; it committed aggression by invading innocent states like Syracuse. Athenian hegemony lasted about seventy years, from 478 to 404 BCE. It was brought down only by its own overconfidence and egotism.

These criticisms of Athens are, in fact, a brilliant caricature. Athens could be severe, exacting, meddling, and cruel. But Athens' hegemony brought such benefits to its subjects as democracy, security, and prosperity. Athenians pursued power less out of greed than necessity. Athens' ultimate failure is attributable more to its indecision than to its arrogance.

Rather than spending their energy agonizing over the moral dilemmas of empire, the Athenians should have focused on the moral disaster that would have awaited had they ceded control of the Aegean back to Persia. If Athens was serious about defending Greece's freedom, it should have been prepared to make difficult compromises. It could not count on the cooperation of the other Greek city-states; on the contrary, Athens had to expect to find chisellers, free riders, rebels, and traitors. It was only to be anticipated that some Greeks would resist Athenian leadership, and resist violently. After all, of the hundreds of Greek city-states in the Aegean basin, only thirty-one *poleis* had united against Xerxes in 480 BCE. As many Greeks fought for the Persians as for the Hellenic League. In order to keep Greece autonomous after achieving victory in 479, therefore, Athens had to deny individual Greeks their autonomy. And it had to be prepared to use force.

Athens' problem in the decades after 479 was not that it used too much muscle against its fellow Greeks; its problem, rather, was that it used too little. And when it resorted to violent force against its obstreperous allies, it could have done so more shrewdly and strategically. But this is to get ahead of the story.

The subject at hand is the rule exercised by Athens between 477 and 404 BCE over a group of between 150 and 250 Greek city-states in and around the Aegean and the straits leading to the Black Sea. Historians refer to this rule as the Delian League and the Athenian Empire. Each, in its own way, is an apt description, but neither term was used by contemporaries.

The word 'empire' comes from the Latin *imperium*, whose original meaning is 'the power to command or the thing commanded.' An *imperium* is a command given by an *imperator* or general. In the Republic, *imperium* included the power of life and death outside the city limits of Rome; within those limits, no Roman could be executed without a trial. In time, *imperium* came also to mean, among other things, the area in which command is exercised; hence, it came to mean what we mean by empire. The Roman Empire, in all its majesty (and misery), was the *imperium romanum*.[1]

The Greeks did not speak of the exercise of state power abroad in the same way. A state that exercised power over other states with their consent was called a *hegemon* – that is, 'leader.' The group of states in which it exercised leadership (*hegemonia*) was generally called a *summakhia*, meaning 'alliance' or, literally, 'common battle.' A state that exercised power over other states against their wishes might be said to be engaging in *turannis*, 'tyranny.' The Athenians referred to what we call today the Athenian Empire as 'the Athenians and the allies' or, more abstractly, as the *arché*. The word has many meanings, among them, 'beginning,' 'origin,' 'realm,' 'rule,' 'magistracy' and 'public office.' Ian Morris prefers to translate it not as 'empire' but as 'Greater Athenian State.'[2] And so it was, but with a definite sting: in their blunter and less guarded moments, Athenians spoke of 'the cities that Athens rules,' using a strong word for rule, *kratos*, which has connotations of force.[3]

Every member of the league had one vote in the league assembly, but Athens was the hegemon and so had additional authority. Each state was required to contribute to the alliance's military needs in one of three ways: by contributing ships, by contributing manpower, or by paying an annual tribute at an assessment rate to be determined by Athens. Most member states preferred to pay tribute, which was cheaper in the long run than either of the alternatives. By mid-century only three states besides Athens were contributing ships and men: the large islands of Chios, Lesbos, and Samos. All of the other ships were Athenian, but not all of the rowers and seamen, many of whom came from the allied states and lived in Athens, where they made a living in the Athenian navy.

Until 454 BCE, the alliance's treasury was kept on Delos. In that year it was moved to Athens, supposedly for safe keeping but in fact as part of a centralizing trend. Within a decade, league monies would be diverted to a vast construction project in Athens – the rebuilding of the city's 'Ground Zero' on the Acropolis, whose temples had been destroyed by Persian invaders in 480 BCE. The most famous result of this project is the Parthenon, completed in 432 BCE. Pericles characterized works such as the Parthenon as 'refinement without extravagance.'[4] His political opponents spoke for many Greeks, however, when they called the Parthenon an abuse of power. They said that Athens' allies would consider the beautiful temple to be 'an act of bare-faced tyranny, when they see that with their own contributions, extorted from them by force for the war against the Persians, we are gilding and beautifying our city, as if it were some vain woman decking herself out with costly stones and statues and temples worth millions of money.'[5]

Indeed, they could point to other examples of Athenian arrogance and high-handedness towards the allies, such as the Long Walls, built under Pericles to connect the city to its ports at Phaleron and Piraeus, about three and four miles away respectively. The Long Walls reflected Athens' determination not to give in to those Greeks who were insisting that Athens make concessions to the allies – what Sparta and its allies called 'freeing the Hellenes.' No wonder Athens' detractors at the time referred to her as the 'tyrant city.'[6]

One of the first democracies in the history of the West, Athens was also its first hegemonic empire. This was the ironic consequence of the founding victory of Athenian freedom and power: the battle of Salamis, the great encounter in September 480 BCE in which the Greek navy, spearheaded by the Athenian contingent, defeated the Persian navy, spearheaded by the Phoenician contingent. It was a clash between the old naval supremacy of the Eastern Mediterranean and the new; a clash between monarchy and democracy; between freedom and obedience; between good order and collapse; and, the Greeks would have added, between civilization and barbarism. The Persians were no barbarians, but they followed customs that were in many ways foreign to Greeks. Or at least customs that were foreign before Xerxes' invasion of

Greece and its disastrous outcome. One of the leitmotifs of Athenian policy and politics in the decades after Salamis was its Persianization.[7]

By 478–7 BCE, Athens had created a new naval alliance of Greek city-states, many of them former subjects of the Great King. From its very founding, the Delian League committed itself to expansion. Not only did its members promise to defend Greece against any new attack by Persia, but they also swore to attack the lands of the Great King in order to avenge the damage done to Greece by Xerxes in 480 BCE and to acquire booty.

For nearly seventy-five years the league succeeded in holding Persia back from the Aegean. But Greek rivalries and divisions destroyed Athens' hegemony. After it disappeared in 404 BCE, the Great King used a combination of diplomacy and bribery to keep the Greeks divided and off guard. Only the rise of a new power, Macedon, led by its kings Philip and Alexander, finally brought the Persian Empire down in 330.

Meanwhile, no sooner had the Delian League been founded than it began to resemble the Persian Empire in certain ways. Persia had required its Aegean (and other) subjects to pay tribute. Athens did the same thing. Athenian allies rose in revolt, just like Persian allies. Athenian generals sailed out with fleets to fight rebels, whom they then executed and enslaved, just as the Persians had tried to do to Athenians at Salamis. Athenian consumers developed a taste for Persian clothes and Persian art – but that only made sense, because imperial powers are naturally attracted to each other. Athenians established settlements at strategic choke points, just as the Persians had. These settlements were called 'cleruchies' or 'allotments,' but the neutral-sounding name cannot hide the reality of confiscated territory. In spite of these settlements, Athens' empire was not primarily a case of territorial imperialism. Rather, it was mainly an example of hegemonic imperialism, to follow Michael W. Doyle's analysis.[8]

Doyle's categories are controversial. Remove the requirement of colonies or provinces from the definition of empire and you open the door to conceptual confusion. A fine line separates hegemony from hegemonic empire. But surely we need a category of empire that takes into account the limited territorial holdings of an imperial state like Athens, so Doyle's distinction is useful enough to be worth keeping. Yet there is a difference between hegemonic empire and hegemonic power, and that lies both in the intention of the hegemon and the restraint with which it exercises power. A hegemonic imperial power intends to exercise control over the states in its influence, and it recognizes few restraints on the use of its power within those states. A non-imperial hegemonic power merely wants to exercise such force as is necessary to protect itself, and it sharply restrains the use of power vis-à-vis other states.[9]

Athens was a hegemonic empire. The Athenians controlled the subject states without actually administering most of them as provinces. There was no Athenian governor of, say, the island of Paros, but there did not need to be, because the system was largely self-policing. The Parians paid tribute, established a democracy, used Athenian weights and measures, sent ambassadors to Athens to polish Athenian apples, and tamely forwarded major court cases to Athenian juries while giving up the right of the Parian people to decide them themselves. If necessary, the Athenians could send a general and a few triremes to tamp down any trouble, as they possibly did under Cimon in the 450s and certainly did in 410 BCE under Theramenes, who overturned an oligarchy in Paros and restored democracy. This was gunboat diplomacy, ancient style, but it was not a territorial empire in the manner of the Romans or the Victorians.[10]

Or the Persians – and there were other significant differences between Athens and its Aegean predecessor as well. Unlike Persia, Athens did not establish tyrannies in the cities it ruled, but democracies. There were no dragnets of conquered territory to find and uproot every last local, nor were there mass deportations of entire populations to resettlement locations a thousand miles or more away. No allies had to watch their sons chopped in half before their eyes; there were few or no eunuchs, and castration was not an acceptable practice. In the years after 478 BCE, Athens perhaps strayed from time to time, but it did not betray the legacy of Salamis.

There is reason to think that Athens attracted ordinary people in its empire as an economic and cultural magnet. The fleet, the ship sheds, and the business of building and maintaining galleys provided employment to tens of thousands of allied citizens every year – most of them, no doubt, poor people. The new temples in and around the city of Athens as well as on the island of Delos, which Athens celebrated as a religious centre, were the foci of feasts and festivals that may also have attracted allied crowds.[11]

Such people may well have thanked Athens for promoting democracy around the Aegean, because ancient democracy meant political power for the poor, which always boosted their morale and usually spelled economic opportunity. The Peloponnesian War included many allied revolts against Athens, but only in the last decade of the conflict, when it looked as if Sparta was the strong horse and oligarchy the coming thing. Earlier in the war, the only revolt, aside from those stirred up by Corinthian agents or Spartan expeditionary forces, was the case of Mytilene. Even at the end of the war, a certain segment of the common people, those of Samos, remained true to Athens.[12]

Yet there is no denying it: many allies, including some staunch democrats, considered Athenian rule oppressive; some would rather have lived in freedom under an oligarchy than in a democracy under Athenian control. The problem with the Athens-as-villain school is its assumption that the alternative to Athenian rule was the freedom of the Greeks: the banner under which, for example, Sparta began the Peloponnesian War in 431 BCE. Actually, the freedom of the Greeks was never a possibility.

Athens was not the first state to centralize political and naval power in the Aegean Sea. Leave aside the question of the degree to which the Minoans or Mycenaeans projected power in the Aegean during the Bronze Age. The first Iron Age state to exercise naval hegemony over a large part of the Aegean was Samos under its ambitious and ruthless tyrant Polycrates (r. ca. 535–22 BCE). Herodotus calls him 'the first of the Hellenes of whom we know who intended to rule the sea,' aside from mythical figures; he was a man with 'many hopes of ruling Ionia and the islands.'[13] The word that Herodotus uses for 'to rule the sea' is *thalassokratein*, the verbal form of *thalassokratia*, the noun that in English is 'thalassocracy.' The *OED* defines the latter as 'a nation's mastery at sea; a nation's sovereignty of large areas of the sea: a maritime empire.'[14]

Polycrates' ambition was probably spurred by a technical innovation that probably occurred around this time: the three-tiered galley, or trireme, a faster and more manoeuvrable warship than its predecessors. No less important was the concentration of wealth needed for sea power, since triremes were expensive to build, maintain, and man and so too were the requisite harbours, ship sheds, and dockyards. As a tyrant of a rich island, Polycrates had many advantages, but they could not compare to those of the empire that ruled the mainland across a narrow strait: Persia.

The Persians not only killed Polycrates but replaced Samos as the Aegean's thalassocrat. The Persian religion, with its abhorrence of salt water as demonic, made this uncomfortable as well as ironic. Surely the landlubbing Persians would have had no easy time keeping their thalassocracy, though it took the genius of Themistocles to wrest it from them in 480 BCE. Athens did not become a great naval power until 483–80, and some other Greek state – Corinth, say, or Aegina – might conceivably have led the naval coalition against Persia. But in the grand scheme of things the Greeks, with their maritime traditions, made a more credible Aegean thalassocrat than the Persians, a land power in the tradition of Near Eastern empires from the Akkadians to the Assyrians.[15]

Persia had the resources to replace Samos, and a Greek coalition had the traditions to replace Persia. All of that makes sense; what would not have made sense was an Aegean without a thalassocrat. Given the technology, the wealth, the commerce, the individual weakness of the island states, and the threat of piracy, it is almost inconceivable that the Aegean basin would have been left without a central coordinating authority after 500 BCE. The question was less whether a naval power would be in charge of the Aegean than what kind of manager that power would turn out to be.

Between 477 and circa 450 the Athenians wrested control not merely of the Aegean but of much of the Eastern Mediterranean from the Persian fleet. After Athens' Sicilian disaster and the allied revolts of 413 BCE, the Persians became competitive again, first through a Spartan proxy, and afterwards without it. Athenian naval power waxed and waned for eighty years after its failure at Aegospotami in 405 BCE; it was only Macedon's victory at the naval battle of Amorgos in 322 BCE that put a period on Athens' prospects for thalassocracy. For the next several centuries other Greek and Macedonian states would vie for control of the Aegean until Rome finally replaced them. At no time was independence for the various Aegean islands on offer – except, that is, for the independence of the disunited victims of piracy. The Aegean Sea was dominated by imperial power before Athens, and it would be dominated by imperial power after Athens.

How cruel could the Athenians be in the exercise of power? It might be instructive to compare Athenian to American actions. When it was discovered in 2004 that American soldiers engaged in abuses and possibly even in war crimes in their treatment of Iraqis rounded up for questioning in the military prison at Abu Ghraib, the American government itself began investigations and prosecutions of the alleged criminals; the American public demanded no less. By contrast, when the Athenian army massacred the men and enslaved the women and children on Melos in 416 BCE, the Athenian government did nothing – but then again, how could it have, since it had authorized the act? Athenian allies who voted to leave the alliance faced military retribution from Athens and sometimes savage punishment: in 427 no less than one thousand Mytilenians were executed, surely a high percentage of the citizen males in that city-state; and it is quite possible that in 440, the marines of Samos were literally crucified – and on the order of no less a figure of enlightenment than Pericles.

But an appropriate analogy to Athens is surely not America but Rome. America is a post-industrial nation-state founded on the Atlantic Ocean in the Age of Enlightenment; Rome, like Athens, began as a pre-industrial city-state in the Iron Age Mediterranean. Both America and Rome are more successful examples of the projection of power than Athens, but whether America is an empire is debatable; Rome, by contrast, is one of history's prime examples of empire. And it offers a striking contrast to Athens.[16]

Rome managed its allies through a combination of generosity and brutality. Rome built bridges to local elites by offering an unprecedented extension of its citizenship, but it did not hesitate to make an example of rebel cities by tearing down walls and by exiling, executing, or enslaving people. Roman roads and colonies around the peninsula guaranteed central surveillance and rapid response to disloyalty. The system was tested to the breaking point by Hannibal's invasion of Italy during the Second Punic War (218–201). In spite of catastrophe on the battlefields at the Trebia, Trasimene, and Cannae, Rome maintained control of the core of its Italian alliance and lived to fight another day – and to conquer. Rome kept allied defections to Hannibal minimal by using its tried-and-true methods of the carrot and the stick.

Most of Rome's allies judged her to be mild and generous as hegemons go. Those who wavered could gauge the price of disloyalty in the savage reprisals inflicted by Rome on cities that had gone over to Hannibal. In the region of Campania, for example, the city of Capua was besieged for two years. When the Romans finally took the town, they killed or imprisoned its leading men, sold the rest of the population into slavery, deprived the city of its independence, and left it to languish until a Roman colony was founded there 150 years later (in 58 BCE). Meanwhile, Rome confiscated about 150,000 acres of territory from Capua and other Campanian towns that had defected to Hannibal: as the *ager campanus*, it represented some of the most fertile farmland in Italy and was under the control of the Roman Senate.[17]

For all their harshness, Athenian punitive measures against rebels did not match Macedonian or Roman standards of repression. It was one thing to carry out the measures mentioned by Thucydides, such as driving the Potidaeans into exile or executing one thousand men from a large state like Mytilene or the adult males from a small state like

Melos; it was quite another thing to destroy Thebes, as the Macedonians did, or to crush Veii (396 BCE) or Carthage or Corinth (146 BCE), as the Romans did, and they sacked each of these cities.[18]

True, Athens lacked its successors' technology of siegecraft and the wealth to pay for it, but there are other ways to be brutal, so one ought to consider moral factors. Cleon argued at the time that fifth-century Athenians were too soft-hearted to crack the whip of empire, but kinship and caution rather than goodness may be sufficient to explain his countrymen's behaviour. Belief in a common Hellenic identity tended to inhibit the abuse or torture of one's opponents. The relative equality of power between the Athenians and the Peloponnesians also placed limits on cruelty, because what one side meted out might be repaid in turn one day. In short, the city-state limited a power's ability to punish or terrorize its opponents.[19]

From the perspective of Thucydides' Greeks, a state faced only two possibilities in international affairs: freedom or slavery. There was no middle ground. For example, consider the words of the Mytilenian envoys to the Peloponnesians at Olympia in the summer of 428. The Mytilenians said that all of the 250 or so city-states of the Athenian alliance who paid tribute instead of contributing their own ships had been 'enslaved' (*edoulôthésan*) by Athens.[20] Because they expected a similar fate for themselves and the Chians – the only two remaining states in the alliance to supply ships – the Mytilenians were about to rebel, they said, and requested Peloponnesian assistance.

On an objective account, the Mytilenian analysis is greatly exaggerated. Merely because they had to tolerate a limited amount of Athenian interference in their affairs, the citizens of the allied states had not been enslaved. Unlike the real slaves of classical Greece, the allies were not subject to torture, rape, sale, the break-up of family, and the denial of elementary freedom. Limited subordination was not slavery. Nor was Athenian brutality much, compared to what Rome would practise.

The freedom–slavery dichotomy of Thucydides is, therefore, wrong. There *is* a middle ground. But what may be more important than the Mytilenians' analysis is their perception. Because it failed to provide incentives for allied elites to maintain loyalty to Athenian rule, Athens faced frequent revolts. Should Athenian power weaken decisively, the whole system might explode, as it did after the Sicilian disaster of 413. The price was the loss of the Peloponnesian War and with it, the *arché*.

What should Athens have done differently? On the one hand, it should have devised a method for extending Athenian citizenship, slowly, selectively, and in piecemeal fashion. On the other hand, it should have used more refined – and sometimes harsher – methods of policing. Mass execution and enslavement gained Athens neither security nor respect. What the Athenians needed instead was to carry out strategic and targeted executions of their worst enemies while extending the olive branch to their friends. But how could they identify those enemies? The best way was by getting reliable local helpers, and the best way to get them would have been to offer the helpers Athenian citizenship. Nothing else would have given enough of a stake in Athenian success to important and powerful people in places like Chios and Byzantium.

Another leaf that Athens could have borrowed from Rome's book (had it been written yet) was to establish colonies. More rather than fewer Athenian military settlements around the empire would have strengthened Athenian security by keeping its enemies close, so to speak. But colonies need soldiers to man them, and that leads to the next step Athens would have needed to take: beefing up its infantry, if necessary, by creating an elite force. Athenians were reluctant to do so for fear of the natural Greek political alliance between infantry and oligarchy. Sea power was democracy-friendly and sea power was Athens' forte, but it was not enough. Without the ability to project sandals on the ground, as it were, Athens would never be able to protect itself against its enemies in Sparta and the Peloponnesian League, since they had Greece's strongest infantry force.

Instead, Athens had built its security on Long Walls at home and peace with Persia abroad. The Long Walls were useful, but they encouraged a false sense of security. The real problem was Persia. Détente after 449 BCE might have been in Athens' interest but only in the short term. In the long term, Persia could not be trusted to keep the peace; in fact, it broke the peace as soon as it got the chance, in 413. Worse still, détente created a superficial logic for breaking up the Delian League. It made it easier for irresponsible politicians around the Aegean to convince their countrymen that Athens was an imperial oppressor rather than the protector of Greek freedom. Meanwhile, the Persian satrap sat in Sardis, the provincial capital only sixty miles from the Aegean coast, and wheeled and dealed with the tyrant of Halicarnassus and other local powers.

Athens should have committed itself to a long-term policy of rolling back Persian power in Anatolia, if not further. Rather than accept the disappointment of its failure in the 450s BCE to drive Persia out of Egypt, Athens should have found a new strategy of attacking Persia elsewhere. A war on Persia would have helped unite the Athenian Empire; it would also have proven to be an investment in Athenian security because it would have weakened a standing threat. Invading Sicily in 415 BCE, as Athens did, was poor strategy; a better target would have been Sardis, Persia's provincial capital in western Anatolia.

Philip and Alexander figured this out in the 330s BCE, but as early as the 390s, Sparta had beaten them to the punch. The Spartan invasion of Persian Anatolia was sound strategy; unfortunately, it would not be backed up by proper alliance management. The Macedonians would do better, though they too would show weaknesses in dealing with allies. But that is another story.

For now, let us think of the Athenian experience less as an example of the evils of hegemonic empire than of the paradoxes of finding security in a hostile world. Athens created a hegemonic empire in the Aegean basin. By doing so, it was not exercising tyranny where there could have been freedom. Because naval hegemony was inevitable in the Aegean, Athens was filling a vacuum, and doing so in a relatively restrained manner.

The Athenian Empire did not fail because Athenian oppression was too great. It failed because Athens had not been shrewd enough in the application of force to its real enemies. If that is a morality story, it is not a comforting one.

NOTES

1 On the nomenclature of imperialism and the Athenian Empire, see M.I. Finley, 'The Athenian Empire: A Balance Sheet,' in *Economy and Society in Ancient Greece*, ed. Brent D. Shaw and Richard Saller (New York: Viking, 1982). For an introduction to the Athenian Empire, see P.J. Rhodes, *The Athenian Empire, Greece and Rome*, Survey 17 (Oxford: Oxford University Press, 1985); or Robin Osborne, *The Athenian Empire*, Lactor 1, 4th ed. (London: London Association of Classical Teachers, 2000); Loren J. Samons II, ed. and trans., *Athenian Democracy and Imperialism: Problems in European Civilization* (Boston: Houghton Mifflin, 1998).

2 Ian Morris, 'The Athenian Empire (478–404 BC),' third draft, April–May 2001. http://www.stanford.edu/group/sshi/Conferences/2000-2001/empires2/morris.pdf, accessed 12.10.06.

3 See the discussion in Russell Meiggs, *The Athenian Empire* (Oxford: Clarendon, 1972), 152–74.

4 Thucydides, *History*, 2.40.1, trans. Robert B. Strassler, in Strassler, *The Landmark Thucydides: A Comprehensive Guide to the Peloponnesian War* (New York: Free Press, 1988), 113.

5   Plutarch, *Life of Pericles*, 12.3, in Plutarch, *The Rise and Fall of Athens*, trans. Ian Scott-Kilvert (Harmondsworth: Penguin, 1982), 177–78).

6   Thucydides, *History*, 1.122.3, 1.124.3.

7   On Salamis, see my *Battle of Salamis: The Naval Encounter That Saved Greece— and Western Civilization* (New York: Simon and Schuster, 2004); on Persianiza-tion, see Margaret C. Miller, *Athens and Persia in the Fifth Century B.C.: A Study in Cultural Receptivity* (Cambridge: Cambridge University Press, 1997).

8   Michael Doyle, *Empires* (Princeton: Princeton University Press, 1986), 54–81.

9   On the difference between empire and hegemony, see Robert Kagan, 'The American Empire: A Case of Mistaken Identity,' in *War and Democracy: A Comparative Study of the Korean War and the Peloponnesian War*, ed. David McCann and Barry Strauss (Armonk: Sharpe, 2001), 49–56.

10 Cimon: see Meiggs, *The Athenian Empire* p. 120. Theramenes: Diodorus Siculus, 12.47.

11 On temple building and the popularity of the Athenian Empire, see Robin Osborne, 'Archaeology and the Athenian Empire,' in *Transactions of the American Philological Association* 129 (1999): 319–32.

12 For an argument in favour of the popularity of the Athenian Empire among the poor, see G.E.M. de Ste. Croix, 'The Character of the Athenian Empire,' *Historia* 3 (1954–5): 1–41; Malcolm F. McGregor, *The Athenians 00 and Their Empire* (Vancouver: University of British Columbia Press, 1987), 166–77. For a counter-argument, see Donald Bradeen, 'The Popularity of the Athenian Empire,' *Historia* 9 (1960): 257–69.

13 Herodotus, 3.122.2.

14 Lesley Brown, ed., *The New Shorter Oxford English Dictionary*, vol. 2 (Oxford: Clarendon, 1993), s.v.

15 Clarisse Herrenschmidt and Bruce Lincoln, 'Healing and Salt Waters: The Bifurcated Cosmos of Mazdaean Religion,' *History of Religions* 43 (2004): 269–83.

16 See my 'The Art of Alliance and the Peloponnesian War,' in *Polis and Polemos: Essays on Politics, War and History in Ancient Greece in Honor of Donald Kagan*, ed. C.D. Hamilton and P. Krentz (Claremont: Regina, 1997), 127–40.

17 See Barry Strauss and Josiah Ober, *The Anatomy of Error: Ancient Military Disasters and their Lessons for Modern Strategists* (New York: St Martin's, 1990), 133–62.

18 Thucydides, *History*, 2.70.3–4, 3.50.1, 5.116.4.

19 Cleon: Thucydides, 3.37.2.

20 Thucydides, *History*, 3.10.5.

Contributors

Laurie M. Johnson Bagby has a PhD in political science from Northern Illinois University with fields in political philosophy and international relations. She is an Associate Professor of Political Science at Kansas State University and author of *Thucydides, Hobbes, and the Interpretation of Realism*; *Political Thought: A Guide to the Classics*; and *Hobbes' 'Leviathan': A Reader's Guide*. Her latest book, *Thomas Hobbes: Turning Point for Honor*, will be published in 2009 by Rowman & Littlefield. Her scholarly articles include 'The Use and Abuse of Thucydides in International Relations,' in *International Organization*; 'Thucydidean Realism: Between Athens and Melos,' in *Security Studies*; and '"Mathematici" v. "Dogmatici": Understanding the Realist Project through Hobbes,' in *Interpretation: A Journal of Political Philosophy*. She is currently working on Hobbes and the desire for glory as a cause of war, Hobbes's political thought in his translation of Thucydides, and Thucydides and the importance of ideology in conflict.

Ryan K. Balot is Associate Professor of Political Science at the University of Toronto. The author of *Greed and Injustice in Classical Athens* (Princeton: Princeton University Press, 2001) and of *Greek Political Thought* (Oxford: Blackwell, 2006), he specializes in the history of political thought. He received his doctorate in classics at Princeton and his BA degrees in classics from the University of North Carolina at Chapel Hill and Corpus Christi College, Oxford, where he studied as a Rhodes Scholar. Balot is currently at work on *Courage and Its Critics in Democratic Athens*, from which he has published articles in the *American Journal of Philosophy*, *Ancient Philosophy*, *Classical Quarterly*, and *Social Research*.

Leah Bradshaw is Associate Professor of Political Science at Brock University. Her work is anchored in the thought of Hannah Arendt. Her book *Acting and Thinking: The Political Thought of Hannah Arendt* (University of Toronto Press, 1989) was selected by *Choice* as an outstanding scholarly book in its year of publication. Her recent work has been on considerations on narrative and theory, comparative accounts of ancient and modern tyranny, and the relationship between emotions and reason in making judgments. 'Tyranny and the Womanish Soul' appeared in David Tabachnick and Toivo Koivukoski, *Confronting Tyranny: Ancient Lessons for Global Politics* (Lanham: Rowman and Littlefield, 2005).

Arthur M. Eckstein is Professor of History at the University of Maryland and a specialist in the history of the Hellenistic world and Roman imperialism under the Republic. He has published four books, most recently *Rome Enters the Greek East: From Anarchy to Hierarchy in the Hellenistic Mediterranean, 230–188 BC* (Oxford: Wiley-Blackwell, 2008), a co-edited collection of scholarly essays on John Ford's film *The Searchers*, and fifty major scholarly articles bridging the fields of political theory, international relations, and history.

David C. Hendrickson is Professor of Political Science at Colorado College, where he has taught since 1983. He received a PhD in political science from Johns Hopkins University in 1982. He is the author or co-author of seven books, including *Union, Nations, or Empire: The American Debate over International Relations, 1789–1941* (2009) and *Peace Pact: The Lost World of the American Founding* (2003). He has written three books with Robert W. Tucker: *The Fall of the First British Empire: Origins of the War of American Independence* (1982); *Empire of Liberty: The Statecraft of Thomas Jefferson* (1990); and *The Imperial Temptation: The New World Order and America's Purpose* (1992). His essays on contemporary American foreign policy have appeared in *Foreign Affairs, World Policy Journal, The National Interest, Ethics and International Affairs, Survival,* and *Orbis.* He was chair of the Political Science Department at Colorado College from 2000 to 2003 and was named Robert J. Fox Distinguished Service Professor at Colorado College in 2004.

John von Heyking is Associate Professor of Political Science at the University of Lethbridge. He is the author of *Augustine and Politics as Longing in the World* (Missouri, 2001), and co-editor of *Friendship and Politics:*

Essays in Political Thought (Notre Dame: University of Notre Dame Press, 2008). He has also written about friendship, just war, Islamic political thought, deliberative democracy, political prophecy, Eric Voegelin, religion and politics in Canada, and the philosophy of the Calgary Stampede.

Geoffrey Kellow is Assistant Professor of Humanities in Carleton University's College of the Humanities, specializing in the history of ideas. In his current research, he is particularly interested in the philosophical and intellectual origins of liberal capitalism and most especially the philosophy of Adam Smith. He has also conducted related research on liberalism, liberal education, and the role of the philosophy of Cicero in Smith's *The Wealth of Nations*.

Toivo Koivukoski is Associate Professor of Political Science at Nipissing University. His first monograph, *After the Last Man: Excurses to the Limits of the Technological System* (Lexington, 2008), explores Hegel's 'end of history' thesis and the available, alternative ways of conceiving progress in an integrated environment characterized more by iterative feedback loops than by linear developments. He is presently working on a book project on the so-called 'wise barbarian,' Anacharsis, towards an understanding of the cultural specificity of notions of barbarism.

Susan Mattern is Professor of History at the University of Georgia, where she has worked since 1998. She is the author of *Rome and the Enemy: Imperial Strategy in the Principate* (Berkeley: University of California Press, 1999) and *Galen and the Rhetoric of Healing* (Baltimore: Johns Hopkins University Press, 2008). She teaches classes on Greek and Roman history, medicine, and law, and on world history.

Waller R. Newell is Professor of Political Sciences and Philosophy at Carleton University in Ottawa. His books include *The Code of Man: Love, Courage, Pride, Family, Country* (New York: ReganBooks/HarperCollins, 2003), *What is a Man? 3,000 Years of Wisdom on the Art of Manly Virtue* (New York: HarperCollins, 2001), and *Ruling Passion: The Erotics of Statecraft in Platonic Political Philosophy* (Lanham: Rowman and Littlefield, 2000).

Clifford Orwin is Professor of Political Science, a Fellow of St Michael's College, and director of the Program in Political Philosophy and International Affairs at the Munk Centre for International Studies, all at the University of Toronto, and a Distinguished Visiting Fellow at the

Hoover Institution of Stanford University and a member of its Task Force on the Virtues of a Free Society. He contributes regularly to the comment page of the *Globe and Mail* (Toronto). He is the author of *The Humanity of Thucydides* (Princeton: Princeton University Press, 1994; rev. ed. 1997) and of several articles on humanitarian military intervention. He is planning a book on Herodotus.

Barry Strauss is the author of five books, including *The Battle of Salamis: The Naval Encounter That Saved Greece – and Western Civilization* (New York: Simon and Schuster, 2004), which was named by the *Washington Post* as one of the best books of 2004 and has been translated into five languages. He is Professor of History and Classics at Cornell University.

David Edward Tabachnick is Associate Professor of Political Science at Nipissing University and a former Fullbright University Research Chair. He has published articles on Heidegger, technology, and Aristotle. He has co-edited three books (with Toivo Koivukoski), including *Confronting Tyranny: Ancient Lessons for Global Politics* (Lanham: Rowman and Littlefield, 2006), and *Globalization, Technology and Philosophy* (Albany: SUNY Press, 2004).

Index